The Lynching of Mexicans
in the Texas Borderlands

The Lynching of Mexicans in the Texas Borderlands

Nicholas Villanueva Jr.

University of New Mexico Press | Albuquerque

First paperbound printing, 2018
Paperbound ISBN: 978-0-8263-6030-4

Library of Congress Cataloging-in-Publication Data
Names: Villanueva, Nicholas, author.
Title: The lynching of Mexicans in the Texas borderlands / Nicholas Villanueva, Jr.
Description: Albuquerque : University of New Mexico Press, 2017. | Includes bibliographical
references and index. | Description based on print version record and CIP data provided
by publisher; resource not viewed.
Identifiers: LCCN 2016039517 (print) | LCCN 2017012169 (ebook) | ISBN 9780826358387 (cloth :
alkaline paper) | ISBN 9780826358394 (electronic)
Subjects: LCSH: Mexican Americans—Violence against—Texas—History—20th century. |
Mexican Americans—Civil rights—Texas—History—20th century. | Lynching—Texas—
History—20th century. | Ethnic conflict—Texas—History—20th century. | Texas—
Ethnic relations—History—20th century. | Mexican-American Border Region—
Ethnic relations—History—20th century. | Mexico—History—Revolution, 1910–1920—
Influence. | BISAC: HISTORY / United States / State & Local / Southwest (AZ, NM, OK, TX).
Classification: LCC F395.M5 V56 2017 (print) | LCC F395.M5 (ebook) | DDC
323.1168/720764—dc23
LC record available at https://lccn.loc.gov/2016039517

Cover illustration: "Six Months Ago and Tonight," *Big Bend*, Jodie P. Harris Collection,
Archives of the Big Bend, Bryan Wildenthal Memorial Library, Sul Ross State University,
Alpine, Texas.
Designed by Catherine Leonardo
Composed in Minion Pro 10.25/13.5
Display font is Bodoni Std. Poster and Bodoni Std.

For
Nicholas Villanueva Sr.
and
Patricia "Patsy" Villanueva

Contents

Illustrations

Acknowledgments

This book would not have been possible without the financial support of the Vanderbilt University College of Arts and Science, Graduate School, and History Department. The following university grants and fellowships enabled me to explore research opportunities in the United States and Mexico: the National Endowment for the Humanities Summer Seminar Grant, the Martha Rivers Ingram Fellowship in History, the College of Arts and Science Summer Research Fellowship, Graduate School–supported travel grants, and the Herbert and Blanche Henry Weaver Fellowship. I am grateful to Vanessa Beasley for providing me with the opportunity to conduct additional research as a postdoctoral fellow in the American Studies Department at Vanderbilt University. I wish to extend my thanks to Arnoldo De León and the Excellence in West Texas History Fellowship board at Angelo State University for the one-year research fellowship that enabled me to conduct valuable research in nine regional archives. Melleta Bell at the Archives of the Big Bend at Sul Ross State University and Suzanne Campbell at the West Texas Collection, Porter Henderson Library, Angelo State University, utilized their extensive knowledge of the files at each archive to help build the case studies in the following chapters.

I wish to recognize Gary Gerstle, who provided me with both professional and personal advice. Professor Gerstle's mentorship was instrumental in transforming me from a graduate student into a research scholar. His attention to detail and high standards never wavered, and he always expected my best work. I owe my gratitude to the following Vanderbilt University professors: Jane Landers, for her sincere interest in my research project; Sarah Igo, for her guidance as the director of graduate studies; Teresa Goddu, for joining my committee at the eleventh hour and providing substantial advice for revisions; Katherine Crawford, for her open-door policy that provided me with an office sanctuary; and Edward Wright-Rios, for his critical eye with regard to the Mexican history within these chapters.

I am grateful for the friends in my life who provide social and intellectual support: Rhae Lynn Barnes, Erin Stone, Angela Sutton, Nicolette Kostiw, Clay Poupart, Chris Brandt, Tom Hodde, Joanne Belknap, and Carol Oyster. I am indebted to Kathy Thoen for her unwavering reliability when I needed a critical eye, to Erica Hayden for being our graduate cohort's forerunner so that we had someone who could answer our questions about the great unknown of academia, to Steve Harrison, who is one of the best friends a person could have, and to Professor Diana Ahmad, my undergraduate adviser, for being an excellent mentor and friend throughout the years. Additionally, I am thankful for the support I received from the College of Arts and Sciences at the University of Colorado Boulder, and my colleagues in the Ethnic Studies Department.

Finally, I would like to thank my family: my sister for being the greatest and most vocal supporter of my career; my father for teaching me how to work hard and never settle for less than my best effort; and my mother, Patricia (Patsy) Villanueva, who inspired me to be proud of the person I am. Most importantly, I wish to thank my best friend and partner, Ryan, for the many sacrifices he made as we followed my career path together, from a river town in Wisconsin to the mountains of Boulder, Colorado. Your support means everything to me.

Rationalizing Hate

IMMIGRANTS, REFUGEES, AND THE INCREASE IN MEXICAN LYNCHING

The history of lynching in the United States is a legacy of racial terror. These bloodstained chapters of our nation's history will forever haunt future generations. One chapter that remains hidden is the history of mob violence against Mexicans in the United States. For over a century, these stories have been lost, the victims forgotten, and, in many cases, the facts distorted. These victims were categorized as enemy others, criminals, and bandits, a false assertion made by the perpetrators of these crimes and a historical inaccuracy that this book seeks to remedy. The murders committed by Texas civilians and armed posses that included officers of the law were celebrated in communities with photographs, heralded in local newspapers, and even encouraged by high-ranking political figures. The alleged criminals were guilty largely of one unifying "crime"—being Mexican.

One hundred years ago, the Mexican Revolution disrupted US-Mexican diplomatic relations. Mexicans living in the United States became targets of violence and unlawful arrests, and in the most severe cases they were lynched on the suspicion that they were part of a criminal element of the revolution. These crimes, motivated by hate and nativist arguments that ethnic Mexicans were not white, were not citizens, and were prone to violence and crime, echo the anti-Latino rhetoric of the twenty-first century. As for retaliation, modern-day perpetrators are not labeled as lynch mobs or posses; their acts of violence, when punished, are referred to as hate crimes. And, similar to the unruly officers of the law a century earlier, often those perpetrators who are armed with a badge go unpunished.

This examination of collective violence against Mexicans in the United States began in the summer of 2007. In the post-9/11 world, hate crimes in the United States, including against Hispanics, have increased each year following 2001. During the early morning hours of April 22, 2006, in Harris County, Texas, David Tuck and Keith Turner viscously tortured a

1

sixteen-year-old Mexican American, David Ritcheson, at a party. The Anglo perpetrators were enraged when Ritcheson was caught trying to kiss the party host's twelve-year-old sister, Danielle Sons. The attack went on for more than four hours. Tuck and Turner stripped and beat Ritcheson, burned him with cigarettes, attempted to carve a swastika into his chest, and sodomized the teen with a PVC pipe, rupturing his bladder. Court testimony revealed that the attackers repeatedly shouted "white power!" throughout the ordeal. Liquid bleach was found on his body and internally. Left for dead, Ritcheson was discovered ten hours later. He remained hospitalized for three months and underwent more than thirty operations. Physically and mentally scarred, the teenager later took his own life.[1]

In May 2010, after being stopped for illegally crossing the border, Anastasio Hernández-Rojas was arrested by border patrol agents. During the detainment process, two days after his arrest, Hernández-Rojas died of heart complications. The agents claimed that he had resisted arrest and become hostile. Eyewitness cell-phone footage taken at the scene revealed a posse of men brutally beating the undocumented immigrant: "All eyewitnesses that we spoke to basically tell the same story of a man hogtied and handcuffed behind his back, not resisting, being beaten repeatedly by batons, by kicks, by punches, by the use of a taser, for almost 30 minutes."[2] However, on November 6, 2015, the US Justice Department cleared all twenty of the border patrol agents of any crime.[3]

Nativist political rhetoric today echoes similar calls to arms of one hundred years ago. Nativist views gained increased traction during the 2015–2016 Republican primary race, with plans to exclude Muslim refugees, repatriate non–US citizens, and construct a wall that would prevent Mexican "killers and rapists" from entering the United States.[4] In the 1910s, hundreds of Mexicans were lynched in Texas, their stories buried by the state's predominant historical narrative. This narrative, which perpetuated the stereotype of Mexicans as suspicious, lascivious criminals, continued to stigmatize ethnic Mexicans throughout the twentieth century. The stereotype was created by nativist Anglo Americans to satisfy their own ethnocentric persona of moral, intellectual, and cultural superiority. They justified their crimes against Mexicans in the borderland with claims that they were policing the border and protecting the national security of US citizens. When we examine this hidden chapter of lynching in the United States, we must answer these two questions: What is the cost of knowing this history? And what are the dangers of not knowing our past crimes?

One thousand nine hundred sixty-nine miles—that is the total length of the border shared by Mexico and the United States. It is the busiest border in the world, with over 350 million crossings per year, forty-six official border-crossing sites, and cross-border trade totaling US$1 billion every day. On January 11, 2010, Mexican president Felipe Calderón and US trade representative Ron Kirk celebrated the opening of the Anzaldúas International Bridge in Reynosa, Tamaulipas. Kirk praised the accomplishment of this new link as a symbol of the connectedness and cross-cultural understanding that the two nations had forged together. Calderón explained: "It's the bridges that unite the people and elevate the competitiveness of economies. . . . [T]he best opportunity we have to create jobs on both sides of the border is to strengthen ties between Mexico and the United States." Kirk added that the bridge was a "potent symbol of our connectedness."[5]

A century earlier, Mexican president Porfirio Díaz and US president William Taft met in Ciudad Juárez. This marked only the second time a US president had stood on foreign soil while in office. The affair was celebrated on both sides of the Rio Grande. In Mexico, the streets were lined with both the Mexican colors and the US Stars and Stripes. A banquet was held at the Ciudad Juárez customhouse. Sparing no expense, the Mexican organizers lavishly decorated the interior of the building. The two leaders enjoyed their dinners on gold and silver plates that had once belonged to Emperor Maximilian. The floral aroma that engulfed the room came from thousands of flowers that had arrived in three boxcars from central Mexico. Díaz made a toast to Taft and the citizens of the United States:

> This visit, which his Excellency President Taft makes to Mexico will mark an epoch in the history of Mexico. . . . [This] proof of international courtesy, which Mexico appreciates and esteems in all of its worth and meaning, will be from today a happy precedent for Latin American republics to cultivate constant and cordial relations among themselves, with us, and with all other countries of the continent.[6]

After two minutes of cheers, Taft responded with equal gratitude and respect for his Mexican hosts:

> I have left the United States and set my foot in your great and prosperous country to emphasize the high sentiment and confidence, the feeling of brotherly neighborliness, which exists between our two great nations.

... I drink to my friend, the president of this great republic to his continued long life and happiness, and to the never-ending bond of mutual
sympathy between Mexico and the United States.[7]

The following year, revolutionary forces demanded the ouster of Díaz,
which led to the outbreak of civil war and the overthrow of the Díaz administration shortly thereafter. The period of peaceful coexistence between the two
neighboring nations, which took sixty years to develop following the end of
Mexican-American War in 1848, drastically transformed as revolutionary
fighting intensified. Civilians from both nations moved from amity to animosity. Violence increased in the borderland, and US-Mexican diplomacy crumbled. By mid-decade, the two nations found themselves on the verge of war. As
the civil war waged on, the revolution spilled over to the American side of the
border in the form of refugees fleeing the war-torn nation. The violence escalated and the lynching of Mexican refugees by Anglo Texans increased, contributing to the dark reputation of the 1910s as the bloodiest decade of racial/
ethnic violence in the United States of the entire twentieth century.

The lynching of ethnic Mexicans was not a new development. During the
decade that followed the 1848 Treaty of Guadalupe Hidalgo,[8] there were more
than 150 known lynchings of ethnic Mexicans in the United States and its
territories, most of which were blamed on property disputes. The cases were
most prevalent in the states of Texas and California, and the territories of
Arizona and New Mexico. Lynchings had declined in number between 1850
and 1910, but the rate spiked again between 1910 and 1920. A pattern of vigilantism developed in southwestern communities, as Anglo Texans increasingly took their interpretation of the law into their own hands. Anglo Texan
men argued that the state and federal governments failed to stop Mexican
rebels from looting their businesses and farms. Anglo Texans' sense that
their manhood was being challenged exaggerated genuine concerns about
the growing lawlessness along the border. They responded harshly, justifying
their actions in the name of Texas and national pride.[9]

This work examines Mexican and Anglo relations in the borderland of
Texas and northern Mexico during the 1910s. The outbreak of the Mexican
Revolution in 1910 was an important event for both nations: it was a civil war
among Mexicans that also triggered hostilities between Anglos and Mexicans in the borderland. This book explores, as no other work has, the dramatic rise in the lynching of ethnic Mexicans in Texas during the decade of
the Mexican Revolution. I argue that ethnic and racial tension brought on by

Mexican revolutionary fighting in the borderland made Anglo Texans feel justified in their violent actions against Mexicans. Using the legal system to their advantage and deploying white privilege, the perpetrators, even when their actions were illegal, often went unpunished. This work contributes to the historical work on lynching, global perspectives on violence, and borderland studies by differentiating between the lynching of African Americans in the American South and the lynching of ethnic Mexicans in the borderlands. I assert that the latter was about citizenship and sovereignty. Moreover, for Anglo Texas, Mexican citizenship also influenced their perception of the "Mexican race," a phrase frequently used to delineate Mexicans as neither black nor white.

In this examination, I also reconstruct some of the earliest, and hitherto hidden, efforts by ethnic Mexicans living in Texas, many of whom were US citizens, to organize a defense of their rights, and show how these efforts drew support from wherever it could be found: among revolutionary groups in Mexico, among sympathetic whites in the United States, and, by the end of the decade, among Mexican American politicians in the state legislature. Out of such resistance, early civil rights protests by Mexican Americans emerged in Texas. This work is one of the first to analyze the earliest stirrings of what we might call the "long civil rights movement" among Mexican Americans in the Lone Star State. In doing so, through the examination of lynchings, I illustrate the backgrounds of the victims, their families, and their capacity to resist racial violence. I avoid resorting to "academic lynching," which, Sundiata Keita Cha-Jua argued, dominates earlier scholarship on mob violence.[10] This work shows that even as the consolidation of the Mexican Revolution eased relations between Anglo Texans and Mexican Americans in the borderland and led to a dramatic decrease in lynchings after 1920, the civil rights movement among Mexican Americans had taken root and would shape future struggles.

While historians have done a great deal of work on the lynching of African Americans, they have only recently begun to examine the lynching of ethnic Mexicans in the United States. Two major factors have contributed to this lack of attention: documents and sources on the lynching of ethnic Mexicans in the United States usually identify victims as "black" or "white," rendering their ethno-racial identity invisible; and, following a strict definition of lynching provided by the NAACP, historians have excluded from consideration hundreds of cases in which law enforcement officials were among the perpetrators.

According to the NAACP, four characteristics must be present to define a murder as a lynching: first, a murder must have occurred; second, there must be three or more perpetrators involved; third, it must occur extralegally; and fourth, the murder must be perpetrated in the name of vengeance or tradition. Herein lies the problem that I address in this book—I argue that law officers acting as jury, judge, and executioner acted beyond their authority. This book seeks to remedy the hidden truth about the lynching of ethnic Mexicans by holding all of the perpetrators accountable for these crimes.

Newspapers and African American institutions led the way in collecting data on lynching cases, with the *Chicago Tribune* publishing cumulative annual totals beginning in 1883. In 1912 the Tuskegee Institute began publishing *Negro Yearbook: An Encyclopedia of the Negro*, which included the annual lynching records collected by the institute since 1892. According to Tuskegee's records, 3,445 of the 4,742 known lynchings that occurred between 1882 and 1964 targeted African Americans. The remaining 1,297 victims are listed as "white." For years no real attempt was made to determine how many of those "white" victims were Mexicans.

Only in 2004 did reliable estimates begin to emerge, most notably in the work of William Carrigan and Clive Webb, which demonstrated that at least 571 ethnic Mexicans were lynched in the United States between 1848 and 1928.[11] Almost 20 percent (124) of these occurred during the 1910s.[12] Alleged murder was the most common justification given by Anglo mobs for targeting Mexicans and African Americans alike. The second most common justification for attacking Mexicans was theft, not the violation of sexual norms that Anglos used to rationalize their attacks on African Americans.[13] Unlike African American men, ethnic Mexican men were not generally viewed by Anglos as sexual predators; Anglo men perceived the shorter, smaller-framed Mexican as a "distinctly effeminate race."[14]

Historians who have looked at the rising number of Mexican deaths during the 1910s have attributed it to the "bandit wars" between suspected Mexican criminals and the Texas Rangers, overlooking the fact that many of the dead were lynched by Rangers and civilians. While the number of Mexican lynchings is unknown, we must include the estimated number killed by the Ranger posses. William Carrigan and Clive Webb point out conservative estimates of "La Hora de Sangre" (the Hour of Blood) in 1915, when "at least 500 Mexicans were hanged, shot, and executed without trial"; such estimates are crucial in understanding how high this death toll could reach.[15] This book seeks to remedy the neglect by focusing on the lynching of ethnic

Mexicans during the decade of the Mexican Revolution, 1910–1920. It also seeks to place those events within a larger political, social, and territorial frame. It illustrates how the Mexican Revolution intensified both anti-US sentiments in Mexico and anti-Mexican stereotypes in the United States. The growing tension led to a decade of disorder, with ethnic and racial violence on both sides of the border and a dramatic rise in the lynching of ethnic Mexicans in the United States.

By examining case studies, this book focuses on several of the most notorious episodes of Anglo-on-Mexican violence. The goal is not to sensationalize the violence but to reconstruct, as fully as possible, the lives of those it touched, and the social and political world in which it occurred. Thus, the chapters that follow focus on the victims themselves, their families, and the communities from which they emerged; on the perpetrators of violence; on efforts to bring the murderers to justice; and on the swirling, violent world of the Mexican Revolution that made the borderland a front line in that revolutionary struggle. The lynching and the disorder of the revolution subsided toward the end of the decade, helped along by the identification of a new enemy to Anglo Texans: German Americans, who now stood accused of aiding America's enemy during the Great War. But the intense strife of the decade left lasting marks on Mexican-Anglo relations in Texas.

This work contributes to the scholarship on lynching by examining lynching in the borderland. Sundiata Keita Cha-Jua recognizes that lynching scholarship in the new millennium explores lynching "beyond the South" and interrogates "antiblack racial violence . . . examining the impact of lynching on Mexican and Asian Americans and tracking it beyond the U.S. racial formation."[16] Michael Pfeifer leads this analysis with his *Rough Justice: Lynching and American Society, 1874–1947*, arguing that the origin of lynching in the United States is not restricted to one region. This book seeks to continue that effort drawing on scholarly work such as Cynthia Skove Nevels's *Lynching to Belong: Claiming Whiteness through Racial Violence*. This work complements Nevels's thesis that those who committed lynchings claimed whiteness through racial violence and makes an argument that Mexican victims were seen as nonwhite. Christopher Waldrep examines the history of the word "lynching," showing that the word's definition is largely associated with the NAACP, and the degree to which US citizens accepted extralegal violence, in his book *The Many Faces of Judge Lynch*.[17] Miguel Antonio Levario's *Militarizing the Border: When Mexicans Became the Enemy* examines Anglo-on-Mexican violence and argues that during the years of the Mexican Revolution, and throughout the twentieth century, "in the southwest United States, 'American' generally meant white, while 'Mexican' referred to race and not citizenship."[18] Ken Gonzales-Day examines the lynching of Latinos, Native Americans, and Asian Americans in his study of California in *Lynching in the West: 1850–1935*. Historian Linda Gordon asserts that, during the nineteenth century, "Mexicans were lynched so frequently" that it appeared "Southwesterners seemed to hold a racial double standard about punishment—white bad men got trials, Mexicans just got hanged." The practice of lynching, Gordon points out, appeared to have a "racial social contract that authorized whites to punish nonwhite transgression"; however, the lynching of alleged white criminals was not socially acceptable. Gordon references sources stating, "You can hang a Mexican, and you can hang a Jew, and you can hang a nigger, but you can't hang an American Citizen," thus equating citizenship with being white.[19] Neil Foley illustrates that white Texans feared that immigration of Mexicans into Texas after 1910 would "destroy white civilization. . . . Regardless of whether one was for or against Mexican immigration, most Texas whites viewed practically all Mexicans as unambiguously nonwhite."[20] Finally, Laura E. Gómez's *Manifest Destinies: The Making of the Mexican American Race* is important in understanding the construction of the "Mexican race" in the nineteenth and twentieth centuries, and this book continues this analysis of Mexican identity in the Texas and Mexico borderland by framing ethnic Mexican and Anglo American relations through lynching narratives.

The lynching of ethnic Mexicans in the Texas borderland was quite different from lynchings in the West and the South. Texas has a unique history, having been a sovereign republic, the frontier West of the United States, and a Confederate state. Three motivating factors led to the rise of a lynching culture in the Texas borderland during the decade of the Mexican Revolution—a racial component, drawing from Gordon, that categorized Mexicans as nonwhite; a national identity that privileged whites with the rights of citizenship and deprived Tejanos, Mexican Americans, and Mexican refugees; and a power struggle over loyalty and sovereign rights within the region that led to xenophobic concerns by Anglo Texans that depicted ethnic Mexicans as an enemy of the state. Anglo Texans did not view ethnic Mexicans as members of Anglo American society during the 1910s and questioned their behavior in terms of loyalty, obligation, and function as "Americans." In short, lynching in the Texas borderland was about citizenship.[21]

Some definitions of terms are necessary. I have chosen to use *Mexican* to refer to Mexican nationals, *Tejano* for Texans of Mexican ethnicity, *Mexican American* when referring to US citizens of Mexican descent who may not identify as Tejanos, and *ethnic Mexican* for individuals whose national origin is unknown or when referring to a group comprising any combination of Tejanos, Mexican Americans, and Mexicans. I use "Anglo" to describe white Texans of English and other European descent.

By *Mexican Revolution*, I refer to the decade of the most intense conflict nearest to the United States in northern Mexico, 1910–1920. I am aware that there are historical arguments that the revolution began decades before 1910, and that historians have argued that the revolution did not really end until the 1940s. Nevertheless, the fighting in the borderland that was most intense in the 1910–1920 period, beginning with Porfirio Díaz's overthrow and ending with the Álvaro Obregón presidency in 1920, is the focus of this examination.

Chapter 1 of this book describes the coexistence of Anglos and ethnic Mexicans in Texas prior to the outbreak of the Mexican Revolution in 1910. Chapters 2, 3, and 4 are case studies that examine episodes of violence against ethnic Mexicans in Texas during the 1910s. Chapter 5 examines the reasons why the violence ended and explores the emergence of a Mexican American civil rights movement in Texas.

More specifically, chapter 1 focuses first on the openness of the border prior to the Mexican Revolution and how the region functioned as a borderland of cultural exchange. An examination of US families in Chihuahua and Mexican families in Texas demonstrates how both maintained patriotism for their respective homelands while maneuvering through the nationalistic cultures they encountered on foreign soil. It was possible for US citizens in Mexico as well as Mexicans in Texas to assimilate into local society and culture while still fostering a love for their former country. But by the 1890s this fluidity had begun to narrow, first through the application of Jim Crow principles to ethnic Mexicans in Texas and then on account of fears generated by the Mexican Revolution. As foreigners fled Mexico to the United States as refugees, their "whiteness" determined their degree of success in crossing the border and finding acceptance in the United States, privileging some while denying others. By the 1910s the fluidity of the borderland had vanished, making ethnic Mexicans prime targets for lynching.

Chapter 2 examines the lynchings of Antonio Rodríguez and Antonio Gómez. The former resulted in anti-US protests in Mexico days before the outbreak of the Mexican Revolution, and the latter occurred months later, resulting in the arrest of four men who were ultimately acquitted. This chapter demonstrates the disruption of Anglo and Mexican relations immediately following the riots, and the fear that arose among ethnic Mexicans in Texas from the realization that white-on-Mexican violence largely went unpunished. Thus, lynching offered Anglo perpetrators an alternative to a time-consuming legal process, promptly providing the verdict and punishment they demanded for alleged crimes. These two events prompted early Mexican American rights groups to announce that their purpose was to protect ethnic Mexicans in the state and to bring the lynchers of Rodríguez and Gómez to justice.

Chapter 3 is a case study about the trial and execution of Leon Martínez Jr., accused and convicted of murdering an Anglo woman. Officially, Martínez was spared a lynching, but the jury that convicted him included members of the mob that attempted to lynch the teenager on the night of the murder. What the mob could not accomplish through extralegal means it achieved through the artifice of legal proceedings. This case study shows the extent to which animosity toward Mexicans ran through all levels of Anglo society. It also demonstrates the stirrings of resistance, evident in a remarkable protest movement that stalled legal proceedings against Martínez for three years. In these moments, one can see a Mexican American civil rights movement taking shape.

Chapter 4 examines the darkest episode of the decade: the lynching of fifteen Mexican men by Texas Rangers and ranchers at the Mexican village of El Porvenir in Texas. This was not a matter of one individual being lynched but of Anglos killing Mexicans indiscriminately. This occurred when the already tense relations between Anglos and Mexicans along the border worsened as a result of World War I amid fears that Germany might seek to open a front against the United States through Mexico. Both Mexicans and Anglos committed violent acts at this time, but Mexicans suffered a great deal more, with Anglo Texans increasingly profiling all Mexican refugees as criminals and "bandits."

Chapter 5 illustrates when and how this transformation took place. Political stability in Mexico was improving. A significant number of Mexican Americans served in the US military in World War I, and they became outspoken in defense of Mexican American rights when they returned. Meanwhile, the war itself caused German Americans in Texas to become the most feared immigrant/ethnic group in the state. German exclusion, ironically enough, facilitated Mexican American inclusion. Violence against Mexicans declined dramatically. Still, the struggle for equal treatment among Mexican Americans remained in its earliest stages.

Towns such as Thorndale, Pecos, and Rocksprings are largely absent from history books. The tragic events that occurred in those towns briefly drew to them national and international attention. The case studies I have executed for each of those obscure towns are meant to render the historical dramas that occurred there in the 1910s in very human terms. By reconstructing the social and political worlds surrounding the lynchings, I have been able to probe Anglo-Mexican relations at their most contested moments of the twentieth century. I have used a wide variety of sources, including newspapers, photographs, court cases, oral history testimonies, diaries, and legislative documents. While I document the rise and fall of lynching, my deeper purpose is to render comprehensible a violent decade of interethnic and interracial relations. And while I argue that a largely disproportionate amount of violence befell innocent Mexicans, I also show how complex, insecure, and uncertain life became for both sides—in Mexico and in Texas—during the decade of the Mexican Revolution.

This book does not make the claim that prior to the outbreak of the Mexican Revolution the US-Mexican borderland was a social, political, and cultural utopia. A century of contestation characterized the borderland region. However, the semblance of a peaceful milieu appeared to foster cultural exchange. The outbreak of the Mexican Revolution brought to light what were in fact the region's fragile cultural ties, reinforced Anglo Texan–held beliefs of the stereotyped "greaser," introduced new pejoratives such as "wetback," and led to the increase in lynchings of ethnic Mexicans at the hands of Anglo Texans. These events revealed what it meant to be Mexican in the United States in the 1910s, and they allow us to understand what it means to be Mexican in the United States today.

CHAPTER ONE

Expatriates, Exiles, and Refugees

SOCIAL ORDER IN THE TEXAS-MEXICO BORDERLAND PRIOR TO THE MEXICAN REVOLUTION

"It was great. We had a wonderful life . . . we had everything we needed."[1] These are the words of Mollie McCallick, a refugee of the Mexican Revolution, reflecting on her life prior to the upheaval of civil war. McCallick remembered a peaceful life in Mexico before revolutionary fighting forced her family to flee the war-torn nation in 1911. Mollie remembered Mexico as a beautiful country where she and her half-Mexican siblings were born but had to flee as refugees once the country erupted in a violent revolution.

Mollie, the daughter of a US businessman, is not the first image that comes to mind when we discuss Mexican refugees. The race, social class, and national origin of refugees from the Mexican Revolution varied. Mexican nationals fled the country for various reasons that differed by social class. Revolutionary factions targeted wealthy landowners because of their connection with the regime of Porfirio Díaz. Many of the poorest Mexicans left the country when mines and haciendas fell under constant attack by rebel forces raiding for food, weapons, and the conscription of males for service. The revolutionary cries called to return Mexico to Mexicans and, most importantly, to reclaim Mexico for working-class Mexicans.

Foreigners living in Mexico found themselves under attack for what they represented—the foreign exploitation of Mexico under Díaz. US citizens made up a majority of these foreigners, who ranged from laborers to wealthy businessmen and banking leaders. Many Anglo American businessmen lived in Mexico with their families in mostly Anglo American communities. Mollie McCallick was the thirteen-year-old daughter of a smelting superintendent, Hugh McCallick, who had been born in Monterrey, Nuevo León, in 1901.[2] The only homeland she knew was Mexico, but when the US Consulate in Monterrey alerted Hugh McCallick that rebels were on their way to raid the operation and kill all Anglo Americans, the families had to abandon their settlement immediately. The young teenager fled with her family to a foreign place—Texas.

In Texas and much of the Southwest at the turn of the century, "Anglo" was synonymous with white and not necessarily indicative of English descent. Most of the European immigrants in Texas—English, French, Scandinavians, and Germans—were part of this "new Anglo America" because of their whiteness, their families' pre-twentieth-century arrival, and knowledge of the English language. Many of the Anglo families in Texas were of varied European descent, often lumped together as "white." In turn, they viewed ethnic Mexicans with their bronze skin as "nonwhite." The wealthy class of Mexicans, the minority elite of the Díaz era in Mexico, often claimed a degree of "whiteness" by virtue of their Spanish ancestry; these families had had very little intermarriage with the indigenous population of Mexico during the generations they had been there. Both Anglo American refugees from Mexico and upper-class Mexican refugees found an easier path toward inclusion in Texas communities than the thousands of working-class Mexican refugees who were arriving each week. Many of these Mexican refugees did not speak English, were not seen as "white," and were associated with the violence of the revolution. Stereotypes about their demeanor, brutality, and susceptibility to diseases became accepted as fact among Anglo Texans.

This chapter traces how the borderland transitioned from a region fostering cultural exchange and tolerance for multicultural societies to a borderline with a nationalistic society on each side, each intolerant of the other. Through this transition, a culture of racial hatred developed among Anglo Texans that combined Mexican stereotypes, with regard to their lack of "whiteness," with the violence of the Mexican Revolution. This transition led Anglo Texans to use brutal force, mob violence, and lynching to maintain a racial order that victimized Mexican refugees in Texas as the decade continued. An examination of US families in Mexico and Mexican families in Texas demonstrates how the two maneuvered on foreign soil prior to the Mexican Revolution. Following the outbreak of the revolution, the question of loyalty presented a problem for the alien populations on both sides of the Rio Grande.

This chapter examines the Texas-Mexico borderland in four parts. First, I document the openness of the US-Mexico border from 1880 to 1900, focusing on Anglo Americans in Mexico and their relationships with Mexicans. US businesspeople and their families lived peacefully in Mexico as they invested in Mexican land and sought economic opportunities. Mormon families established colonies in Mexico to escape persecution by Anglo American nativists because of their culturally "foreign" lifestyle. Next, I identify Mexicans in Texas who found inclusion through assimilation and acceptance by Anglo Texans because of their ability to claim "whiteness." Then I examine a period of intensifying discrimination against newly arriving ethnic Mexicans on the US side of the border during the first decade of the new century. Here, I analyze how the degree of "whiteness" among Mexicans became more important as the Anglo population increased in West Texas, bringing with them Jim Crow–era practices of racial segregation that they applied to ethnic Mexicans. Finally, I illustrate the impact that the outbreak of the Mexican Revolution had on both groups attempting to cohabitate in the borderland. I show how cultural exchange and plurality along the border became stigmatized and forbidden at this time. As refugees arrived in Texas following the outbreak of the revolution, inclusion or exclusion by US citizens varied depending on their socially constructed identity: Mexicans who were once favored as immigrant laborers were now undesired refugees; Mormon exiles living in Mexican colonies for decades were now America's wayward children in need of protection; and white American expatriates were privileged in their ability to return home unhindered.

US CITIZENS IN MEXICO

The pre–Mexican Revolution borderland was an open door of exchange, and the fluidity of the border allowed for the movement of people seeking opportunity, refuge, and entertainment in Mexico. During the dictatorship of Porfirio Díaz, 1876–1910, the period known as the Porfiriato, Mexico went through a period of modernization that saw the development of a vast rail system. The network of interconnecting rail lines throughout the country linked up with US lines in places like El Paso. In 1876, railroads were still negligible, but by 1910 they stretched over more than fifteen thousand miles of the Mexican countryside. Modernization was financed through large-scale foreign investment in mining, farming, and oil exploration, which brought thousands of US businessmen and their families into Mexico.[3] By 1910, there were seventy-five thousand US citizens living in Mexico.[4] Initially, support was strong for Díaz among middle- and upper-class Mexicans, but as the economy began to suffer by the turn of the century, Díaz's middle-class support waned.

Mollie McCallick's father, Hugh, worked on the railroads in Mexico during the Porfiriato. Born in Wilkes-Barre, Pennsylvania, in 1865, he was the son of Irish immigrants Charles McCallick and Mary Rose. By his early twenties, Hugh had left Pennsylvania for a job building a rail line from Eagle Pass, Texas, to Monterrey, Nuevo León. In Eagle Pass, McCallick met Santos Peña, a Mexican woman, and in 1888 they married—Hugh was twenty-three and Santos was fifteen.[5] The two left for Mexico for the infinite financial opportunities they believed awaited their family.

The McCallick family was one of three hundred American families living in Torreón, Coahuila, in 1910. The families included both Anglo parents and families with an Anglo father and a Mexican mother like the McCallicks. Mollie McCallick described her life in Mexico with her siblings as "wonderful." They were educated in both English and Spanish. During this time, the illiteracy rate of the Mexican population was 81 percent, as opposed to 7.7 percent in the United States.[6] The McCallick children and their Anglo American friends had private tutors who taught in English in the morning and Spanish in the afternoon. It is unknown how or when, but Hugh McCallick had moved up in the company and become a manager. The family lived in a fourteen-room house with beautiful furniture and two living rooms. Mollie's mother imported all of their furniture for the master bedroom from Germany. Most impressive was the red velvet canopy bed. The exterior of the house had a garden and a lavish water fountain.[7]

The McCallick family showed the kind of upward mobility that could occur for US citizens living in Mexico during Díaz's presidency. The McCallicks enjoyed lush decor in their homes and bilingual education by tutors. Most of the men who brought their families over the border were in management, supervisory roles, or skilled positions that provided favorable living conditions.[8] In Monterrey, US laborers working for the American Smelting and Refining Company lived in substantial brick quarters built exclusively for them, while Mexican laborers of the same class lived outside of the fenced-in compound in "mud huts and shanties made out of slabs and tin cans and brush, with no floors."[9] Anglo American families lived well above the average standards in Mexico, while the masses of Mexico's poor struggled to put food on their tables.

Lucrative opportunities in Mexico were plentiful for foreigners with the wealth and means to invest in oil and real estate. San Diego, Texas, attorney William Frank Buckley moved to Mexico City during the Porfiriato with his brother Claude. Together, the two founded the firm Buckley and Buckley, which represented North American and European oil companies. The Buckley brothers made major real estate investments and profited considerably from their interests in Mexico.[10] The Díaz administration strongly encouraged foreign capitalists to come to Mexico; critics charged that these investors were exploiting poor Mexican workers.

Dr. James M. Taylor, one of the secretaries of the Board of Foreign Relations of the Methodist Church, spent several years as a Methodist missionary in Monterrey, Tampico, Mexico City, Puebla, and dozens of smaller towns. He said that prior to his initial visit to Mexico he believed the stories he had heard about the exploitation of Mexicans by foreigners. However, after living in Mexico, he argued that expatriates were actually helping the poorer class of Mexican citizens by modernizing the nation, and he even described their involvement as quasi-missionary work because of efforts to disseminate modern sanitation techniques, "better modes of living, compelling the children to go to school, and things of that kind."[11] This was a common defense made by foreigners who lived in Mexico.

Tourism was another pull factor that brought foreigners, mostly US citizens, to Mexico. Local and state governments lobbied for the building of railroads to isolated regions of the Yucatán Peninsula (as far as modern-day Cancún), in an effort to generate revenue for the government.[12] Tourism brochures circulated by the National Railways of Mexico urged foreigners to explore Mexico (fig. 1.1). Many of the brochures described Mexico as having a history as "sophisticated" as that of the ancient Egyptians and with cities that rivaled Europe's finest. One flyer described Mexico as "the Egypt of the New World" and claimed that once "the ruins of old Mexico are explored, greater discoveries will be made than those made in Egypt."[13] The captivating rhetoric targeted Anglo Americans in an effort to present Mexico in a culturally sophisticated light. The National Railways of Mexico encouraged tourists to take an entire month off and travel in first-class cabins. A March 1908 flyer described Mexico as a "Mecca for Tourists," and Mexico City tourism referred to the city as "the Paris of America" because of the city's historical parks, parades, outdoor concerts, and numerous cafés: "To no other metropolis can Mexico City be so aptly compared, yet it possesses a charm distinctly apart from that fashionable metropolis of Europe."[14] Mexico City was advertised as having a mild climate during the summer months; "even in July and August, one welcomes a blanket for bed covering."[15] Additionally, President Díaz encouraged restaurant and hotel owners to hire light-skinned Mexican workers in these high-traffic tourist locations, preferably of "Spanish and European" origin.[16] The National Railways of Mexico became the vehicle that US tourists used to explore their neighboring country, and the Mexican government under Díaz welcomed tourism as an emerging industry.[17]

Anglo Americans were comfortable visiting the neighboring country prior to the outbreak of the Mexican Revolution. Howard and Mary K. Quinn, for example, enjoyed spending their summers in Mexico when Mary was a college student during this time. Howard recalled in an interview how Mary loved Mexico and the Mexican people, and even more so the spending power of the American dollar. He described that the suite they often rented had a sitting room, an entry hall, two bedrooms, and a balcony. The Quinns felt safe traveling throughout Mexico, and Mary spent one summer studying at a Mexico City university unaccompanied. Howard asked a family friend living in Mexico to "keep an eye on her," but Mary responded that nobody could keep track of her.[18]

Border towns became Mexican attractions for Anglo Americans, who traveled across the country to El Paso with the intention of experiencing Ciudad Juárez, El Paso's "cosmopolitan" sister city. The center of town included both Mexican- and US-owned businesses. Here, visitors could experience Mexican culture, eat exotic foods, and take in a local bullfight while still enjoying familiar intoxicants—whiskey and gin. On Comercio Street in Ciudad Juárez, Jimmie O'Brien owned O'Brien's Bar and Café, where a standard drinks delivery included one hundred barrels of "American whiskey" and two hundred cases of gin—saturating the Mexican city with "American liquor." The Manhattan Café was a popular bar for American businessmen, where the slogan read: "Some spend their evenings at home but we spend ours with one foot on the rail where we can spit on the floor." However, most appealing to both Anglo American men and women was Lobby Café no. 2 in the heart of Ciudad Juárez (fig.1.2).[19] Men and women mingled in the border town, escaping from the Victorian rules and traditions that prevailed on the northern side of the border. Visitors interested in the darker side of Ciudad Juárez referred to it as an "open town," because it was easy to find a gambling establishment, a house of prostitution, or an opium den.

Social conditions in the United States also contributed to the movement of Anglo Americans to Mexico during the Porfiriato. During the late nineteenth century, Mormon families fled the United States and its territories, specifically Utah Territory, after the US Congress enacted antibigamy laws. Individual states had antibigamy laws, but in 1862 Congress enacted the

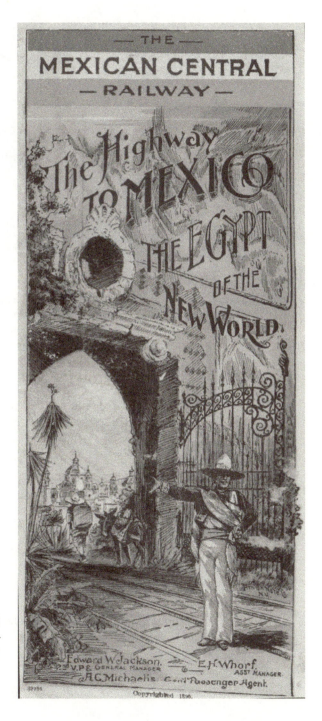

Figure 1.1 Mexican Central Railway, Russ Todd Collection, box 3, file 13, courtesy of West Texas Collection, Angelo State University, San Angelo, Texas.

Figure 1.2 Lobby Café no. 2, Russ Todd Collection, courtesy of West Texas Collection, Angelo State University, San Angelo, Texas.

Morrill Anti-Bigamy Act, which criminalized bigamy in US territories, setting the penalty at five years in prison.[20] The Morrill Act failed, however, to end the practice of plural marriage because it was too difficult to enforce. Couples were not required to file for marriage licenses in Utah Territory, and if questioned, wives were uncooperative with authorities. Mormon women, Nancy Cott has argued, believed that polygamy was "the only safeguard against adultery, prostitution, free-love and the reckless waste of pre-natal life [abortion]."[21]

In 1882 Congress passed the Edmunds Anti-Polygamy Act, making plural marriage a felony rather than a misdemeanor. Moreover, the legislation facilitated the federal government's effort to target bigamy by making bigamous cohabitation a misdemeanor. In addition to increasing the severity of the crime, the Edmunds law threatened offenders with the loss of voting rights and prohibited those convicted from ever serving on a jury or holding political office. An estimated 1,300 Mormon men were jailed as "cohabs" the following year (fig. 1.3).[22] Five years later, the Edmunds-Tucker Act added a fine of up to $800 to a polygamy conviction and dissolved the corporation

Figure 1.3 A group shot of Mormon men in prison stripes, standing in front of the Sugar House Penitentiary in Utah Territory. The prison was located in the Sugar House neighborhood of Salt Lake City. In the photograph, on the far right is John Henry Bott. Seated in the center is George Q. Cannon, who served a six-month sentence under the Edmunds-Tucker Act for having five wives. Courtesy of L. Tom Perry Special Collections, Harold B. Lee Library, Brigham Young University, Provo, Utah, MSS P-365.

of the Church of Jesus Christ of Latter-day Saints. The Edmunds-Tucker Act allowed the federal government to seize all church property valued over $50,000.[23] The LDS challenged the constitutionality of the seizure of church property only to see the US Supreme Court uphold the Edmunds-Tucker Act on May 19, 1890.[24]

John Henry Bott, the man pictured first from the right in figure 1.3, is known to have married three women. Bott married Maria Hadave Jensen on October 13, 1876. On January 1, 1880, he married Susan Reeder. Following Reeder, he married Cecelia Rasmussen. In 1885 Bott fathered a child with each woman, welcoming Brigham, Ester, and Susan into their family. In 1887, Bott fathered Charlottie, Jesse, and Mary Ellen, one with each of his three wives. Ultimately, Maria Bott gave birth to seventeen children. In total, John Henry Bott's wives gave birth to thirty children between 1877 and 1902.

The question of Utah statehood became a sensitive issue, with Protestant Americans arguing against admitting Utah into the union. The leaders of Protestant churches went so far as to say that Mormons should be barred from immigrating to "our shores," depicting them as dangerous foreigners. They also opposed Mormon missionaries, who went to Europe in search of Mormon converts to bring to the United States, many them young women from northern Europe. Mormon interest in Europe began as early as 1840, when Brigham Young and four of his colleagues traveled to England to spread their faith. That country was in the midst of a depression, and "government authorities had recommended migration to America."[25] During their year abroad, Young and his companions successfully converted more than eight thousand people to Mormonism, and many women converts returned as Mormon wives to the United States.[26] The church creed stated, "Increase and multiply, and raise up a generation unto the Lord."[27] Heber Chase Kimball, one of the original twelve Mormon apostles, went so far as to scold missionaries for marrying the foreign women before returning to the United States. He claimed, "The brother missionaries have been in the habit of picking out the prettiest women for themselves before they get here, and bringing on the ugly ones for us; hereafter you have to bring them all here before taking any of them, and let us all have a fair shake."[28] The *New York Times* reported that Kimball "offered a father a yoke of oxen and a wagon for a sixteen-year-old girl."[29] Critics of these missions and of polygamy argued that these women were similar to slaves, and one unidentified daughter of Brigham Young told a *New York Times* reporter, "If Salt Lake City was roofed over, it would be the biggest whore house in the world."[30]

International pressure fueled immigration concerns. By the late 1880s British newspapers began reporting stories of Englishwomen being lured by American Mormon missionaries back to Utah. One of these women, Elizabeth Rutter, told a terrible story about women being brought to Utah under false pretenses and subjected "to fearful indignities . . . by the elders." Rutter escaped and made a four-day trip from Ogden, Utah, to Chicago without anything to eat or drink, and was found by authorities lying on a street unconscious.[31] British officials likened what Mormon missionaries were doing in Europe to slave trafficking. Stories circulated in the papers estimating that "an average of

3,500 girls, most of whom are English and Swedish, leave Liverpool annually for Utah," often describing the church as a "cult" that allegedly went from house to house offering money to bribe the girls to emigrate.[32]

In their *1890 Manifesto*, the LDS bowed to antipolygamy pressure and officially banned the practice of plural marriage. Although individual Mormons practiced polygamy well into the twentieth century, it was no longer official church policy. In a Protestant Episcopal paper, *Standard and the Church*, published in Philadelphia, a writer argued that Mormons were only pretending to outlaw polygamy in order gain statehood for Utah and that Mormon judges and Mormon juries would not enforce the law. The author argued that "Gentile Americans" would be outcasts in a Utah state and likened the idea of Protestant Americans living in Utah to that of abolitionists in antebellum days living in the South.[33] By prohibiting Mormon missionaries from foreign recruitment and rigorously enforcing the Edmunds Act, the author argued, "Utah, in time, will accumulate a sufficient Gentile American population to outvote the Mormon adherents. Then, and not till then, will it be safe to consider the matter of statehood for Utah."[34] Federal pressure on the Mormon Church and anti-Mormonism by nativists made expatriation to Mexico an appealing alternative.

Mormon interest in Mexico began in the 1870s when Brigham Young began sending Mormon missions there. Their goal was to spread their faith to the indigenous population—specifically the Yaqui Indians.[35] The Mormon missions that arrived in Mexico in the 1870s were successful in spreading the word of the LDS, and they informed Mormon communities in western US territories of their general acceptance in Mexico, leading many Mormon families to seek refuge there. By 1910 there were more than four thousand American Mormons living in nine colonies: six in Chihuahua and three in Sonora. Their influx brought a new religion into the country that reached as far inland as Mexico City.[36]

Memoirs and journals by Mormon exiles detail stories of hardship during the early years of expatriation.[37] Many colonies were twenty to thirty miles from the nearest town, and resources were scarce. Colonists endured a hot, dry climate in some regions while they searched for a location with fertile soil and fresh water. Mary Ann Black recalls finding one such location in Cove Valley and quickly abandoning it when the community realized that they were outnumbered by rattlesnakes.[38] Thomas Cottam Romney was a teenager in the late 1880s when his family left Utah for Colonia Juárez in Chihuahua. Romney later wrote that their homes were adobe-style buildings with dirt roofs and dirt floors. Most Mormon boys attended school no more than three months of the year, rarely reaching the eighth grade. Romney described how they went months without white flour and that his diet consisted of redroots and pig-weed—commonly used today by farmers as pig fodder. When the plant grows to full maturity it becomes less edible, forcing Romney's mother to serve alfalfa as the family's principal meal. After several attempts to adapt to this diet, Rom-ney declared that he had "no objection to competing with pigs in the consump-tion of weeds, but in eating of alfalfa I must draw the line."[39] His dissatisfaction went beyond the living conditions: "Worst of all," he wrote, "our neighbors for miles around were Mexicans—a people, up to this time, whom I profoundly disliked."[40] Romney, like most Mormon refugees, considered himself a US citizen and white, doubly different from the dark Mexicans.

Nelle S. Hatch moved to Colonia Juárez as a young girl and was twenty-three years old when the Mexican Revolution began. Hatch helped to care for George Romney, son of Gaskel and Annie Romney, relatives of Thomas Rom-ney. When she played with the Mormon children, she was instructed to keep them separated from the Mexican children. When asked if she ever dated Mexican boys, she replied that it was never officially prohibited because Mor-mon girls never desired to do so on their own—"Why should they? There were plenty of white boys. Why become a poor Mexican?"[41] Thomas Romney's dis-like of Mexicans was not shared by all Mormon exiles. In memoirs and jour-nals, these men and women recalled a satisfaction with their new compatriots because of the religious freedom they found in Mexico. Protestants and Catho-lics in Mexico objected to the practice of polygamy, but with nowhere near the size and scope of the persecution they had endured in the United States.

Some Mormon families welcomed Mexican converts into their communi-ties. Manrique González, who fled peonage conditions on a hacienda north of Mexico City, found refuge in the Mormon colony of Colonia Juárez. Mor-mon families raised the young Mexican boy in their community and edu-cated him through high school. At the age of sixteen he was baptized and became a member of the LDS. Hatch reminisced about the spiritual moment:

I'll never forget the day, it was so important to us. As soon as they are baptized, then they're confirmed and made members of the church. In the meeting where that happened, we had an old patriarch there who stood up and spoke in tongues, and had us all spellbound. . . . He told him [González] what an influence he was going to be among his own people.[42]

González's conversion changed his religious identity, which superseded his ethnic identity, allowing him to gain acceptance in the community.

After high school, González married a white Mormon girl and went to college in Logan, Utah. When he graduated, the LDS wanted González to help them spread their faith to ethnic Mexicans living in the United States and abroad. Church officials were impressed with how well he assimilated into their "white" world, and in deciding where he would settle down, they remarked, "Why, we can place you anyplace. We can put you any one of six places when you get through here [college]."[43] However, this was not the case. After five job placement rejections in the United States, he met with a sixth and final Mormon employer who had no intention of hiring him. On that occasion, González remarked, "You don't need to tell me . . . I know why they don't hire me, I'm a Mexican."[44] González left Utah with his family and settled in New Mexico; he believed that inclusion in the ethnic Mexican community there would be much easier to achieve. However, both Protestants Anglos and Catholic Mexican Americans took issue with his Mormon faith and once again ostracized his family. Unable to bear this discrimination, Gomez's white wife left him and moved with their seven children to a Mormon colony in Arizona. After their departure, González wrote in his diary: "Well, I've been denied a position once because of my race and another one because of my religion. I think I'll go back to Mexico, where I came from."[45] The Mormon families who lived in Mexico and had introduced their faith to González were more accepting of cultural exchange, possibly because they were on the fringes of society or because of a strong desire to convert the Mexican boy to their faith. In their Mexican colony González was accepted because he assimilated into their world, but the greater "white" Mormon world was not as accepting of the young Mexican Mormon, especially after the turn of the century as racial lines throughout the United States hardened.

MEXICANS IN TEXAS

Mexicans in Texas made up a highly diversified group. Those from the wealthier class found inclusion much easier than the poor did, especially those of Spanish descent and "whiter" in appearance. These upper-class Mexicans chose assimilation as a necessary step toward inclusion. Anglo Texans began to exclude poor Mexican Americans and Mexican immigrants as the southern segregation system of Jim Crow, or Juan Crow, was established in Texas and applied to ethnic Mexicans. There was a tension among Anglos in Texas between those who sought to assimilate and those who sought to segregate ethnic Mexicans in their state. Inclusion or exclusion by Anglo Texans depended on multiple factors including skin color, class standing, and the ability to speak English.

In Texas, Anglo Americans grouped Mexicans with African Americans near the bottom of the racial hierarchy. This racial order ranked working-class Mexicans, referred to as "peons," at the bottom. Derived from "peonage," the word "peon" described a lower-class Mexican worker, subjugated by Anglo society and hired to do work that was "beneath" whites. Additionally, the word "greaser" was commonly used to identify poor Mexicans. It also had its origin in the mid-nineteenth century. Historian Arnoldo De León explained that the term most likely arose from an effort to link Mexican skin color to the color of grease and to the filth associated with dirt.[46]

In Mexico, Mexicans were grouped into three main categories: European in origin, mestizo, and Indian. At the top of the social hierarchy was the European stock, which usually had Spanish heritage and mixed little with Indians; they represented less than 15 percent of the country by the turn of the century. The mestizos, with a mixture of Spanish and Indian blood, constituted the largest group, making up over half of the population. The remaining 35 percent of the population was Indian.[47] When US employers sought laborers, a vast majority of the recruits who came to work in mining, agriculture, and railroads were mestizos.

The color line separating Anglos and Mexicans in Texas was complex because it was based not only on skin tone but also on class standing. Manuel Gamio was one of the first to examine the color line between Anglos and Mexicans in the 1930s. According to Gamio, Anglos in Texas accepted Mexicans into their communities only when they possessed a light skin color and a high class standing. Darker-skinned Mexicans experienced the same degree of "restrictions as the Negro, while a person of medium-dark skin can enter a second-class lunchroom frequented also by [white] Americans of the poorer class."[48] A Mexican of "light brown skin" could not enter a high-class hotel, but "a white cultured Mexican [would] be freely admitted to the same hotel, especially if he [spoke] English fluently."[49] The treatment of Mexicans by Anglo Texans differed from the treatment of African Americans, all of whom were completely excluded from all-white establishments. However, the willingness of Anglo Texans to assimilate light-skinned and higher-class

Mexicans into Anglo society declined somewhat over time, and a preference for segregation increased.

Fair-skinned, wealthy, upper-class, English-speaking Mexican immigrants found inclusion into Anglo society. Many of these men and women were tied closely to US business investors in Mexico and moved to the United States as the Mexican economy declined near the end of the nineteenth century. Assimilation was not necessarily forced on these light-skinned Mexicans claiming Spanish heritage as much as it was embraced by them. Such was the case with Mexican immigrant José Robles, who had light-brown hair and light-brown eyes. Robles arrived in Texas with his wealthy Mexican parents as a teenager. In Dallas he studied English and enrolled in a local business college. He eventually met a German American girl, and the two were married in a Baptist church. Regarding assimilation, he stated, "I am now following American customs in everything that I can. . . . My wife prepares my food and even though she is German she learned to cook American Style."[50] Robles and his wife found that assimilation helped them maintain a level of acceptance among Texans, who considered them to be "white."

Upper-class Mexican women who displayed "white" attributes found relatively easy entry into Anglo Texan society. Ruhe López, a native of Mazatlán, Sinaloa, was the daughter of a Spanish woman and Austrian man. Before her arrival in Texas, her father owned a prominent hotel that permitted only "Europeans, Americans, and prominent persons in Mexico." She studied English, and at the age of seventeen her father introduced her to an Anglo American mining engineer staying at the establishment whom she later married.[51] Upper-class Mexicans of Spanish descent believed that they were white; by quickly demonstrating American cultural characteristics following their arrival, they found inclusion into Texas communities much more easily than working-class Mexican immigrants.

Anglo Texans believed in the importance of acculturation as a necessary step to possible inclusion into the dominant society. To discourage affluent ethnic Mexicans from reading Spanish-language newspapers from Mexico, Texas presses began printing editions of their own daily papers in Spanish. The *El Paso Morning Times* learned the importance of employing a native Spanish speaker as its translator when the paper ran an ad for a clearance sale at the City of Mexico Store that read "Gran Venta de Deficación" instead of "Gran Venta de Evacuación." The former announced, "Big Sale of Shit."[52] In the borderland region of Texas and Mexico, assimilation into US culture occurred on both sides of the border. On the Mexican side, the so-called *fronterizos*, those living in northern Mexican communities, were seen by Mexicans in central Mexico as having assimilated into Anglo American culture.

From 1880 to 1900 the population of Texas almost doubled from 1,591,749 to 3,048,710. During the same twenty-year period, Mexican laborers arrived in unprecedented numbers: the Mexican-born national population in Texas increased from an estimated 43,000 to over 70,000. By 1910 the population of ethnic Mexicans in Texas reached 367,000, with 125,000 of them being Mexican-born nationals.[53] Mexican immigrants to the United States fared better when they settled into already established communities, many of which had been part of Mexico before 1848 and of Spain before that.

The West Texas town of San Angelo is a community with a Spanish-Mexican history. Prior to European arrival, Jumano Indians inhabited large parts of the region. In 1632 a Spanish mission led by Friars Juan de Ortega and Juan de Salas arrived in the region. The Jumanos eventually integrated into the Apache and Comanche tribes after disease and warfare had decimated their population by the late eighteenth century. Anglo American settlers began arriving in the region in the 1860s, and they clashed violently with Native Americans. The US Army soon arrived and established military forts to provide protection for the settlers. San Angelo was first established as a town to serve the needs of Fort Concho, built along the Concho River in 1867. With an abundance of water and plenty of liquor, sex, and gambling, it had become indispensable to the 450 soldiers posted at Fort Concho by 1875.[54] Bartholomew DeWitt officially established nearby Santa Angela as a trading post in 1883, the name memorializing his late wife, Angela. It quickly became a West Texas center for farming and ranching. In 1888 the Santa Fe Railroad arrived, making the town a fast-growing center for shipping as well.[55]

Tejanos who had lived in Texas for decades were not necessarily welcomed into Anglo circles, but some factors led to better relations between the two groups. Some of the Tejano men spoke English, were educated, and had fought for the Confederacy in the Civil War. Those who were bilingual could more easily maneuver through Anglo society. In 1888 a group of Tejano men organized the Juntá Patriotica, the first Mexican patriotic organization in San Angelo. Their goal was to establish a civic group that would honor Mexican Independence Day on the sixteenth of each September.[56] Manuel Trevino was the secretary of the organization and kept detailed notes of its plans for the festivities, as well as a list of the group's official members. Their first meeting was conducted at the office of the justice of the peace, Charles E.

Dubois. The chairman of the organization, Zenon Ramírez, reported that a great number of Tejanos were in attendance to discuss the celebration. The records list the following officers of the committee: Froilan Guerra, president; Manuel Trevino, secretary; Felipe Alderete, treasurer; and Felix Flores, sergeant at arms.[57]

Forty men and three women pledged a total of fifty-six dollars to pay for the upcoming festival.[58] The celebration was open to everyone in San Angelo. Twenty-two-year-old Froilan Guerra, a photographer who had immigrated earlier that year and was fluent in written and spoken English, became the organization's president.[59] Fifty-eight-year-old Felix Flores, the sergeant at arms, was a Tejano farmer who spoke only Spanish and could neither read nor write. Yet Flores had fought in the Confederate Army as private in the Thirty-Sixth Regiment, Texas Cavalry, which had engaged in combat during the Red River Campaign battles at Mansfield and Pleasant Hill.[60]

The festivities began on Friday evening, September 14, 1888, at 10:00 p.m., with bands playing traditional Mexican music in the center of town. At 11:45 p.m., Trevino read the *acta de independencia* to the crowd in Spanish. After the short oration, the band played music until 12:30 a.m., packed up for the night, and reconvened after sunrise. The committee organized a parade honoring the flags of both the United States and Mexico, which concluded in the town park, where a barbeque awaited local residents. The most important part of the celebration began around 4:00 p.m. when Guerra welcomed guest speaker Rafael Duarte, who, sixty years earlier, had fought as a teenager against Spain in the Mexican war for independence. Following their speeches, numerous other ethnic Mexicans came to the podium to speak proudly of their love for Mexico and the importance of honoring the sixteenth of September. Music played and dancing went on throughout the night. Flores was responsible for the evening's refreshments—beer, cigars, and fruit.[61]

Trevino not only helped organize the celebration, he also helped create San Angelo's Mexican Dramatic Company. On January 18, 1896, the *San Angelo Standard* published a favorable review of one of the company's first performances, *In the Hilt of the Sword*. The *Standard* described the performance as a Mexican opera infused with humor. The report praised the acting ability of the local Tejano performers, male and female.[62] The existence of this organization demonstrates that a more culturally sophisticated Tejano community had emerged in rural West Texas by the late nineteenth century. These productions featured large casts and elaborate costumes (fig. 1.4) and

THE ACTORS IN FULL COSTUME, EXCEPT THAT THE DEVILS ARE WITHOUT THEIR MASKS

Figure 1.4 Mexican Actors in Full Costume, Arnoldo De León Collection, box 3, file 16, Photos of Hispanic Influence in San Angelo, courtesy of West Texas Collection, Angelo State University, San Angelo, Texas.

were well received in the Anglo parts of town. *In the Hilt of the Sword* was performed at the Pickwick Theater in the center of town on the same stage as Anglo performances. The *Standard*'s reviewer marveled at the lavish costumes and noted that the play was a financial success.[63] Most importantly, the reviewer reported that the play "indicated the high degree of intelligence of our Mexican friends."[64] The audience likely included sizeable numbers of local Anglos, one sign of how well the Anglo and Tejano communities had accommodated themselves to each other and how willing they were to cross cultural borders. This cultural openness would not survive long into the twentieth century.

Juntá Patriotica was the first ethnic Mexican civic organization in San Angelo. Other organizations, like the theater group, formed thereafter. After the turn of the century, new organizations appeared, including the Club Latino Americano (1906), which aimed to celebrate Mexican heritage and provide a physical location in San Angelo exclusively for ethnic Mexican social entertainment. Ethnic Mexican organizations began to meet exclusively in the Mexican district in town. In their inaugural celebration, the forty-member Club Latino Americano hosted an event honoring the memory of don Benito Juárez, a former president of Mexico who had resisted the French occupation of his country. According to the *San Angelo Standard*, the group was "made up of the best class of the Mexican citizenship of this city." Invitations were sent to more than three hundred people for an event that included dancing and patriotic speeches.[65] Also in 1906 the Spanish-speaking citizens of San Angelo gained enough of a presence to attract the attention of Amado Gutiérrez, the publisher of *El Liberal*, a Spanish paper in Del Rio, Texas; Gutiérrez announced plans to issue a weekly version of the paper in San Angelo.[66]

After the official establishment of San Angelo in 1883, ethnic Mexican families moved to the town and began working on the neighboring ranches and farms. These families organized a school for their children in the early 1880s. In 1886 as many as sixty children attended the ethnic Mexican school. A reporter for the *San Angelo Standard* made an unannounced visit to the school during the winter of 1886, unsure of what he would find. He reported that, to his surprise, the ethnic Mexican children were "very bright"; all of the students from the oldest to the youngest were put through a series of intellectual "exercises" to demonstrate their ability.[67] He wrote that "they looked neat, clean, and happy" and that they demonstrated an eagerness to learn English and "American methods."[68] The students were learning English and following daily routines that were similar to those of Anglo children; they were assimilating at a young age.

By the turn of the century, the openness of the border had allowed many Mexican workers to seek better employment in the United States; many found communities like San Angelo an appealing place to live. Historian George J. Sánchez examined the economic push-and-pull factors that influenced this mass movement and illustrated how the main railroad lines in Mexico served as a vehicle for migration. Mexican laborers sought better-paying jobs in the United States, where they could earn "between $1 to $2 a day" in railroad and agricultural positions as opposed to the "12 cents a day paid on several of the rural haciendas."[69]

Labor recruiters from the United States traveled south on the central railroad deep into Mexico for recruitment purposes.[70] The press questioned this tactic of seeking foreigners for employment in the United States. A *Dallas*

Morning News article raised the question, "Who pays the fare of the hundreds of Mexican peon laborers that continually come into the United States?" The article pointed out that "the average peon seldom accumulates more than $5, but these Mexicans are coming in droves from the interior of the southern republic on tickets that cost as high as $20."[71] The railroads that carried investors, businessmen, and their families into central Mexico now became a vehicle for the recruitment and movement of Mexicans into Texas. Migration increased as the cost of living in Mexico began to rise while wages remained low. As the movement of Mexican immigrants into Texas increased, Anglo Texans grew less tolerant of ethnic Mexicans already in their midst, especially those who celebrated their ancestry. By 1900 a shift in a preference advocating the segregation of Mexicans occurred among Anglos in Texas.

The population of San Angelo grew quickly due to the sheep and cattle industries, with sheep shearing providing work for many working-class Mexicans in the town (fig. 1.5).[72] Some areas of town soon became segregated districts; the north side near the railroad tracks became known as the Santa Fe barrio. Isolation within a barrio encouraged ethnic Mexicans to live in the manner to which they were accustomed in Mexico and to preserve their culture, customs, and traditions. However, living conditions for ethnic Mexicans were primitive in the early days of settlement (fig. 1.6). And as the Anglo population grew, brick buildings largely replaced wooden ones for the Anglo residents by 1900, and the disparity in living conditions between Anglos and Mexicans became more apparent. San Angelo's population grew from 4,510 in 1890 to 10,321 in 1910. With the arrival of more Anglo settlers, the ethnic Mexican presence decreased from 40 percent of the city population in 1890 to 7 percent in 1910.[73]

Texas as a whole became more difficult as an environment for ethnic Mexicans. Increasingly, the poorest ethnic Mexicans were discriminated against and confined to poorer neighborhoods.[74] It became impossible for migrant workers and the illiterate to assimilate or otherwise be included in the growing Anglo population. Their fears deepened as, despite the shifting demographics that began favoring large Anglo majorities in some towns like San Angelo, thousands of single Mexican laborers nevertheless arrived in Texas looking for work. These newcomers were dark, poor, and without the anchor that families offered. If they could not be kept out, they had to be kept separate from the white population. Anglo Texans believed in the importance of segregating poor ethnic Mexicans from Anglo Texans, and some of the first examples of official segregation involved schools.

Figure 1.5 Sheep Shearing, Arnoldo De León Collection, box 3, file 16, Photos of Hispanic Influence in San Angelo, courtesy of West Texas Collection, Angelo State University, San Angelo, Texas.

"JUAN CROW" IN TEXAS

The segregation of ethnic Mexicans in Texas occurred as early as the late nineteenth century. Initially, segregation appeared in residential districts of Texas cities—which featured an African American section of town, a Mexican quarter, and the remaining area for the white population. By the late nineteenth century, ethnic Mexicans were encountering segregation in public institutions such as schools, restaurants, and hotels. Schools began following Jim Crow practices in most Texas cities by dividing into all-Mexican, all-black, and all-white schools. By the early twentieth century, Anglo businesses posted signs with such warnings as: "No Mexicans and Dogs Allowed."[75] Anglo Texans redoubled their efforts to segregate those seen as nonwhite. Mexican Americans in Texas were especially offended. Their determination to protest inclined them to emphasize the "American" dimension of their identity rather than the "Mexican" dimension. They also emphasized that they were white by US law. Thus Anglos in Texas had no right to impose segregationist ordinances and practices upon them.

At the turn of the twentieth century, "whiteness" in Texas was not

Figure 1.6 *Views of the Concho Country*, Arnoldo De León Collection, box 3, file 16, Photos of Hispanic Influence in San Angelo, courtesy of West Texas Collection, Angelo State University, San Angelo, Texas.

ultimately determined just by the color of one's skin but rather by a formula derived from a medley of categories regarding one's race, ancestry, and cultural characteristics and from the vagaries of American law. By most Anglo standards, Mexicans were found to be nonwhite. In one respect, however, they had an exceptionally strong case to be considered white. The Treaty of Guadalupe Hidalgo (1848) declared that Mexican citizens who found themselves on the US side of the border following annexation had the option to remain in the country and become US citizens. At the same time, US naturalization law declared that anyone born on foreign soil desiring to become a citizen had to be free and white. Thus, if Mexicans were declared eligible for citizenship by the Treaty of Guadalupe Hidalgo, then they must be white—at least by law. This is exactly what a US federal court ruled in 1897.[76] Ethnic Mexicans lost no time declaring that their eligibility for US citizenship and their whiteness rendered segregation measures passed against them inappropriate and illegal. This meant that Anglo Texans had to find a nonracial basis and justification for segregating Mexicans.

In 1893 Texas enacted the Public Free Schools Act, which allowed for the segregation of children in public schools based on their race and color. The act defined "colored" as being "of mixed blood descended from Negro ancestry."[77] By this definition under the law, Mexicans were considered "white." Anglos, however, were simultaneously pursuing the segregation of Mexican children on linguistic grounds: Spanish-speaking immigrant children had to attend separate schools to help them learn English without holding back English-speaking children. Texas passed English-only laws in 1893 and 1905, targeting not only Mexican children but also the arrival of large numbers of new immigrants from eastern and southern Europe. The new laws provided guidelines for the proper use of English in the classroom: "All lessons, instructions, recitations, songs, etc., were to be conducted in English."[78] The rationale for separating Mexican and white children also extended to economics: proponents argued that Mexican children needed separate schools in order to cater to the seasonal labor needs of migrant families. Segregationists claimed that Mexican children reached puberty sooner than Anglo American children, another reason why they had to be kept separate from white children.[79] All of this contributed to the widespread segregation of Mexican children and subjected them to the many difficulties associated with segregation: poor facilities, poor resources, and fewer teachers.

Throughout the state of Texas, Mexican schools were often the last to open and the first to close. Attendance at the beginning of the fall term usually lagged behind that of the winter months as young boys worked in seasonal positions with their brothers, fathers, and uncles. From Galveston to El Paso, segregated schools had many deficiencies relative to their Anglo counterparts. In Kerr County, a heavily German American region, both Mexican and German American students attended the same schools in 1902–1903, but Mexican students were restricted to a single building.[80] In Lockhart, school boards allocated funds for the following improvements: a general overall improvement to the Anglo high school, a second room for the Mexican school, and "the negro building [to] be worked on later in the season."[81] The additional room for the Mexican school improved the facility from the previous school year, when the city of Lockhart had failed to hire a teacher for the Mexican children until well into November.[82] In Alpine, town administrators segregated Mexican children as early as 1910 when they erected the Madero Ward School, an all-Mexican school on the corner of West Avenue G and South Tenth Street.

In San Angelo, as a revolution brewed south of the border, ethnic Mexican families organized to challenge the segregated educational system of their community. The segregation of ethnic Mexican children began there in the 1880s, primarily for the Mexican children who could not read or write English. Over time, as the state implemented the English-only laws in the schools, Mexican families attempted to send their children to the white schools and were met with resistance. School districts like San Angelo applied the same restrictions to Mexican students as to black students. School officials argued that segregation began as a way to provide Spanish-speaking Mexican children with an opportunity to learn English without interfering with the education of English-speaking children. However, over time, the segregation of Mexican children became the unwritten rule in San Angelo and much of Texas for linguistic and ethnic-racial reasons.

Few historians have examined school desegregation efforts by ethnic Mexicans in the Southwest during the early twentieth century.[83] The San Angelo protest of 1910 successfully brought awareness to ethnic Mexican communities across the state that the practice of unequal education of their children should not be tolerated. These men and women fought the segregation of Mexican children in San Angelo on their own, without the support of a national civil rights group. This may have been the first Mexican American civil rights challenge to segregation in the schools, in Texas and nationwide.

On June 7, 1910, the Mexican population of San Angelo, represented by an attorney and a committee of four, began its protest against the inequality of the local school system by formally addressing the school board. Representatives of the Mexican community presented a formal application requesting that the board either integrate the Mexican children of San Angelo into the all-white classrooms or relocate the students to some section of the main white building. They demanded that the Mexican children be educated on the same physical grounds as whites. The group of parents prepared for two weeks and hired attorney J. P. Dumas of the Anderson and Dumas law firm to represent them. The San Angelo School Board recognized that the Mexican school facility was unsatisfactory, "and that in the future the Mexican children will have public school facilities equal to the white schools."[84] But school board chairman Sam Crowther also stated that the children should not integrate. The board was unanimous in its opposition to "placing the two races on the same playgrounds."[85]

The board believed that they met the demands with an acceptable compromise by promising to move the Mexican children to a better facility—an abandoned building once used to school Anglo children. They believed that

Mexican parents would not press any further. What the board did not understand was that the protest was not merely a spontaneous reaction but rather a calculated plan with a sophisticated fiscal argument. Months earlier, Patrick Dooley, an enumerator for the 1910 census, encountered stubborn protest while gathering population data. Several Mexican parents withheld the names of their school-aged children "claiming that they did not receive the benefit of the Mexican apportionment."[86] They believed that withholding the names and number of children in their families from the census taker would be a silent protest—the additional head count of Mexican children provided the San Angelo School District with additional money for the school system, which would most likely benefit only the all-white facility. Perhaps the white school board would notice the drop in school district funds, and, in an effort to recover those funds, address Mexican school grievances. This information was brought to the school board's attention and appears to be the reason that it quickly agreed to improvements of the Mexican school. One week after the meeting, the *San Angelo Standard* announced that the 1910 census would be retaken in the Mexican portion of the city. As a result, the original number of 154 Mexican children increased to 200. The successful maneuver initially reduced the amount of state funding the city of San Angelo received for operating public schools, a financial burden for the school board and a strong statement that the Mexican families were no longer going to cooperate with Juan Crow.[87] Based on these new numbers and the demands of the Mexican parents, the board selected new teachers for the Mexican students and promised that they would soon make a decision regarding a new location for the school. Ten days after the formal protest, the members of the board believed that the issues regarding the Mexican school were settled.[88]

The Mexican families rejected the offer and called an emergency meeting for the following Sunday at Turn Verien Hall. An estimated three hundred Mexican men, women, and children met and listened to Florentino Muñoz, chairman of the Mexican committee, deliver a speech urging them to boycott the Mexican school. One after another, participants joined Muñoz at the podium and delivered enthusiastic speeches about their rights under the law and how they intended to secure those rights. Most importantly, they agreed not to accept the board's decision: "We repudiate the school board's offer and demand our rights."[89] The families did not want yet another abandoned building that had once schooled Anglo children; they wanted integration, because they believed that the Anglo students had better teachers and facilities. Some of the speeches were in English, while others were delivered in

Spanish. The diverse group included all classes of ethnic Mexicans living in San Angelo—skilled workers, unskilled workers, sheepherders, and some of the wealthiest members of the city.[90]

Attorneys for the Mexican families informed school board chairman Sam Crowther that they were prepared to mount a legal challenge that would cost the city dearly. Crowther was unrelenting, arguing that he had offered the Mexican families "a square deal" but warned that "we will not think for one moment of admitting them into the white schools and thus demoralizing our entire school system. I won't do it and it won't be done."[91] Mayor Joseph D. Hassell supported the decision: "I want to say right here that I am strictly in favor of their action and were I in Mr. Crowther's position, I would follow in his footsteps exactly and see that the Mexicans are not admitted into the white schools. Such a move would be absolutely a lightning strike to our school system as it stands and demoralize it altogether."[92] Hassell, a Democrat, was born in Hamburg Landing, Tennessee, in 1863. Both his maternal and paternal extended families were planters and slaveholders. Hassell's father had been a soldier in the Confederate Army and spent the final eleven months of the Civil War as a federal prisoner at Camp Morton in Indianapolis. Following the war, his family lost everything and suffered greatly. As a young man, Joseph Hassell heard stories about the prosperity of his family before the Civil War. His family left its Tennessee home in 1886 when Joseph was a child, loaded up a wagon drawn by oxen with all of their remaining possessions, and migrated to North Texas. Hassell was educated in an all-white school and matured during the Jim Crow era in which "separate but equal" was the status quo; he viewed Mexicans as nonwhite.[93] The Hassell family believed that the integration of the races had destroyed their life in the Old South.

By late June 1910 it appeared that the Mexican community of San Angelo was ready to challenge the Anglo-imposed social order—a dangerous thing to do in the early twentieth century. Muñoz, the most vocal leader of the group, declared, "We have the right to put our children in the white schools and we are going to do it if we have to go to the highest authorities in the state."[94] Talk of a mass meeting of the white community of San Angelo began in early June. Crowther invited "every loyal citizen of San Angelo" to attend.[95] The San Angelo Standard urged "the white citizens of San Angelo to endorse the action of and support the school board in whatsoever manner it may be deemed best." The article included a subtle threat to Mexican readers: "It is murmured quietly that if the Mexicans do not come to an agreement . . . stringent methods will be brought into action."[96]

The Mexican committee in San Angelo was successful in getting the attention of local government leaders and, at the very least, demonstrated a willingness to fight racial inequality in the public schools. Their protest and resistance demonstrates that Mexicans in San Angelo believed that, as US citizens, they had the right to send their children to attend school with Anglo children. Moreover, they used all available resources to protest inequality. When classes began in the fall of 1910, two students attended the Mexican school; in a bold display of protest, seven other Mexican pupils marched up to the North Ward white school and attempted to register for classes but were refused entry. The school board, determined to demonstrate the workability of Juan Crow at all costs, had to maintain a separate facility for the Mexican pupils and pay the salary for a teacher who only taught a few students.[97]

The *San Angelo Standard* reported that many of the Mexican families who boycotted the public school enrolled their children in the local Catholic school, the Immaculate Conception Academy. Academy officials separated the white children from the Mexican children and provided different teachers to the two groups. This appeared to be an improvement in the eyes of the Mexican families, because at least their children attended school on the same grounds as white children. However, rumors quickly spread throughout San Angelo that white children mingled with Mexican children at the academy. In an official statement, academy administrators reported that these rumors were unfounded. The mother superior confirmed this when she declared, "The Mexican children have never been taught in the same room with whites and they never will."[98]

The reaction of the school board reveals how Anglo Texans perceived Mexicans as nonwhite. The Mexican committee followed through on its threats to take the school debate to a higher authority in the state; as a result, this became, for a short time, a question with international ramifications. Muñoz appealed to the Mexican consul in San Antonio, Enrique Ornelas, for advice on how he should proceed with his fight against the school board. Muñoz stated, "We think we are in the right and are going to stand up for entrance into the white schools."[99]

Ornelas was aware of a similar situation in San Francisco with Japanese schoolchildren. Nativists in California convinced the San Francisco School Board in 1905 to segregate Japanese children from white children. Chinese laborers had been barred from immigrating since the passage of the 1882 Chinese Exclusion Act, and nativists were arguing for the exclusion of Japanese laborers as well. The incident became a foreign relations concern between the United States and Japan. Historian Gary Gerstle explains that President Theodore Roosevelt viewed Japan in higher regard than China and other Asian nations. Gerstle explains that Roosevelt was impressed with Japanese success in foreign market competition and territorial expansion, and with the country's victory in the Russo-Japanese War of 1905. Roosevelt negotiated a resolution to end the international controversy. The Gentlemen's Agreement of 1907 restricted the immigration of Japanese laborers to appease the nativists but required the San Francisco School Board to end its policy of segregating Japanese schoolchildren.[100]

From his posting in San Antonio, Ornelas was determined to stir the diplomatic pot, so to speak, by making the San Angelo school segregation topic one of international importance in Mexico and the United States. Ornelas took up the matter with the government of Mexico, Texas governor Thomas Campbell, and President William Howard Taft. "The dispute," the *San Antonio Light* reported, "promises to become as serious and important as when California excluded the Japanese."[101] It would appear that Ornelas had the upper hand, since a precedent had been set in the Gentlemen's Agreement halting the segregation of children of foreign-born parents. Ornelas stated, "I believe the San Angelo board to be clearly in the wrong. . . . The Mexicans pay taxes to the state, county, and municipalities and their children are entitled to the same educational advantages as the children of Anglo American parents."[102] Unfortunately for the families fighting the school board, the Mexican government had no grounds for appeal to the United States because an earlier petition by Muñoz, the head of the Mexican committee in San Angelo, argued that every signatory was a legalized voter in Texas and "to all intents and purposes American citizens."[103] Muñoz attempted to recant the previous statement, but the damage had already been done. Diplomacy could not help with the Mexican fight for desegregation because it appeared that the protestors had renounced their Mexican citizenship.

The San Angelo school protest made headlines across the state, and families continued their protest beyond 1910; Mexican organizations in other Texas cities were encouraged to raise the issue of segregated education. In 1911 Mexicans in Laredo organized to protest the segregation of Mexicans from Anglo children in their public schools. The local Mexican group there, the Congreso Mexicanista, was more interested in discussing the education debate than planning for the September sixteenth festivities. Outlining six grievances with the local school board, the group stated that its number one

priority and the priority of Mexicans across the state should be the "education of the Mexican children in the state of Texas." The Congreso Mexicanista threw down the gauntlet to Anglo Texan authorities: "Is it, or is it not our
duty to protect against exclusive schools for Mexican children, wherein they
are separated from the American children?" Citizens concluded their meeting with a few remarks about the admission of other foreign children in
Texas schools, thus questioning the legality of prohibiting Mexican American children from attending the same schools.[104]

The case of education in San Angelo provides an example of how Anglo
Texans viewed ethnic Mexicans, and how ethnic Mexicans viewed themselves as American citizens with civil rights. The *San Angelo Standard*
reported how the local ethnic Mexican population protested segregation
while maintaining a desire for peace in their city. An anonymous ethnic
Mexican stated to a reporter, "I am a Mexican by blood, but by birth I am an
American, and I want to see things peaceful in San Angelo."[105] However, the
racial hierarchy in Texas did not permit integrated education. Anglo Texans
viewed ethnic Mexicans as poor, prone to disease, primitive in their living
conditions, and dangerous. It is unlikely that a Mexican government, even if
it took a close interest in the events in San Angelo, would have produced a
different outcome for Mexicans living in the United States. As San Angelo
Mexican families were challenging the local school board, an even greater
international event dwarfed their debate. A revolution brewing in Mexico
would soon change the Anglo-Mexican racial divide in Texas from one of
discriminatory social rules to a violent period of chaos in the borderland that
quickly turned deadly.

THE OUTBREAK OF THE MEXICAN REVOLUTION

President Porfirio Díaz continued his close ties with foreign investors and
world leaders while discontent among Mexican citizens intensified. In 1909
President Taft visited Ciudad Juárez to meet with Díaz and reinforce the US
commitment to Mexico and the Díaz administration. Privately, Taft was
growing concerned that an upheaval in Mexico would have an adverse effect
on US financial interests. In a letter to his wife after meeting Díaz in El Paso
and Ciudad Juárez, Taft commented on how remarkable the eighty-year-old
leader was in his "agility, quickness of perception, and dignity of carriage."
But he cautioned,

There is great fear, and I am afraid a well-founded fear, that should he
die, there will be a revolution growing out of the selection of his succes-
sor. . . . It is inevitable that in case of a revolution or internecine strife we
should interfere, and I sincerely hope that the old man's official life will
extend beyond mine, for that trouble would present a problem of the
utmost difficulty.[106]

A social revolution was on the horizon by 1910. Only 2 percent of the Mexican
population owned land, one of every two houses in the country were deemed
unfit for human habitation, and the average life expectancy was thirty years,
compared to fifty years in the United States.[107]

The Porfiriato had taken a toll on the masses of the poor in Mexico, and
Taft's premonition of revolution would prove to be true, even before Díaz
died. Francisco Madero ran against Díaz in the 1910 election. Madero, an
upper-class politician, sold much of his property in 1909 to fund his election
campaign, which sought to reclaim "Mexico for Mexicans." Madero warned
against Porfiriato propaganda and voter fraud. Díaz jailed Madero in 1910 to
silence him. When Díaz again "won" the presidency in 1910, hostility grew to
a point of no return. Mexicans knew that the election had been fixed. Madero,
after being released from his jail cell in San Luis Potosí, fled across the border
to San Antonio, where he issued his proclamation—"the Plan of San de
Potosí." The plan, which Madero had written in his jail cell, declared the 1910
election to be null and void, called for the uprising of the Mexican people to
overthrow the Díaz presidency, and urged Mexicans to restore democracy
through whatever means necessary—including violence. The plan called for
an armed uprising to begin on November 20, 1910, at 6:00 p.m.

Revolutionary leaders recruited soldiers in Mexico and working-class
Mexicans in the United States. The Mexican Embassy in Washington warned
the Taft administration to monitor the Texas towns of Mesa, El Paso, Presidio, Boquillas, and Eagle Pass for recruiting efforts and arms smuggling.[108]
Revolutionary leaders recruiting in Texas found many of the working-class
Mexican laborers loyal to their cause. Anti-American sentiments were present among these workers long before the outbreak of revolution. They criticized Anglo Texans for the poor treatment they received, while foreigners
were welcomed in Mexico during the Porfiriato. An anonymous advocate for
these workers argued in the *Monitor Democratico*, a Spanish-language newspaper in San Antonio, that "our countrymen abandon their homes and come
[to] this side of the Rio Grande to beg," even though there was an abundance

of bread in Mexico; however, that was for "foreigners, and more particular for the Yankees."[109] Anti-American feelings were strong among some of the Mexican population prior to the revolution, but Anglo-on-Mexican violence in the borderland during the 1910s intensified that sentiment.

Over time the revolution devolved into a bloody civil war. Revolutionary armies fighting federal soldiers used every means to support themselves— forced conscription of peasants, raids of industries and haciendas in Mexico, and theft of property in close proximity to the border. Mexican men and women fought in the revolution, as did young boys forsaking their childhood. Tomás Zepeda and two childhood friends in their early teens were working on a hacienda in December 1910 when revolutionary soldiers approached them. Tomás remembered trying to avoid the Mexican federal army draft, but when approached by a general of Venustiano Carranza's revolutionary forces, Pablo González, the boys eagerly joined the ranks of the resistance. The three boys fought that very first day against the government forces—the Federales. With the exception of the captains and generals, "every soldier in his regiment was under sixteen."[110]

The Mexican Revolution would, by its conclusion, claim over one million Mexican lives. Zepeda told a gruesome tale of military warfare that often turned to savage hand-to-hand combat. War even made enemies of various revolutionary factions. Yet, more hated were the US military forces along the border. "Everyone," he said, "hated the US soldiers." Zepeda recalled stories about how Mexican women who traveled with the regiment preparing food, the *tortilleras*, "had even killed a few American soldiers."[111] Zepeda lost his stepfather and both of the childhood friends he'd signed up with in the three years he fought for revolutionary forces, before fleeing to Laredo. Mexican soldiers such as Zepeda were poor peasants thrust into battle; many told similar stories of fighting, movement over the border, and hostility toward Anglo Americans and other foreigners in Mexico.

As the fighting during the early years of the revolution intensified, foreigners fled Mexico. The revolutionaries made many demands on Mormon colonists. Prior to the revolution, Mexicans and Mormons had lived peacefully among each other, with only minor disputes about petty thievery.[112] Thomas Cottam Romney echoed the words of young Mollie McCallick when reflecting upon his life prior to the Mexican Revolution: "We had about all we could wish for."[113] Following the outbreak of war, Mormon colonies were seen as sources of equipment, funds, and livestock by revolutionary leaders. Mormon historian Irene Hatch Redd recalls her uncle, George Redd, complaining that Mexican rebels would sneak into his barn and milk the cows at 4:00 a.m. One morning, George waited outside the barn to catch the thieves in the act but fell victim to his own trap when a startled Mexican thief fired a shot that pierced his leg. The bullet severed his femoral artery, and he bled to death before sunrise.[114]

Colonists fell victim to extortion and theft by revolutionaries. First, they were ordered to provide leather goods and supplies in exchange for receipts for reimbursement if the revolutionary cause succeeded. Uncooperative colonists were threatened with force.[115] In extreme cases, the raids ended with the colonists being killed. In Colonia Díaz, citizens caught several Mexican men looting the Union Mercantile bank. After a brief chase and an exchange of gunfire, a Mexican raider was shot during his escape. The following day, a posse of Mexican men retaliated and shot colonist James Harvey while he worked in his field. Junius Romney feared that the event would precipitate more racial violence and bloodshed "owing to the strained condition now existing between the Mexican people and foreigners."[116] Thus, many of the exiled Mormon families in Mexico made plans to return quickly to the United States.

Reports of revolutionary armies raiding Mormon colonies spread throughout the Mormon network in Mexico and to LDS members in Arizona and Utah. In the wake of the violence, Bishop Bentley at Colonia Juárez called upon his community and warned that "political conditions have taken an unhoped-for turn. Perilous times no doubt lie ahead." Yet he urged the Mormon followers to have faith:

> Though they may despoil us, deprive us of our property and misuse us in many ways, let us not forget that the despoilers, though ignorant and depraved, are still God's children, and that our mission in this land is to be a link in the chain of their salvation. Who knows, we may be hastening the day when they shall become a white and delightsome people?[117]

Bishop Bentley prayed that peace and goodwill would prevail over violence and lawlessness—that Mexicans "shall become white." But just the opposite happened: the violence intensified, and Anglo Texans increasingly viewed Mexicans as dark and dangerous.

Immediately after the outbreak of fighting in November 1910, news reports reached the United States that Mormon colonies were under attack.[118] Anglo American women and children would soon be engulfed by the savagery of revolutionary fighting. The *Coshocton (OH) Daily Tribune* reported that colonists, under a flag of truce, offered to give the rebels food and horses in exchange for their safety, and declared that they would remain neutral in the fighting. The rebels agreed to no such terms, pillaging the community and threatening to burn down buildings. Siding with the expatriate Americans, the Ohio newspaper reported on how the four thousand members of the colony had spent a quarter of a million dollars improving the land, building schools and churches, and implementing an irrigation system.[119] Almost overnight, Mormons ostracized from the United States for their culturally un-American practices became America's children in grave need of assistance.

Bishop Bentley's Colonia Juárez fell under multiple rebel attacks as the revolution raged on. Dynamite explosions destroyed homes and drove cattle off the ranches. In nearby Colonia Díaz, rebels burned every home and business to the ground.[120] Bentley might have urged church members not to engage in fighting, but it appears that Mormon colonies in Mexico participated in weapons smuggling operations across the border. These weapons were for protection but perhaps also for profit. An investigation in Ogden, Utah, revealed an unusual demand for .30 caliber rifles four months prior to November 1910, and a man who represented himself as a "salesman" in Salt Lake City made large purchases in both cities. Whether these weapons were for colonists' protection, extortion, or profit is unknown.[121]

Five months into the fighting, news filtered into the United States that several Mormon colonies had all but lost hope of remaining in Mexico. An Associated Press report from Agua Prieta announced,

> The determination of the Mormon colonists of Colonia Morelos and Colonia Oazaca, coupled with the Mormon appeals to Washington presented a menacing situation today. . . . Mormons have been killed by rebels since the revolution began five months ago. Most of the Mormons are American citizens. . . . A few of the Mormons are naturalized Mexicans and great fear has been expressed that this circumstance might compel the rebels to assume they were justified in attacking the colonists if they resist demands for supplies.[122]

The destruction of property and the burning of homes and businesses were explained as part of the rebel forces' hatred of foreign investment and ownership of Mexican property during the Porfiriato. Early colonists had reported that amity prevailed with their Mexican neighbors when they first arrived, possibly because the two groups lived in similar conditions and worked tirelessly to survive. Over time, however, as the disparity of wealth between Mexicans and Mormons increased, Mexicans "begrudged" their new neighbors, and Mormons "viewed Mexicans as lazy and primitive."[123] Thomas Romney blamed this on his belief that Mexicans did not share the genetic legacy of "Nordic stock" that largely made up the ancestry of the Mormons.[124] One colonist of Colonia Chuichupa, Chihuahua, alleged that native Mexicans were jealous of the living conditions of the Mormon colonists. The commander of rebel forces that attacked Colonia Chuichupa, José Inés Salazar, declared: "The time had come when the Mexican citizens were going to live in good houses, and American citizens were no longer to be allowed to live in good places [while] Mexicans live in out-of-the-way places."[125]

Mormon colonists began their flight to the United States with women and children fleeing first; as the revolution continued, the men followed and found refuge north of the border. In El Paso, hundreds of Mormon families initially took shelter in temporary housing such as lumberyards (fig. 1.7). In time, the US federal government paid for the cost of relocation, and Mormon refugees resettled in various western states.[126] Mormon colonists had once again been driven from their homes, this time into an Anglo Texas world growing hostile toward ethnic Mexicans, not Mormons. As the white refugees arrived, they told stories of barbaric revolutionary fighting that became the image Anglo Texans held of their southern neighbors.

US businessmen who had flourished in Mexico during the Díaz presidency now found themselves in a hostile environment, often leading them to flee the country. In Zacatecas, Mexican rebels attacked the family of John Hoffman, a mine superintendent, repeatedly firing shots at the family's home. Mrs. Hoffman and her daughter hid in the storeroom of a local shop until they fled by carriage, being cursed at and stoned by angry Mexican men.[127] Another US refugee, Miss Gladys King, gave details of a mass exodus of Anglo American women and children from Torreón. She traveled with 134 US refugees on a train northbound to the United States. Along the way, she observed a distant train wrecked by rebels and noted that every bridge was damaged. She remembered looking from the rear of the train and watching a band of armed men burn one of the bridges they had just crossed.[128] The wife of a US dairyman in Ciudad Juárez, Mrs. H. M. McClure, fled across the river to El Paso in February 1912 without any intention of returning. She described herself as a longtime resident of Ciudad Juárez and that in all her

MORMONS LVING IN LUMBER YARD EL PASO.

Figure 1.7 Mormons Living in Lumberyard, El Paso, Library of Congress Prints and Photograph Division, Washington, DC, call number LC-B2–2765–6.

years prior to the revolution she had never received verbal abuse or threats to her life. She told a story about a gun-wielding Mexican woman who chased her home, where she barricaded herself inside until the threat subsided.[129]

As the stories became more violent, editors amplified their headlines to include every gruesome detail and warned that several classes of Mexican citizens held animosity toward Anglo Americans. One El Paso construction worker warned fellow citizens in Mexico that "peons" were "worked up" to a threatening attitude, and that middle-class Mexicans held the same hatred toward US citizens but that they were in a better position to control themselves. He believed that Mexican authorities were losing control of the working class and feared that the growing number of rebels had become too large to control. Their hatred for foreigners, especially US citizens, was life threatening.[130] Stories such as these were commonly published in local papers, damaging the already tattered image Anglos had of working-class Mexicans.

The revolution uprooted the McCallick family. Businessmen who had settled in Mexico with their families had established communities in Mexican cities near Mexican haciendas and other industries. The violence of the revolution forced their exodus. Mollie McCallick remembered the American consul coming to her family's home in Torreón and informing them that there was no time to pack; within two hours, rebels would attack their smelting community. The US government funded special train transport out of Mexico for the McCallick family and other US citizens. Rebels attacked this transport on several occasions and seized the refugees' rations, leaving the families with nothing. As a result, the refugees bathed in muddy ditches along the tracks and on one occasion stopped to kill a bull for meat. They made soup from the remains.[131]

Refugees witnessed terrible violence, including federal soldiers hanged by their necks from trees, known as Pancho Villa's "fruit trees."[132] Mollie and her older brother, desensitized by the violence, made a game of this by challenging each other to see who could count more bodies hanging from the trees. At times their train stopped because revolutionary fighting blocked its passage. Rebel leaders boarded the train and cautioned the passengers not to harbor federal soldiers, tossing amputated body parts onto the train as a warning. Mollie's older sisters hid during these intrusions for fear that they would be kidnapped and raped. Mollie remembered her father telling the two girls, "If some of these bandits get on this train, I'm going to have to shoot you both," rather than have the men take the girls.[133]

The refugees had to abandon their exit route when they reached a bridge near Monterrey that had been destroyed. They traveled east toward Veracruz on the Gulf Coast, where they boarded the SS *Texas* for Galveston. The passenger manifest lists Mollie's parents, two brothers, and two sisters.[134] After ten days of quarantine in Galveston, Mollie and her siblings set foot on US soil for the first time. Exhaustion got the better part of Hugh McCallick's health, as he rarely slept or ate while protecting his family during their journey. He continued on to El Paso, where the smelting company that employed him was headquartered. Within a few days McCallick had a stateside job and had secured a small three-room house for his family. One week after arriving in Texas, Mollie remembered her father coming home early from his new job. Not feeling well, he went to bed and never woke up again. Mollie, her siblings, and their Mexican mother were refugees in an unknown place. In an interview years later, she tearfully recalled how much she loved her life with her family in Mexico. "It was great. We had a wonderful life . . . we had everything we needed."[135] Mollie remembered how the revolution destroyed their home, took the life of her father, and left the remaining family members strangers in a foreign land—Texas.

CONCLUSION

Prior to the revolution, Mexican workers came to the United States for work, and some brought their families with them. Mexican communities that formed in the late nineteenth and early twentieth centuries developed civic groups in association with ethnic Mexicans already living in Texas. Mexican Americans believed in their rights as US citizens: equal protection under the law, the right of their children to be schooled with Anglo children, and the right to no longer be considered as second-class citizens.

Many of the first refugees who fled during the early years of the Mexican Revolution were Anglo Americans, but poor Mexican families soon joined in the flood of people crossing into Texas. The fluidity of the border once seen as a vehicle for cultural exchange was now viewed as a threat. Disturbing reports similar to those of the McCallicks poured into the United States with the refugees. The US press circulated stories about anti-American protests and indignities carried out against Anglo Americans in Mexico. During the 1910s US citizens became targets of violence in Mexico, more than any other foreigners. Forty-six US citizens died from revolutionary violence in Mexico, compared to just one of any other nationality, apart from the Chinese, who were a special case.[136] These events led Anglo Texans to see Mexican males as unscrupulous characters associated with the revolution, or with criminal activity such as banditry.

As the decade progressed, thousands of Mexican refugees arrived in Texas. According to census data, the Mexican immigrant population in the United States doubled during the 1910s, a pattern that was certainly reflected in Texas. The 1910 census lists 125,827 Mexican immigrants living in Texas. That number grew to 251,827 by 1920.[137] As the revolution intensified, the Mexican population in Texas surged. Anglo Texans became irritated and anxious, referring to this population surge as the "Mexican problem." The problem had two characteristics. First, Anglos believed that the "quality" of Mexicans entering the state declined during the 1910s. Those who came seeking labor prior to the revolution were preferred because of their willingness to perform undesirable jobs. The refugees were less desirable, because Anglos believed that the best of the Mexican working class was either already in the United States or was fighting on one side or the other in the revolution.

The homeless status of the population surging into Texas border towns became another aspect of the "Mexican problem." Refugees arrived by the hundreds and thousands, creating processing delays at the border and leaving entire Mexican towns deserted. Within a three-day period, the border town of Del Rio, Texas, received over two thousand Mexican citizens from Las Vacas (today, Ciudad Acuña). Upon arrival, these homeless foreigners waited for US immigration officials to clear them for entrance.[138] Part of the inspection included a health and physical examination for potentially life-threatening and communicable diseases. At Eagle Pass immigration officials identified three cases of smallpox among the six thousand detainees. The officials ordered the entire group of refugees to be deported.[139] The combination of news reports describing diseases among the refugees, and public opinion arguing that Mexicans arriving in the wake of the revolution were less desirable than those who had come earlier, led more Texans to resent the growing presence of Mexicans in their state.

In El Paso citizens did not believe that the "Mexican problem" would be temporary. Anglos believed that the large number of Mexican migrants would depress the wages of working-class whites, creating financial problems for Texan families. Frustrated El Paso citizens believed that at least one thousand Mexican laborers who lived across the border in Ciudad Juárez and worked during the day in El Paso were stealing $1,500 per day in wages from their own pockets. They described the men, women, and children crossing the border each day as a "silent invasion . . . before El Paso is hardly astir and the workers return to their homes after dark."[140] Anglos resented the labor that Mexicans toiled at during the day and despised the "degenerate" behavior they saw in Mexican men at night.

Border crossing sites such as El Paso were full of bars and saloons eager to get a cut of the Mexicans' wages. Gambling, prostitution, and alcohol abuse flourished, with nativists blaming all of these ills on the presence of Mexican "peons." As one nativist reporter for the *El Paso Morning Times* declared, "The lower class of Mexicans have no more control over their passions than an angry beast and in their ignorance they are just as unreasonable."[141] Newspapers dwelt on the arrests of Mexican men for crimes of murder, theft, abuse, and even the use of strong language toward Anglo women.[142] Anglo men responded with threats to punish those who violated the color line through legal or extralegal means.

The increased presence of poor Mexican men combined with rumors of the barbaric savagery of the revolution created a panic in Texas. Over the next ten years, innocent Mexican lives would be taken by mob violence, Texas Rangers, US soldiers, and the bloodstained hands of judges, lawyers, and jurors. The next chapter examines two lynchings that occurred in Texas.

Weeks before the outbreak of the Mexican Revolution, the murder of twenty-year-old Antonio Rodríguez became the center of an international controversy. In Rocksprings, Texas, a group of Anglo men lynched the Mexican migrant worker; no arrests were made, and an international protest erupted. Mexicans desecrated the American flag; US citizens attacked and threatened Mexicans on both sides of the border. The young man's death was buried in the ashes of the revolution. His death exemplifies the rough justice carried out by Anglo Texans against ethnic Mexicans. It set a precedent for the years to come: mob violence could supersede the law, and violence against Mexican refugees in Texas would go unpunished. Within a year after the Rodríguez lynching, a mob of men in Thorndale, Texas, lynched fourteen-year-old Antonio Gómez. With dozens of witnesses to the crime, and pressure from the governor on officials to make an arrest, the lynching of Gómez tested the Rodríguez precedent.

CHAPTER TWO

Out of the Ashes

THE BURNING OF ANTONIO RODRÍGUEZ AND
THE HANGING OF ANTONIO GÓMEZ

The iron hoof of the Texas "Yankee," in his barbarous and savage sentiments of race-hatred, is no not trampling upon the Negro, but the rottenness of its core has spread out so as to wound and even kill a Mexican by the iniquitous method of lynching. Lynching is not practiced by the blond "Yankee" except upon beings whom, for ethnic reasons, he considers his inferiors. When a Mexican is immolated, it is to be inferred that the social conscience of the state of Texas, in her loathsome scorn, compares the sons of Negroland with the descendants of Cuauhtémoc. Our race is in no way inferior to the Anglo-Saxon. Our ancestry is more glorious than that of the pork-dealers of Chicago. Our traditions are more splendid and heroic than those of the Quakers of Philadelphia.

—*El Debate, 1910*[1]

O n November 5, 1910, the article "La Pezuna de Dollaria" (translated in the US press as "The Hoof of Nobility") headlined the front page of the Mexico City newspaper *El Debate*. This bold article lambasting the United States targeted Anglo men living in Texas for the lynching of Antonio Rodríguez. Two days earlier, an Anglo mob had seized Rodríguez from a jail cell in Rocksprings. The vigilantes broke down the jail doors and took the twenty-year-old Mexican migrant worker to a fire prepared beforehand, and after each member of the mob took a turn at striking the young man, Rodríguez was doused with oil and set ablaze—still conscious.[2]

Historians who have examined the Rodríguez case tend to place it within the context of the origins of the Mexican Revolution, arguing that the lynching, and the consequent rioting throughout Mexico, was a driving force for the revolution. What historians have failed to consider is that the riots in Mexico in turn contributed to increased Anglo resentment and mob violence in Texas toward Mexican refugees. This chapter addresses what is missing from the literature. Rodríguez's murder established a prec-edent that Anglo-on-Mexican violence would go unpunished during the 1910s, setting into motion a race war that intensified during the decade of the Mexican Revolution. This undeclared war between Anglos and Mexi-cans in the Texas-Mexico borderland would be the bloodiest conflict between the two nations since the Mexican-American War, deepening an already oppressive racial order in Texas that privileged Anglos over Mexicans.

Mob violence against Mexicans increased during these years as Anglo Texans addressed the "Mexican problem." I use this phrase to refer to Anglo frustration with revolutionary fighting along the border, massive waves of refugees entering the United States, and an overall tension that existed between Mexicans and Anglo Texans. Conflict raged between citizens and aliens, Texas Rangers and Mexican revolutionaries, and Anglo mobs and alleged Mexican criminals. The battles were fought on farms, in the streets, and in courtrooms. The larger story is not simply one of Anglo aggression toward victimized Mexicans; it is also a story in which both races justified their actions by their belief in their own superiority and sovereignty in the border region. The Antonio Rodríguez lynching marks the turning point in the early twentieth century when violence against people of Mexican descent began to increase in Texas. Anglo attacks on ethnic Mexicans grew more severe at this time partly out of Anglo panic that the Mexican Revolution would destabilize the entire region and disrupt the racial order that stood at its core. Furthermore, Anglos justified their actions with arguments about national pride and the need to protect America from Mexican revolutionar-ies, bandits, and other undesirables.

This chapter reconstructs the rise of Anglo vigilantism in the early years of the Mexican Revolution and the turning point that this rise marked in Anglo-Mexican relations. First, I reconstruct Rodríguez's lynching and the subse-quent rioting in major Mexican cities. Next, I examine the racial stereotypes that Anglo Texans held of Mexicans and how the Mexican Revolution intro-duced new ones. Then, I examine how worsening race relations in Texas led to the lynching of fourteen-year-old Antonio Gómez only months after Rodríguez's burning. Finally, I analyze how Gómez's killers, despite the testi-mony of eyewitnesses who reported having seen them hang the boy, were acquitted, and how this verdict imbued Anglos in Texas with the belief that their crimes against Mexicans would go unpunished. Out of the ashes of the burning of Antonio Rodríguez emerged a privileged society determined to protect a racial order in Texas that was threatened by the events of the Mexican Revolution.

THE BURNING OF ANTONIO RODRÍGUEZ

In the Southwest, lynching has a long and dark history. Michael Pfeifer explains that collective violence within the borderland region after the 1840s "stemmed from white Americans' efforts to achieve a racial and cultural conquest of Native Americans and Hispanics that consciously supplanted recently established American criminal justice institutions as inadequate instruments for racial mastery."[3] Carey McWilliams believes that this lawlessness resulted in "more Mexicans [being] lynched in the Southwest between 1865 and 1920 than blacks in other parts of the south."[4] Historians William Carrigan and Clive Webb create a database listing all known lynchings of ethnic Mexicans in the United States between 1848 and 1928. They argue that the lynching of ethnic Mexicans in the United States far exceeded that of any other immigrant group and is comparable with African American lynchings, "at least on a per capita basis."[5] Carrigan and Webb found that mobs believed they were policing the region and targeted Mexicans for suspected crimes of murder or theft more than any other reason.[6]

The decade of the 1910s witnessed more lynchings of ethnic Mexicans than the previous thirty years combined. Historians claim that this increase correlated with the increase in the number of migrant laborers arriving in the United States during those years; however, the first decade of the twentieth century witnessed an unprecedented influx of Mexican migrant workers into the United States, and the number of known lynchings of ethnic Mexicans actually decreased from 24 cases in the 1890s to 8 in the years between 1901 and 1910, only to spike during the decade of the 1910s to 124 known cases.[7] Thus, something much more powerful was responsible for the violence that ensued between 1910 and 1920, some factor that infuriated Anglo Texans sufficiently to persuade them to revert to a nineteenth-century strategy of frontier justice—lynching.

Initially, the lynching of Rodríguez escaped local and national attention. Only the story that Rodríguez had murdered a well-known rancher's wife, Mrs. Lamuel Henderson, was covered in the local papers. After his capture, police reported that Rodríguez confessed to having committed the crime because "she had talked mean" to him when he approached her for food.[8] The press first reported the murder of Mrs. Henderson with an article encouraging local men to seek out the wanted man. The *Waco Times Herald* reported that a battle was to be expected when the posse located the "greaser."[9]

In the town of Rocksprings, where Rodríguez was lynched, most Mexicans were sheepherders. Mexican investigators, recruited by the Mexican consulate in San Antonio to look into the case, questioned these locals in the wake of the Rodríguez murder and reported that they were mostly satisfied and generally well paid. None of those questioned knew Rodríguez, and they speculated that he was a drifter from Las Vacas, Mexico (present-day Ciudad Acuña), just across the border from Del Rio. Immediately following the violent evening, the Mexican American community appeared to have accepted the fate of the alleged killer. Rather than investigating who had burned Rodríguez, the press appeared to be more concerned with the young man's mental state.[10] In a special report to the *Waco Times Herald*, the press reported,

> Acting Adjutant General Phelps today said that state authorities will take no action toward identifying and arresting members of the mob which burned at the stake an unknown Mexican recently at Rocksprings, Texas, after he had shot to death the wife of a prominent ranchman.[11]

Convinced of Rodríguez's guilt, the Anglo community believed that his execution had served the cause of justice. But reactions to the killing in Mexico made it clear that the door to this episode with respect to Mexican-American relations could not be so summarily shut.

When the news of Rodríguez's lynching reached his hometown of Guadalajara, an international crisis developed. Mexicans wanted their president, Porfirio Díaz, to demand that the US government investigate the crime, arrest the men responsible for the slaying, and guarantee the safety of Mexicans living in the United States. Protests erupted throughout Mexico and quickly turned into anti-American riots. The Mexican press fueled the fire that burned within the protesters with details of the lynching. Most of the articles explicitly attacked the US government for not pursuing the men responsible. Several days of riots produced numerous editorials in Mexican papers full of anti-American rhetoric.

Mexican newspapers reported the lynching in Texas as a direct attack on Mexicans, and the initial response by Texas officials not to investigate the crime infuriated native Mexicans in the United States and abroad. US officials falsely reported that Rodríguez might have been born in New Mexico and requested that the Mexican government therefore rescind their request for an investigation and reparations.[12] In the end, no member of the mob was ever questioned or charged with a crime, a breakdown in justice that infuriated Mexicans. Public protest in the streets of the Mexican capital began with college students who had read about the lynching. It then spread like brushfire across the countryside. Anti-American protests were reported by all of the major Mexican newspapers, with many supplying their own anti-American rhetoric. The student protesters urged their compatriots to boycott American businesses in Mexican towns in order to make a political statement. In the days following, the riots grew more violent.[13] Tempers were pushed to their limits. Police, attempting to maintain order, arrested hundreds of protesters who had become violent and even shot several students. Crowds chanted "Death to Americans!," "Down with the gringos!," and "Death to the Yankees!"[14] On the second day of rioting, an American living in Mexico City, Carlos B. Carothers, manager of the West End Realty Company, fired his pistol into the crowd of anti-American protesters, killing a fourteen-year-old Mexican boy. As a mob of Mexican protestors sought Carothers and his wife, who was a Mexican national, Mrs. Carothers called to an officer for protection: "I am a Mexican protect me."[15] The officer replied: "You married an American, you don't deserve protection." Mexican police arrested Carothers, leaving his wife alone fearing her safety.

The boy's death worsened the situation in Mexico. In Chihuahua a mob that had assembled at Hidalgo Plaza in the center of town divided into three groups, which then marched separately through the streets and shouted, "Remember Antonio Rodríguez!"[16] The protesters in Guadalajara tore through the American section of the city and shattered the windows of the American Banking Company, the Cosmopolitan Hotel, American-owned hardware stores and drug stores, and American-owned restaurants. C. E. Myers of Joplin, Missouri, and Cliff Munger of York, Pennsylvania, were beaten in the streets by the rioters. These stories made their way back to the United States, as did reports that in each city the American flag was spat upon, burned, or both.

Anglo Texans already believed that extralegal violence was necessary to protect Americans from the "peon class." The Rodríguez riots in Mexico now led Anglos to believe that middle-class Mexicans were also incapable of controlling their anger. Anti-American demonstrations in Mexico began with

college students protesting the American response to the lynching. The
crowds, which included both lower- and middle-class Mexican citizens, grew
to great numbers as they listened to speeches. The press identified the students as largely middle-class Mexicans. As middle-class protesters informed
the lower class of the atrocities that had occurred against their fellow countrymen north of the Rio Grande, the two classes united in common cause.
The *New York Times* reported that the real danger was with the students: "As
a class," the *Times* noted, "they are not likely to attempt any overt acts against
foreigners or their property, but, by initiating demonstrations, they may put
into motion a mob which would soon get beyond their control . . . [composed
of] of the lower classes."[17]

Americans who witnessed the violent demonstrations firsthand sent letters to family members in the United States reinforcing the claims that all
Mexicans—young and old—were threats to Americans abroad:

> [Mexican] children from the working class have told our children "when
> President Diáz dies there won't be an American left in this country."
> Children do not invent such ideas. There have been threats to take the
> penitentiaries, turn loose the prisoners, poison [American] water sup-
> plies, cut telegraph wires, tear up the [railroad tracks]. I am frightened.[18]

The American press released these reports, creating an image that most
Mexicans of any class other than the elite were anti-American and prone to
violence.

The events of the Mexican Revolution, a few weeks after the Rodríguez
protests, had a similar effect. Mexicans once again took to the streets in protest. This time, however, Mexicans wanted to see President Díaz removed
from power. During his years in office, the dictator had formed close ties
with the United States, and US businesses were heavily invested in Mexico.
Associating Díaz with the United States, protesters shouted anti-American
slurs such as "Kill Díaz and his Yankee friends."[19] However, there is little to
directly connect the Rodríguez lynching with the outbreak of the Mexican
Revolution. Although the riots that accompanied the two events were barely
a week apart and in cities like Rodríguez's hometown of Guadalajara there
was hardly a break in the rioting, they were separate in their intentions.
While the Rodríguez riots intended to send a direct message to Washington
that Mexicans deserved better protection in the United States, the revolutionary riots were directed toward the Mexican government, demanding

political change. In Texas, however, Anglo Texans saw only one common denominator—they perceived the Mexican population as violent and anti-American. The anti-American rhetoric of the revolution fueled anger among Anglos toward people of Mexican descent, and toward any persons they believed to be disloyal to the Stars and Stripes.

Meanwhile, south of the border, in the Rodríguez case, one journalist reported that "the spirit of nationalism runs high in that ancient city [Guadalajara] and is quickly expressed for small cause."[20] The conditions in Mexico worsened during the early months of the revolution, and tensions rose as refugees flooded border-crossing checkpoints in Texas. American refugees fled the country into cities like El Paso, bringing stories about brutal attacks on Americans. Anglo Texans justified their violence against Mexicans living in the United States by highlighting the anti-American threat that the revolutionaries represented. Mexican newspapers circulated in Mexican neighborhoods in San Antonio, Waco, and El Paso, featuring cartoons like one in the Mexico City paper *El Diario del Hogar* showing Mexican people clubbing Uncle Sam, while in the background Rodríguez was being burned.[21] During the early years of the Mexican Revolution, Texans wrote to their political leaders urging them to protect the state and the nation from a perceived Mexican threat. This letter to Texas congressman John Nance Garner exemplified what dozens of people expressed about Mexican-American allegiance:

> The fact remains, and will ever remain, that the Mexican, whether he be naturalized, native-born Mexican-American, still retains and stubbornly maintains race prejudice against the American People. It is innate in them and Hell can't eradicate it. This feeling has existed with that nationality ever since . . . the treaty of Guadalupe Hidalgo of 1848 when the territory . . . was ceded to the United States. . . . Mexican children have been taught that this territory was STOLEN from them by Americans—Mexican histories repeat it, their statesmen herald it, and their priests communicate it.[22]

Letters from concerned Texans questioned the motives of ethnic Mexicans in the state. By mid-decade, rumors of armed uprisings and manifestos to kill Anglo Texan males and reclaim the region for Mexico were made public in the American press. Such rumors led law enforcement and political figures to require ethnic Mexicans to provide documentation that they remained loyal to the United States.[23] People of Mexican descent living in Texas during the 1910s were under constant surveillance by Anglos for signs of disloyalty or criminality. Anglo Texans believed that taking up arms against Mexicans in the United States was their duty as America's first line of defense. At a time when nativists in America were celebrating new immigrants from southern and eastern Europe who were attempting to "successfully" Americanize, people of Mexican descent were caught between two fires: a revolution in their homeland that brought devastation to family and friends, and an intensified hatred in the border region of Texas.

THE ROOTS OF ANTI-MEXICAN PREJUDICE

Claims of Mexicans' inferiority came in many forms. Anglos argued that Mexicans were intellectually inferior, largely because the Mexicans they most frequently encountered in border society were migrant workers, whom they referred to as peons. Anglo Texans subjugated these workers in Anglo society, yet at the same time they needed their labor. These workers built the increasingly important railroads that connected the eastern seaboard to the mineral-rich western frontier, implemented new irrigation technology for agriculture, and performed dangerous mining jobs. Most of these men and women spoke very little English, and some were not literate in Spanish either. As late as 1910 only 32 percent of adult Mexicans in Mexico could read.[24]

Many Anglo Texans also viewed Mexican migrant workers as unhealthy, unsanitary, and susceptible to communicable diseases. The press often reported cases of smallpox among Mexican migrants as a warning, and concerned citizens wrote to newspapers, their congressmen, and the state's governor. In June 1911 people wrote to Governor Oscar B. Colquitt demanding that he reconsider the state's plan to establish a leprosarium at Fort Ringgold, Texas. The citizens of the nearby town of Rio Grande adamantly opposed this colony due to the large number of Mexicans in the region who, Anglos believed, would be vulnerable to infection. Starr County Judge J. R. Monroe charged that his county had spent over $8,000 in the previous four years defending "this border against the influx of every contagious disease coming to us from Mexico."[25] In a separate letter, Judge Monroe argued that it was common knowledge that Mexicans were highly susceptible to contagious diseases and that the "ignorance and superstition prevailing among the lower class of the Mexican people . . . [lead them] to have no fear or dread of any contagious disease."[26] These fears reached a concerned Governor Colquitt. In August 1910 Colquitt's own son became ill with typhoid fever.[27] Another letter to Colquitt, which included a petition signed by more than one hundred citizens of Starr County, made a similar claim about Mexicans as carriers of deadly diseases. Moreover, the petitioners warned that the county's dense population of Mexicans posed a high risk of disease to everyone who lived in the area.[28]

These border communities in Texas usually had "sister" towns directly across the Rio Grande in Mexico. These twin cities witnessed the majority of the migration into the United States from Mexico, and inspections at these border-crossing sites were routine. Part of the inspection included a health and physical examination for potentially life-threatening communicable diseases. At Eagle Pass, the Department of Immigration identified three cases of smallpox among the six thousand detainees. Immigration officials ordered the entire group of refugees deported.[29] By mid-decade, the US Public Health Service (USPHS) had implemented the practice of branding Mexican laborers who passed immigration inspections with the word "admitted," justifying this as a procedure to guarantee public safety from diseases carried by "Mexican paupers."[30] When criticized by the Mexican consul, USPHS medical inspector H. J. Hamilton defended the practice as necessary for the safety and well-being of Texans. News reports of disease among migrants, and later among refugees during the Mexican Revolution, led more Texans to resent the growing presence of Mexicans in the state.

During his campaign of 1910 prior to the outbreak of the Mexican Revolution, Governor Colquitt embraced the Mexican American voter. Francisco A. Chapa of San Antonio, a good friend of Colquitt and a member of the Mexican American elite, reached out to the Tejano community to support Colquitt's campaign. With Chapa's help, Colquitt carried the Tejano vote, and he later appointed Chapa to one of twelve advisory positions. He only began to distance himself from the Mexican American community as the years of the Mexican Revolution brought increased resentment among Anglo voters toward ethnic Mexicans. Colquitt was known as the "pardoning governor" because of the symbolic pardons he granted on various holidays; however, during his second year in office, 1912, he refused pardons for ethnic Mexicans on Mexican Independence Day because of the criticism he had received for pardoning them the previous year.[31]

In response to the previously mentioned letters from border communities, Colquitt attempted to show sympathy for Mexicans while at the same time expressing certain nativist convictions. In one letter, he attempted to defend himself from being considered "terribly prejudiced against the Mexican" and claimed that this "is not an accurate conception" of his position. He expressed sympathy for Mexican refugees because of their "inability to take care of [themselves]."[32] However, in another letter drafted only a few days later, he displayed greater prejudice about the status of Mexicans in the racial hierarchy. In response to a letter that praised how Texas Rangers policed the border and protected Texans from Mexican bandits, Colquitt stated: "Our Texas Rangers are very valuable to us, and are worth a great deal more than 500 Mexican horses. As a matter of fact, I think every Texas Ranger is worth more than 500 Mexicans."[33] Colquitt perhaps had always held such a low opinion of ethnic Mexicans, but it took a more negative turn as a result of the Mexican Revolution. New charges against Mexicans because of their behavior during the revolution now developed alongside old stereotypes in the minds of Colquitt and others.

Theft by revolutionaries, bandits, and refugees increased substantially in the early years of the revolution and intensified Anglo hatred of the Mexican people. Letters to the governor announced that thieves stole horses, mules, wagons, buggies, cows, hogs, chickens, farming implements, "and in fact everything that is not tied down and watched with a shot gun."[34] Rancher J. R. Axsom reported with disgust that one of his cows had been butchered and only the hindquarter taken; his cow, valued at one hundred dollars, was "left to rot so that the thieves could enjoy one steak."[35]

The most damaging claim of inferiority was that Mexicans lacked the ability to control their anger, which threatened the safety of Americans in the United States as well as in Mexico. The events in Mexico that followed the Rodríguez lynching reinforced this claim in the minds of Anglo Texans. Not since the mid-nineteenth century had Mexicans appeared to pose a threat as a group to the United States. While Anglos had long believed that working-class Mexican men could not control their anger, many now charged that all classes of Mexicans were prone to violence. These claims increased after the riots that followed the Rodríguez lynching.

THE LYNCHING OF ANTONIO GÓMEZ IN THORNDALE

As described earlier, the outbreak of the Mexican Revolution in November 1910 triggered a rush of Mexican refugees into Texas; the *San Antonio Light and Gazette* reported that, as early as December 1910, a refugee colony had

Figure 2.1 Charity House Refugees, Robert Runyon Photograph Collection, "The South Texas Border, 1900–1920," Center for American History and General Libraries, University of Texas at Austin. Digital ID: txruny 02467.

been established within the city limits.[36] Those who had denounced Porfirio Díaz began fleeing even earlier, months before the start of the revolution. Disguised as a priest, Juan Sánchez Azcona crossed into Texas at El Paso. Azcona left Mexico in July after federal authorities shut down his printing press, which had published the periodical *México Nuevo*, because of his seditious remarks about the Mexican government and his affiliation with revolutionary leader Francisco Madero. While political exiles, wealthy Mexicans, and American expatriates populated a percentage of the refugee stream, the majority of those fleeing for Texas were the Mexican poor, who lost jobs and means of sustenance. When fighting broke out in Matamoros, women and children fled across the Rio Grande into Brownsville, overwhelming the Charity House of Brownsville, a shelter (fig. 2.1).

Anglo Texans were concerned not just about the refugees but about

reports of the violence unleashed by the revolution in Mexico. Texas newspapers reported the events of the revolution daily, focusing especially on
reports of Americans being mistreated in Mexico. In March 1911, for example, the *New York Times* reported on an American sentenced to ten years in
a Mexican prison for being an accessory to the murder of a laborer. Criminal
Judge Marentes of Zacatecas, the presiding judge, was notoriously known to
be antiforeign, and he displayed a strong bias throughout the trial.[37] However, it was the murder of Americans that most enraged Anglo Texans, and
as the first few months of the revolution progressed, the names of Americans
killed in Mexico made front page headlines:

> Samuel Hidy, murdered at the Los Plátanos colony, in the state of San Luis
> Potosí, in May, 1911; George W. Crichfield, shot from an ambush near Tux-
> pán, in the state of Vera Cruz, and who died on April 7, 1911 . . . Patrick
> Glennon, A. L. Foster, and John G. D. Carroll, who were killed at Alamos,
> Lower California, on June 11, 1911 by Mexican Federal soldiers . . . [and]
> William W. Fowler, who died as the result of wounds inflicted by a Mexi-
> can peon near Tuxpán, in the state of Vera Cruz, June 18, 1911.[38]

Wanting President William Howard Taft to intervene, F. W. Meyer of
Bonney, Texas, offered his suggestion as to what to do about the murder of
Americans in Mexico. Meyer proposed that "every time an American gets
murdered in Mexico, by Mexicans, let this Gov. collect, besides other
indemnification, one million dollars for every American life . . . and take
one million acres off of Mexico, adjacent to Texas."[39] Meyer was one of hundreds of Texans who wrote to Taft about the "Mexican problem," and most
shared the opinion that some form of intervention in Mexico would be necessary. Two days of violent disturbances beginning on May 8, 1911, produced
thirty-one casualties, including American citizens from El Paso. Following
the death of five Americans in Ciudad Juárez, the *El Paso Herald* printed an
editorial that criticized President Taft and his failed diplomacy with Mexico, stating: "The attitude of the American national administration with
reference to the protection of American rights in Mexico and along the
border is shameful, disgraceful to the last degree, and deserving of open and
unreserved censure."[40]

The murders of Americans in Mexico along with the negative stereotypes
that Anglos held of Mexicans exacerbated Anglo Texan and ethnic Mexican
relations. In May 1911 a mob of Anglo Texans in Barstow, Texas, lynched a

Mexican man.[41] Rumors of possible lynchings increased as the year continued, and alleged crimes by ethnic Mexicans against a white Texan brought the fear of "Judge Lynch" to the scene. In Thorndale, on the evening of June 19, 1911, hundreds witnessed a mob of German American men take the life of a fourteen-year-old Mexican boy. By June, only seven months after the Rodríguez lynching, Texas had recorded two additional lynchings of ethnic Mexicans—nearly the total of four known lynchings of ethnic Mexicans that had occurred in the state during the previous ten-year period.

Established in 1879, Thorndale was not the most desirable location for migration in southeastern Texas. The town derived its name from the surrounding landscape. It was a railroad employee's comments about the "abundant thorny vegetation—mesquite thorn, prickly pear, and sagebrush"—that led to the town's naming.[42] Coal had been discovered in the 1860s in Milam County, and once the railroad lines began running through and stopping in locations such as Rockdale and Thorndale, mines such as the Black Diamond and Santa Fe belonging to companies like the Texas Coal Company arose and attracted businesspeople, laborers, and their families.[43] The first businesses to arrive in Thorndale were a hotel and dry goods store, and the town was selected as a strategic shipping point for Milam County farmers. A boxcar served as the railroad station in 1883, and by 1884 "Thorndale had a church, a school, and 130 residents."[44] By 1910, 811 people lived there. Of these residents, 523 were fourteen years of age or older, and 90 percent were white (neither African American nor of Mexican descent).[45]

With the new railroads cutting through Milam County and stopping in Thorndale, many people came to the county in search of work in the newly opened mines. The majority of these new miners were Mexican migrant workers. During the second half of the nineteenth century, immigrant laborers had helped build the transcontinental railroads, mine valuable raw minerals, and work the fields. After 1890 Mexican workers arrived in ever-increasing numbers in Texas. A majority of these migrant workers were young men, both single and married, but married men often arrived without their families and sent their earnings back to Mexico, creating an imbalance of men and women in these towns. The new ethnic demographics led to increased fear of ethnic Mexicans among Anglo Texans because of cultural differences and traditions. To nativists, Mexican workers appeared to pose a threat. Defenders of Mexican labor argued for their usefulness, conceding that they could easily be sent home once that usefulness had been exhausted.

In Thorndale, there were only eighteen ethnic Mexican residents in 1910.

Most ethnic Mexicans lived outside of town or near neighboring Rockdale, where the coal mines were located. Those who lived in Thorndale were general laborers or worked on farms.[46] As in San Angelo, Milam County did not integrate Mexican children into the county schools. Mexican children attended La Eschelita (the little schoolhouse), where they were taught English and not allowed to speak in Spanish. However, in this overwhelmingly German American town, speaking German was unofficially allowed in the public schools.[47] Mexican children were segregated from the white children in Thorndale until 1944.[48] Many of the single ethnic Mexican males in Milam County worked as sharecroppers or in the mines. These employees lived on property belonging to Emory A. Camp, a lawyer who was active in politics, and were paid in tokens that could only be used at the mine commissary, where they could be swapped for sharecropper food or medical treatment. The town's German American community managed to re-create the peonage system that was notorious in Mexico and use it to hold Mexican workers captive yet again. This Mexican community of laborers became known as La Recluta (the recruitment).[49] German Americans in Thorndale defined Mexicans as nonwhite. Thorndale residents segregated Mexicans from the start and barred them from voting in the Thorndale Democratic primary.[50]

Gabriel Gómez, Antonio's father, arrived in Texas as a seasonal laborer in 1867 at the age of eighteen.[51] Like many seasonal laborers, Gómez sought the higher wages offered to migrant workers in Texas. Gómez met his wife, Amelia, in Mexico and continued his seasonal work in the United States, returning to his family during the winter months. Amelia, who was Mexican-born, was twenty years younger than her husband. In 1889 she gave birth to their first child (Emma). She would have four more children (Dolores, María, Appilones, and Antonio) before emigrating to Texas in 1900. In 1908 she gave birth to Josephia, their only child known to be born in the United States. It is unclear whether Antonio Gómez was an American or Mexican citizen. For the 1910 census Gabriel reported that his children had been born in "Tex. Spanish." Possibly Gabriel wanted his children to be listed as American citizens, but since Amelia listed her arrival year as 1900, it would seem that their first five children, Antonio included, had been born in Mexico.[52] All of the children understood and spoke English, but none could read or write. The Gómez family rented a house near Thorndale, and Gabriel worked on a nearby farm.

A racial hierarchy existed in Thorndale, and the dominant German American population viewed Mexicans as nonwhite and racially inferior. The local press perpetuated this prejudice by reporting extensively on the poor living conditions of the Mexican migrant workers as well as their alleged poor hygiene, susceptibility to disease, addiction to alcohol, and criminal inclinations.[53] Following the outbreak of the Mexican Revolution, the two local newspapers, the *Thorndale Thorn* and the *Rockdale Reporter and Messenger*, continued their negative portrayal of ethnic Mexicans and printed stories about the fear that plagued border towns—that they were "the last line of defense." These two papers provided daily reports about the Mexican Revolution as well as editorials about ethnic Mexicans living in Texas. The reporters and editors often referred to any criminal activity as "banditry" and grouped all people of Mexican descent—Tejanos, Mexican refugees, and Mexican Americans—under that label. During the months that followed the outbreak of the revolution, Thorndale citizens read headlines such as "[Mexicans] Seek American Captives," "American Planter Slain," "American Women Captives," and "Americans Face Peril in Mexico" in the two local papers. In April and May 1911, the two papers described how a group of Americans were held captive in Álamos, Mexico. The reports detailed how women, children, and the elderly were attacked by Mexican "bandits." Thorndale citizens grew suspicious of their Mexican neighbors.

The newspaper reports about alleged crimes against Americans by Mexican revolutionaries both in the United States and across the border reinforced negative stereotypes about ethnic Mexicans and raised questions about the Mexicans living in Milam County. Anger, frustration, and fear harbored by Anglo Texans toward Mexican refugees triggered "rough justice"; the record of daily violence by Mexicans in Mexico became Anglo justification for anti-Mexican violence. The ethnic division in Milam County appeared to be an "us" versus "them" scenario pitting German Americans who had embraced American nationalism and nativism against ethnic Mexicans who had been stigmatized with stereotypes of inferiority, banditry, malice, and anti-Americanism.

On the evening of June 19, 1911, eyewitnesses in Thorndale reported that a young Mexican boy, Antonio Gómez, was whittling a piece of wood with his pocketknife outside of the Old Bank Saloon around 7:00 p.m. when the saloon's owner, William Stevens, exited the establishment and, annoyed by the presence of the boy, took the piece of wood he'd been whittling and tossed it into the street, shouting that "the sidewalk was no wastebasket." Stevens grabbed the boy, scuffled with him, and tossed him to the ground. Two groups of men, one drinking in the saloon and the other out in the street, began to ridicule the boy. At the scene were Charles Zieschang, Constable Bob McCoy, Johnny Davis, and Wallace Young. Retrieving his wood carving, Gómez attempted to leave the scene. But Zieschang, declaring that he could "make the damn little skunk quit whittling," snatched the wood from the boy and began to whip him with it while the crowd of men continued to berate the boy. In an act of self-defense, Gómez stabbed Zieschang in his chest with his pocketknife. Almost instantly, Zieschang bled to death on Main Street in Thorndale.

At the trial, another version of these events emerged. In this version, Zieschang was reported to have grabbed the wood out of the boy's hand and then returned to the saloon. When he exited after a few minutes, Gómez was waiting for him and lunged toward him with his pocketknife, stabbing him below his clavicle and instantly killing him. We cannot know for sure whether Gómez acted in self-defense or aggressively attacked Zieschang, but what is certain is that a mob of men hunted the young boy with an appetite for blood.[54]

The stabbing of Zieschang occurred at the intersection of First and Main Streets. No other place in town could have been more central and in plain view than this spot, in front of the Old Bank Saloon. Constable McCoy immediately apprehended Gómez and marched him north up Main Street to the calaboose—a typical one-horse-town jailhouse with a single cell. Along the route, Thorndale citizens exited buildings to see what the commotion was about and watched as Constable McCoy marched the murderer to jail. Many of these citizens offered themselves as witnesses, but they had only secondhand knowledge of the stabbing. Nonetheless, they talked freely to the press, further distorting the events of the evening. As he sun descended, Gómez settled into a state of fear. Darkness introduced the sinister "Judge Lynch."

McCoy was well aware of the necessary ingredients for a lynching and attempted to prevent such action. He knew that the town's citizens would want the harshest punishment meted out to Gómez, but the fourteen-year-old was too young for capital punishment in Texas. Only three years prior, Alex Johnson, an African American man, allegedly attacked Birdie Haley, an Anglo woman in Mayfield, a neighboring town north of Thorndale within Milam County. Since a rape did not occur, Johnson was tried for assault with the intent to rape. Outraged Anglos sought a more severe punishment and took the man from jail, beat him to near death, and hanged him from a tree near the courthouse. The headlines of the *Rockdale Reporter and Messenger* read, "Negro Brute Hanged by a Crowd of Incensed Citizens."[55] Since the death penalty was not an option due to his age, and because the boy's attorney might argue self-defense and thus take a murder charge clear off the table, Gómez became a prime target for a lynching. For these reasons, and given the intense fury that he could see developing, McCoy demanded that all saloons shut their doors for the night, hoping that clearer and cooler heads would prevail. When more citizens descended onto Main Street, however, the commotion only grew in intensity. Now, more than one hundred people crowded the streets.

A discussion about what to do with Gómez quickly turned into a decision to summarily execute him for the murder of Zieschang. McCoy knew that the calaboose could keep Gómez locked in but could not keep an angry mob, hell bent on lynching the boy, locked out. At approximately 8:00 p.m., McCoy took Gómez from the cell, tied a small chain around his neck, and led him, with the help of Wilford Wilson, to the home of G. W. Penny. Wilson stayed there with the boy as McCoy left the house to secure transportation to convey their prisoner to the county jail in Cameron, another town in Milam County.[56]

Somehow, before 9:00 p.m., members of the mob learned the whereabouts of Gómez and made their way to the Penny house. Penny and Wilson kept their prisoner hidden as a group of men arrived demanding that they surrender the boy. Gómez sat in the small house no longer as a prisoner but rather as prey. While Penny informed the men that Gómez would not be released, Wilson led Gómez out the back door into an alley, and the two fled under the cover of night. They were headed to the oil mill, a rendezvous point where McCoy had planned to have a transport waiting to take the three to Cameron. However, lurking in the shadows were three men on foot and one on horseback who blocked Gómez from the only route to the oil mill.

When Gómez faced the four men in the darkness of the alley, the terrified boy circled around behind Wilson, using the man as a shield. The horseman, Ezra Stephens, grabbed the chain secured to the prisoner's neck and rode east toward Main Street, dragging the boy along the way. Rather than taking Gómez to the site of the murder, the four men took him to the corner of North Railroad and Main Street—the location of the calaboose. When Wilson arrived, Gómez was falling from a ladder that had been leaned against the telegraph pole from which the mob had initially tried to hang him. This was the mob's first attempt at hanging the boy as he tried to kick his way free. Wilson watched as the four men circled Gómez's nearly lifeless body, which lay on the ground. Witnesses reported hearing the whistling sounds of the boy gasping for air. Finally, an enraged Stephens repeatedly kicked the boy's head. Unable to prevent the inevitable death, Wilson reported what he had seen to Woodbury Norris, the justice of the peace. Wilson named

Z. T. Gore Jr., Garrett Noack, and Harry Wuensche as Stephens's accomplices. The first lynching attempted failed, so the determined mob pulled Gómez up once again and hanged him from the telegraph pole. While the lifeless body of the fourteen-year-old boy dangled above, witnesses reported having overheard the men congratulating one another and even asking the young corpse if he "wanted to kill any more Germans" as they left the scene.[57]

News of the Gómez lynching quickly spread through the American press. "The News is not capable of producing anything that could express the horror and humiliation that it feels because of the crime committed by a mob at Thorndale," wrote the editors of the *Dallas Morning News*.[58] The press lambasted the actions of Thorndale citizens whether they participated actively or simply witnessed the lynching. Newspapers in Dallas and San Antonio reported the lynching as a dark episode of Texas history, and national news outlets reported a similar tale of "Thorndale's finest" taking matters into their own hands.[59] The mob, whose actions were witnessed by over one hundred citizens, believed that it was necessary to override the law and carry out swift "justice." However, the subsequent condemnation of their crime conveyed the growing sense among Anglo citizens in the state that no act left a "deeper stain" than lynching. "Even those mobs that have resorted to fiendish torture have not brought so foul a disgrace on Texas," noted the *Dallas Morning News*.[60] The Thorndale mob—the four men who beat and hanged the boy as well as the onlookers who did nothing to prevent it—had reached a new level of cowardice.

After the Texas press condemned Thorndale citizens, the original report was recanted by the *Thorndale Thorn* and a new statement was made that Gómez, without provocation, had murdered Zieschang. The town, unable to suppress its anger, then reacted to the crime. A witness came forward to rebut this new account, which led to the arrest and prosecution of the four Thorndale men responsible for the Gómez's murder. The witness, Antonio Álvarez, was a Mexican laborer. Colquitt sent a Texas Ranger to Thorndale to secure the witness and escort him from the town to San Antonio, due to fear that he would meet the same fate as Gómez.[61] The first report appears to be the most accurate depiction of the events. Most newspapers reported these to be the events that led to the lynching, and the trial records indicate that Gómez was provoked and not "insane" as local reports later claimed to be the case. The trial records further indicate that a considerable amount of time passed from the moment of the initial stabbing to the parading of Gómez's near-lifeless body in the center of the town.

In neighboring Rockdale, the *Rockdale Reporter and Messenger* received national criticism for its reporting of the event. The weekly publication initially appeared to be in support of the mob that had taken Gómez's life. The following week, the paper printed the semblance of an apology on page 2:

> It is the duty of every newspaper, in the interest of good government, to denounce mob violence wherever found under the guise of punishment for crime. Our report of the Thorndale lynching as it appears on the first page of this issue was written Tuesday and was as complete a report as we could get at the time. Subsequent reports, however, as published in the large dailies of the state, the dispatches being sent direct from the scene of the tragedy, indicated that the Thorndale mob probably overstepped all precedent in the line of lynchings, and has brought the fair name of Milam County and all Texas down to disgrace. There are, of course, two sides to all questions and the Thorndale mob may have been as much justified in their actions as any mob heretofore guilty of a similar offence.[62]

Constable McCoy arrived late that evening to find Gómez hanging lifelessly in the air by the chain he had fastened around the boy's neck hours earlier. McCoy removed the chain and lowered Gómez to the ground. Shortly before midnight, several German American men went to the house of Gabriel Gómez, Antonio's father, and ordered the family to leave Thorndale immediately or suffer the same fate. Fearing that the mob would return and "kill the whole family," Gabriel went into town and retrieved his son's body. Sometime in the early morning hours, Gabriel buried his son, and then the Gómez family gathered their belongings and left for San Antonio.[63]

San Antonio was a safe place for the Gómez family to relocate. A large ethnic Mexican community resided there, and, more importantly, several San Antonio organizations advocated for better treatment of ethnic Mexicans in Texas. Donaciano Davila, the president of La Agrupacíon Protectora Mexicana, testified before the US Commission on Industrial Relations about peonage conditions, describing how Mexicans were defrauded out of their earnings in various ways.[64] In 1911, in light of the Gómez lynching, La Agrupacíon Protectora Mexicana shifted emphasis from labor rights to the protection and safety of ethnic Mexicans "whenever they faced Anglo-perpetrated violence."[65]

In July 1911 the organization's members attended the first Mexican Congress—Congreso Mexicanista—in order to give more exposure to violence and

injustice against ethnic Mexicans. Activists who opposed these atrocities organized the annual meeting, which began in the summer of 1911. When news of
Gómez's lynching reached San Antonio, members of La Agrupacíon Protectora Mexicana quickly responded to the events, providing his family with protection and organizing a mass meeting, making the following proclamation:

> The society has for its general purpose the protection of Mexican citi-
> zens throughout the state of Texas, and for the specific purpose bringing
> to justice the perpetrators [of] the lynching of Antonio Gomez at
> Thorndale and Antonio Rodriguez at Rocksprings.[66]

Flyers were distributed throughout San Antonio announcing the
urgency and importance of this June 29 meeting. The flyer explained that
the purpose of the general meeting was to develop a response to the infamous and cowardly lynching of a fourteen-year-old boy in Thorndale.
Mexican consul Miguel E. Diebold pleaded with Davila not to hold a large
event. Nevertheless, more than three thousand attended the meeting. Tensions ran high; some participants wanted to avenge the boy's death. The
group's leaders had all attendees sign a petition for Governor Colquitt to
intervene and see that those responsible were arrested for the murder of
Gómez. Colquitt responded that it was his "desire to do what is right at all
times."[67] On behalf of La Agrupacíon Protectora Mexicana, Emilio Flores
drafted a letter about the event and sent it to the US Department of State
and the Department of Foreign Affairs in Mexico City.[68] Colquitt wrote to
Diebold promising to send "an experienced Ranger to Thorndale to look
further into the matter, and to talk to the witness who appeared against
those now incarcerated."[69]

THE ACQUITTAL

Persons suspected of complicity in the lynching . . . have been arrested. While
indignation is running high, it is a ten to one shot nothing is ever done to them.
From all records of the past this seems to be the most probable outcome.

— *San Antonio Light, 1911*[70]

As Mexicans united in the wake of the violence, the German American community of Thorndale came together in defense of the men who were now

charged with the murder of Antonio Gómez. Twenty-three-year-old Garrett P. Noack was one of the men who had sought retaliation for the fatal stabbing of Charles Zieschang. Noack was the son of one of the founders of Thorndale who had deeded land for churches and schools.[71] Harry Wuensche and Ezra W. Stephens, both twenty-one, had joined Noack as leaders of the mob. Wuensche was a grocery store clerk and the son of a lumberyard owner who employed many of the men who were later called to testify in court to what they had witnessed that evening. Z. T. Gore is the only one of the four arrested who may not have physically assaulted Gómez; his role was to prevent interference. All four men were descendants of prominent German American families who had lived in the Thorndale area for two or three generations, known as Thorndale's "finest" men. These prominent and tightly knit families intended to fight to get their sons acquitted.

Twenty-six year old Charlie Karl Gottlif Zieschang was a first-generation American born to two German immigrants—Johann Traugott Zieschang and Maria Theresia Jannasch. Johann emigrated to the United States in 1869 at the age of eleven with his parents, August and Annie. Theresia left her hometown in Saxony in 1875 with her family. Four years after her arrival, Johann and Theresia married in Serbin, Texas, in Lee County, just south of Milam County. The couple started a family, and Johann took to his agrarian roots and began farming.[72] By 1900 they had nine children who had survived past infancy (seven boys and two girls), and by 1910 Johann owned "free" the farm he operated.[73] The farm was in neighboring Williamson County, which would serve as a change of venue for one of the convicted men to ensure an "impartial" jury selection.[74] Charlie was the oldest son and worked on the farm as a young boy. He left the farm in his early twenties and moved to Thorndale, where he worked as a mechanic at a garage alongside twenty-six-year-old Chas Fonner. The American-born men shared German heritage and advanced laboring skills, and both had recently married Thorndale women—Charlie married Annie in 1905, and Chas married Bertha in 1908.[75] Upon his death, Charlie left behind his wife and four children—Adala, five; Alvin, four; Alvinia, three; and Amanda, two.[76]

Before German immigrant families established the Thorndale community, they had settled in the northeastern United States. Eighteenth-century German immigrants settled along the East Coast in New York and Pennsylvania, but not until the mid-nineteenth century did a mass migration occur. Intellectuals and adventurers arrived in the United States and surveyed this new country. One such German scholar was Gottfried Duden, who visited

St. Louis, Missouri, and upon returning to Europe published *Report on a Journey to the Western States of North America*, which encouraged Germans to immigrate to this region of the country. The landscape and soil, he argued, were similar to conditions in Germany.[77] This began a chain migration of Germans to the rural Midwest.

Many who arrived were farmers and skilled laborers. These men and women left behind their homeland but brought with them their culture and traditions. German immigrants assimilated into American society over time while maintaining some of their unique cultural characteristics, which brought on intense xenophobia against German Americans during World War I. By 1915 the National German-American Alliance, an organization that sought to preserve German language and culture in the United States, had over two million registered members. Furthermore, towns throughout the Midwest had German phonic names, and it was common to have the German language taught in schools. However, assimilation during the early years of the twentieth century penetrated the German communities relentlessly. German Americans were becoming culturally and politically "American" and appeared to be genuinely accepted by nativists. Thorndale exemplifies this image of a community transplanted in the nineteenth century and coming to fruition by the 1910s.

Thorndale is the quintessential example of an American town influenced by chain migration. US Census records indicate that most of Thorndale's second- and third-generation German Americans had ancestors from northern German towns. Historian George Nielsen explains that the German Americans in Thorndale had a much more complex ethnic heritage as Wends, a general term for West Slavic peoples who lived in German lands. However, on US immigration records they were listed as German, and on the 1910 US census they all listed their country of origin or the country of origin of their parents as Germany.[78] It could have been their history as outsiders, as minority Slavs on the fringe of German society, that led to their desire to belong, and in the United States at a time of intense nativism they found comfort in identifying as Americans. Thorndale citizens were 74 percent native-born Texans, and one in every four of those citizens had a parent born in Germany.[79]

Assimilation occurs over time, and German Americans in Thorndale adopted an American nationalist identity. American nativists have a long tradition of being WASPs. Historian John Higham explains that nativists' "initial distaste for German customs had rapidly worn away," and by the

1910s they agreed that German immigrants—whether of Germanic or Wendish ethnic heritage—were among "the most assimilable and reputable of immigrant groups."[80] Germans were genuinely accepted as "white," although those who traditionally practiced Catholicism suffered some discrimination on religious grounds. Thorndale's first two churches were Lutheran. The first was Saint Paul Lutheran Church, established in 1890, with sixty-nine communicants.[81] A church and school were built on ten acres of land donated by local resident Karl Michalk, and in November 1893, twenty-six-year-old Adolf Kramer became the first official full-time pastor.[82] Kramer lived in Thorndale with his wife, Emma, and their children. Emma died in 1908, one month after giving birth to their tenth child, and Adolf continued as the minister until his death on August 7, 1920.[83] By 1911 church membership had grown to 654.[84]

On County Road 437 a historical marker and a cemetery with 175 graves are all that remain of Thorndale's second church—Saint John Lutheran Church. Built on land deeded by Carl Tick, August Boening, and Ernst Richter in 1900, the wording on the marker celebrates the Germanness of the agricultural community of Detmold and Milam County's immigrant past. (Detmold is located outside the Thorndale city limits, and Tick, Boening, and Richter, as well as many of the church's congregation, were Thorndale residents.[85]) Saint Paul Lutheran Church remains an operating church in Thorndale today, and the cemetery, located off North Fourth Street, is where Zieschang was laid to rest on June 21, 1911.

Based on the eyewitness testimony of Wilson on the night of the crime, arrests were made and Noack, Stephens, Wuensche, and Gore were charged with Gómez's murder. On July 31 bail was denied for all except Gore. On October 24 the Milam County grand jury in Cameron indicted all four for first-degree murder.[86]

Each of the four accused men faced trial separately for the lynching of Gómez. Jury selection proved to be problematic at the first trial, for Z. T. Gore, which was held in Milam County. The selection process took three days, and it is believed that racial prejudice against ethnic Mexicans was the primary reason that the prosecution was unable to secure a fair and impartial group of jurists. A reporter for the *San Antonio Express* detailed the selection process and expressed the belief that it was nearly impossible to find a group of men that did not harbor ill will toward Mexicans. Potential jurors were asked whether the same standards should be applied to a Mexican defendant if the circumstances were reversed, and whether the punishment for the murder of a Mexican person should be more or less severe than that for the murder of a white person. One by one, the potential jurors either balked in their response or clearly exhibited a racial bias for white men.[87]

Each man was tried individually. The first to stand trial was Z. T. Gore on November 11, 1911. The accused admitted to being at Penny's house, but only out of curiosity to find out what had caused such a commotion in Thorndale. Gore testified that he had left the house and returned home, and he provided an alibi for the time the lynching occurred. After an hour of deliberation, the jury acquitted Gore. Following this first trial in Milam County, the venue was changed to Williamson County in an effort to secure a more impartial jury; however, this county was home to one of the three remaining accused, Garrett Noack, whose trial began on February 26, 1912. More than 150 family members and friends of Noack arrived for the first day of the trial. The state's case crumbled over time as witness testimonies changed. Witnesses who were originally called to help the prosecution ultimately became either unhelpful or uncooperative when called to testify. None of the witnesses placed Noack at the scene of the crime, and Noack argued that he had been at the Old Bank Saloon and not at Penny's house. On March 1, after only twenty minutes of deliberation, the jury found Noack not guilty. Next, it was Ezra Stephens's turn to argue his innocence in court, on May 1. Two days later, the jury deliberated, and two jurors initially found Stephens guilty. Following a recess and a second vote, however, the defense received an acquittal. The German American community of Thorndale believed that the three men were being held in the county jail for unjust reasons. They had convinced themselves that no crime had been committed, and Thorndale's finest were privileged to escape punishment.

Lost in the news reports on the trial was the fact that a group of men had lynched a fourteen-year-old boy. Nearly one year after the event, all the testifying witnesses claimed to have seen only the stabbing of Zieschang, and they provided alibis for the accused. Shortly after Stephens's acquittal, the trial judge, a man named Wilcox, released the final defendant, Harry Wuensche, from custody. By early June the charges against Wuensche were dropped. Neither Williamson nor Milam County wanted to spend the time and expense for another trial that would most likely end in another acquittal. "Not guilty" was the verdict for three of the four men charged with the lynching of Antonio Gómez.[88] The *San Antonio Light* had predicted it correctly—the lynching of the Mexican boy went unpunished.

CONCLUSION

The growing reality for ethnic Mexicans in Texas was that white perpetrators of mob violence against them were above the law. As the violence of the Mexican Revolution escalated, so too did Anglo-on-Mexican violence. The Mexican consul in San Antonio, Miguel Diebold, criticized Thorndale citizens and Texans alike for the crime, declaring that "Texas is Hell." As a result of these remarks, he was recalled by Francisco Madero, who had recently claimed the presidency of Mexico. Madero remarked that the comment was "ill-advised and not tending to promote peace and friendly relations between Mexico and the United States." Most likely, though, Diebold was on his way out anyway due to his personal ties with former president Porfirio Díaz.[89]

Hundreds of newspapers around the country had originally declared their outrage about the heinous lynching of Antonio Gómez. One year later, very few papers followed the trials; news of the acquittals was absent from the national press. Within Texas, all of the major newspapers announced that jurors had cleared the accused of wrongdoing. Scattered reports were included in papers throughout the United States; the *Anaconda Standard* of Anaconda, Montana, explained that the jury had deliberated for only twenty minutes before Noack's acquittal, making the case appear to be clearly an unnecessary waste of time for "Thorndale's finest."[90]

The not-guilty verdicts demonstrated that the lynching of ethnic Mexicans in Texas would most likely go unpunished during the decade of the Mexican Revolution. The death of Antonio Gómez brought ethnic Mexicans together and altered their political agenda to one of safety and protection within the United States. During the first two years of the revolution, accusations about suspected Mexican criminals led Anglo Texans to seek out the wanted men themselves, bypassing legal authorities. Announcements in the newspapers read like outlaw posters of the Old West frontier. In San Antonio the press reported that "a hundred ranchmen are in the field, and a battle is expected hourly" after a Mexican gun smuggler fired on Dimmit County officers. The headlines read, "Hunt Mexican Murderers."[91] In Marfa and Valentine, in the state's Big Bend region, a mob of sixty cattlemen and ranchers banded together to seek out the suspected murderers of Texas Ranger E. D. Hulen and customs inspector Joe Sitter. The men vowed to hang the suspects and declared that they would even cross into Mexico for the chase.[92] Texans developed an appetite for blood during the early years of the Mexican Revolution, taking the lives of hundreds of ethnic Mexicans before the end of the decade.

At the same time, La Agrupacíon Protectora Mexicana would be at the forefront of advocating for the rights and security of ethnic Mexicans in the United States. One of the cases it took was that of Leon Martínez Jr., a young Mexican boy who stood accused of murdering a white woman, Emma Brown, in Pecos, Texas. Martínez was aware of the lynchings of both Gómez and Rodríguez, which may have influenced his decision to "admit" to killing Brown. This admission of guilt saved him from the mob but put him on a path toward execution. At fifteen, he was just one year older than Gómez, but he faced a similar Anglo mob hundreds of miles away from Thorndale in a West Texas town. The Gómez lynching and the Martínez trial revealed a dilemma for Mexicans suspected of committing a crime in Texas— punishment would be at the hands of either a lynch mob or an unjust legal system, neither of which provided equal protection before the law for ethnic Mexicans in Texas during the decade of the Mexican Revolution.

CHAPTER THREE

The Legal Lynching of Leon Martínez Jr.

I listened again to this list with a profound interest at the mixture of names, for the names bear the marks of the several national stocks from which these men came. But they are not Irishmen or Germans or Frenchmen or Hebrews any more. They were not when they went to Veracruz; they were Americans, every one of them, and were no different in their Americanism because of the stock from which they came.

—Washington Post, 1914[1]

On May 11, 1914, President Woodrow Wilson read this tribute to the nineteen servicemen killed in action at the Mexican port of Veracruz weeks earlier. A memorial procession bearing the dead soldiers traveled through the streets of New York City. The parade of vehicles passed one million people, and cities across the country conducted their own ceremonies of honor. In concluding statements, Wilson announced, "We have gone down to Mexico . . . to serve mankind."[2]

In Pecos, Texas, on that very day, a ceremony of a different type occurred. Citizens came to the county seat to witness the execution of Leon Martínez Jr., a Mexican teenager, for the murder of Emma Brown, a young Anglo woman. Newspaper reporters across Texas had followed the case for nearly three years. Citizens raised concerns about the inferiority of Mexican migrants and the increasing number of undesirable aliens entering the country. An informal racial order that privileged Anglos over Mexicans had long existed in Texas, but new developments were threatening to marginalize Mexicans even further. The presence of anarchism and "un-American activity" among some ethnic Mexicans increased Anglo hatred during the decade of the Mexican Revolution. Anglos viewed these men and women as uncivilized and intellectually inferior. The influx of Mexican refugees into Texas during this decade further intensified Anglo antipathy toward Mexicans, who became increasingly vulnerable to verbal and physical attacks. This case study of Leon Martínez Jr. provides a window into the life of one such ill-fated Mexican.

Wilson's speech identified Irish and Jewish servicemen who risked their lives at Veracruz as American citizens, and he welcomed them into the American family. The status of Mexican immigrants, by contrast, remained uncertain. During the 1910s Mexican refugees fled to the United States and increased their presence particularly in Texas. When the United States verged on war with Mexico in 1914, US troops along the border clashed with Mexican rebels, and Texas Rangers, border patrolmen, and American servicemen lost their lives. At odds with native-born Texans, Mexicans during these tumultuous years appeared dangerous. Anglo Texans questioned the national allegiance of newly arrived refugees.

After the murder of Emma Brown, Anglos considered Martínez a predator who could not control his sexual drive because of the savage nature of his race. They argued that Martínez murdered the young woman because she refused his sexual advances, even though no witnesses could testify as to what actually happened. The jury dehumanized Martínez and convicted him of murder. Local journalists portrayed Martínez as a brute. His father, deemed a Mexican radical, linked the family with anarchist factions of the revolution that frightened people in Texas and Arizona as well as US citizens in Mexico. During the final weeks of Martínez's life, US-Mexican diplomatic relations were strained, and newspapers posted warnings in US border towns that lives were at risk by Mexican rebel raiders.

This study of the Martínez case examines the fate of ethnic Mexicans living in Texas during the early years of the Mexican Revolution: Were Mexicans accused falsely of crimes? Did they receive equal treatment under the law? Was Martínez innocent but unable to receive a fair trial in this hostile environment? In contrast to the Gómez case study in the previous chapter, Martínez escaped lynching and received his day in court for the murder. However, an Anglo community that sought revenge made a mockery of the legal system by conducting a criminal trial within days of the crime and securing a guilty verdict with a death sentence. Moreover, the guilty verdict was handed down by a jury that included members of the lynch mob that had sought out Martínez for the murder. Martínez may not have been lynched the night of the alleged crime, but the community used the legal system to secure a death sentence for the boy.

According to the NAACP, for a killing to qualify as a lynching, it must be carried out illegally. Martínez was "legally" executed, but it may be argued that a blatantly unjust execution itself qualifies as a lynching. Thus, I argue that the Martínez execution qualifies as a legal lynching. This chapter demonstrates how the Texas legal system, from the local level up to the appellate courts, did not guarantee Mexicans a fair trial or equal protection of the laws, and how the turmoil of the Mexican Revolution worsened the image of Mexican refugees among Anglos in Texas.

THE MURDER OF EMMA BROWN

Leon Martínez Jr. was born in the state of Durango in 1896. His parents, Leon Sr. and Sidra, also had a younger son named Manuel; the father and older boy soon moved to El Paso. As a boy, Leon Jr. attended El Paso public schools. His father spoke English and Spanish and raised his son in Texas, while Sidra and Manuel remained in Durango. Neither father nor son applied for naturalization papers. The Martínezes left El Paso when young Leon became old enough to work. They moved to Toyah, a West Texas town in Reeves County eighty miles north of the border. Toyah was "a typical rail-road town composed almost entirely of saloons and restaurants . . . a rendez-vous [place] for gamblers . . . a town in which six-shooters, shot-guns and dirks [a dagger with a long straight blade] were standard equipment and carried ready for use at any time."[3] Martínez Sr. worked for a Spanish-language newspaper, and his son worked in a neighboring town at Saragosa Mercantile Company, owned by Floyd Crenshaw. The company owned a warehouse, a post office, a Western Union office, and a general store. An intelligent boy who spoke Spanish and English, Martínez Jr. worked in both the general store and the post office. He appeared lighter skinned than most Mexican migrants, who generally had darker complexions. The week before the murder, the boy met twenty-six-year-old schoolteacher Emma Brown.

Brown traveled from her home in Austin, Texas, to Saragosa in June 1911 to spend the summer with her sister, Mrs. H. C. Copper.[4] On the afternoon of July 22, 1911, after picking up supplies from the mercantile company, she traveled back to her sister's home east of town. Her four-mile trip stretched along the lime-rock foothills of the Davis Mountains. Her path crossed a pasture belonging to "Stump" Robbins, a pioneer rancher who later found her body. Beyond the pasture, the path entered a valley with fields of grass four to five feet in height. Travelers on this half-mile stretch were barely vis-ible from the surrounding area, and it was here that Brown's murder occurred.[5]

The physical evidence collected at the scene provided enough information to retell the events as follows. Hoofprints from the murderer's horse indicated that the attacker came toward Brown from the east, not from the direction of Saragosa. The tracks from her buggy almost reached the far end of the valley, where they converged with those of the single horse. An abrupt change in direction of the buggy indicated that something or someone had startled the woman, and the tracks ran back and forth throughout the hidden valley. Bullet holes lined the rear of the buggy, and one pierced Brown. After falling from her buggy, Brown was stabbed several times in the chest. Emma Brown died in that field, lying face up to the stars all night, until ranchers discovered her body the following morning.[6]

The discovery of the young woman's body shocked townspeople and prompted an immediate search for the killer. Several people had seen an unusual suspect having an intimate conversation with the young woman on the morning of the murder. That person was Leon Martínez Jr., who became the first and only suspect in this crime.[7] Martínez owned a pistol, had the use of his employer's horses, and, most damaging of all, was seen by shoppers at the general store speaking with Brown on the day of her murder. Someone alleged that the two were planning a private rendezvous together.[8] Both legal and extralegal posses began hunting for Martínez. He was easy to find, as he did not run or hide. He continued with his weekly routine, and on Sunday afternoon, the day after the murder, he saw his boss, Floyd Crenshaw, traveling toward town. Crenshaw stopped Martínez and informed him that a young woman had been found murdered several miles from Saragosa. Crenshaw asked if he knew anything about it, and Martínez said no. The boy continued on his way to a watermelon patch, and a group of men surrounded the boy as he was eating a melon.

Pecos merchant Jim Mayfield led the posse, which grew in number as the evening progressed. The men demanded that the Mexican boy confess to the crime. Martínez protested his innocence, and the angry mob threatened that they would hang him if he did not confess. The distraught boy cried for his mother and father to help him, and Mayfield responded, "You are not worthy of it." Martínez confessed after they promised not to hang him until after Sheriff Brown (unrelated to the murder victim) arrived.[9] Upon his arrival, Brown took Martínez to the Pecos jail, where he ordered the boy to confess or he would release him to the men waiting for him outside. As dawn approached, District Attorney Will P. Brady held up a written confession to the crowd outside the jail.[10] Only the signed confession, not the events of that evening, were introduced at Martínez's trial as evidence.[11]

Two conflicting stories about the events developed from Martínez's written confession and an interview he did with an El Paso reporter. The first story, from the signed confession, stated that on Saturday morning, the day before his arrest, Martínez and Brown met at Crenshaw's shop. Martínez was working at the time, and the two had a conversation in which the young Anglo woman promised Martínez sex, an unusual move for a young lady of that time. Later that afternoon, around 4:00 p.m., they met two miles outside of town. He asked her to do what she promised; she refused his advances and shouted, "You sonofabitch, I am going to have you arrested." He said that was not necessary; he only wanted her to do what they had planned. She rose up on her buggy, told him she would kill him, and then reached for her hip. Alarmed by this, Martínez pulled his weapon out and shot her in the chest. He returned to Saragosa, ate supper, and went back to Crenshaw's shop to do his evening shelf stocking.[12]

It is difficult to determine the validity of a confession made under duress by someone who is the target of a lynch mob. Quite often an alleged criminal, being sought by a posse of men, believes that a confession to the sheriff is his only option for safety. Historian Paul J. Vanderwood provides a rich analysis of the making of a Mexican folk hero in Tijuana who might have suffered the same fate. In his account of the execution of Juan Soldado, Vanderwood states, "It was said that more than anything else he feared being turned over to the mob, of literally being torn apart, limb by limb, kicked and trampled, by enraged townspeople."[13] Only six months prior to Martínez's arrest, Antonio Rodríguez had been burned alive by a mob for allegedly killing a rancher's wife. Martínez knew that if he were handed over to the mob, death would be certain. Thus, it is probable that his confession was coerced by the sheriff and influenced by the fear that his executioners awaited him. Following his arrest, the boy's father reported to the *El Paso Morning Times* that he feared for his son's safety even in his jail cell because mobs in other cases had stormed prisons to seize prisoners and dispense their own justice. The *Times* reported that he begged that "the people of Pecos and vicinity will not descend to lynch law, as has been the case in two other sections of Texas lately," namely Rodríguez in Rocksprings and Antonio Gómez in Thorndale.[14]

The second account of the events developed from an interview by an unnamed reporter accompanied by Sheriff J. F. Franks of Caldwell County, where Martínez was moved in late August 1911. The reporter described the boy as four feet, ten inches in height and weighing 116 pounds, with "great inquiring brown eyes . . . and he smiles often." From his jail cell, Martínez explained the events that led to his arrest as follows:

I am fifteen years and two months of age. It is not true that I am eighteen years old. I was born in 1896. I did not kill Miss Emma Brown. I
knew nothing of the murder until a Mexican told me about it, shortly
before my arrest. I never had any relations with Miss Brown. I worked in
the store and post office at Saragosa and often waited on her, selling her
some goods on the morning of the killing. I placed her goods in the
buggy and untied her horse. That was the last I saw of her until I viewed
the body. They made me sign that confession. I told them I was innocent
but they told me they would kill me if I didn't sign a confession. I was
frightened and did it. They said that Miss Brown was killed at about five
o'clock in the afternoon. I could have proved that I was in the store at
that hour, but they wouldn't let me.

As the sheriff and the reporter exited the cell, Martínez called out, "Honest, I don't know anything about the killing."[15] The differences between these
two conflicting stories went unresolved. The majority of Anglos preferred the
story in the confession to that of the interview.

Shortly before midnight on Sunday, Reeves County court judge S. J. Isaacks learned of the murder of Miss Brown and the arrest of the young Mexican teen. The county court had recessed, and Judge Isaacks was at his home
in Midland, about one hundred miles east of Pecos. Sheriff Brown informed
Isaacks that anger was growing toward the murderer, and he needed to
depart for Pecos immediately. In the early morning hours, Isaacks boarded
a train for Pecos, and he arrived shortly after dawn. He went directly to the
Oriental Hotel, which was owned by his friend, F. W. Johnson. The hotel was
a central location in town where the county's elite gathered. Isaacks and
Johnson met with the district attorney and two of the wealthiest men in
Pecos, W. D. Cowan and B. R. Stein, vice presidents of the local bank and
financiers of the newly chartered Pecos Valley Southern Railroad.[16] Their
order of business was to discuss the "excited condition" and "threatening
attitude of the citizenship" toward Martínez and to determine what would
be in the best interest and safety of the town.[17] They decided that Sheriff
Brown should escort Martínez to a jail in Midland until trial. This was the
only time in his official career that Isaacks sent a prisoner to another jail for
protection.[18]

On Monday, July 24, 1911, Isaacks convened a special session of the court
in Pecos. The judge's order stated that the reason for this unusual and urgent
procedure was "that a horrible murder had been committed." By the end of

the day, he had summoned a grand jury and secured an indictment for murder. Isaacks notified Sheriff Brown that a murder trial would take place on Friday, July, 28, 1911. Confined in the Midland jail, Martínez did not meet with his defense attorneys until mere hours before the trial. Two attorneys were selected by Isaacks to defend the Mexican boy: George Estes, a former district attorney from El Paso, and R. L. Parker, a former Reeves County judge and friend of Judge Isaacks. The trial began Friday morning, with Martínez entering a plea of not guilty. The prosecution read Martínez's signed confession but omitted the statement indicating that he was fifteen years old. Before noon on the following day, the jury returned a guilty verdict and sentenced Martínez to death.[19]

Judge Isaacks gave the defense until 3:30 p.m. to prepare a motion for a new trial. Isaacks ordered Texas Rangers to escort Martínez back to the county jail in Midland while his attorneys went to Parker's office and prepared an appeal. Angry citizens wanted an execution, and it is unclear what prompted Estes and Parker to appeal. The court has no record of Martínez's request, but months later Martínez stated that his father had requested an appeal because there should have been a change of venue. Martínez's Anglo attorneys possibly believed that they had to do everything in their power to defend their client; Parker was a former judge and Estes a former district attorney. News that these men were attempting to save the convicted teen spread rapidly. Shortly before 3:30 p.m., Estes and Parker left for the courthouse to file an appeal with Judge Isaacks. Meanwhile, F. W. Johnson, Jim Mayfield, and Sheriff Brown met with Cowan and Stein at the bank to gather up men. The purpose of this mob was to prevent an appeal. Johnson reported that from the front door of the bank he could see Parker and Estes going toward the courthouse. The angry men shouted for the attorneys to stop. The mob met them "one hundred and fifty feet from the court house door."[20] Fifty men, including several who served on the jury, stood between Martínez's attorneys and the courthouse. Mayfield, who had been present on the night of the arrest and had threatened to hang Martínez personally, was part of a growing mob that sought these attorneys.

A. W. Hosie, the local justice of the peace, stood up on a box and shouted that the crowd would not permit an appeal.[21] Hosie, born of Scots-Irish immigrants, had a reputation in Reeves County as roughneck fighter able to take care of himself.[22] Parker became concerned about public safety. Months later, he stated, "I felt that if they undertook to take the Mexican from the rangers, some of them [citizens and Rangers] would get killed . . . and we could not well scrap a whole county, or what looked like a whole county to us at the time."[23]

Estes was less concerned about the safety of the citizens than he was for his own life. As Johnson argued with Parker, four or five persons were shouting their disapproval. Members of the mob began to yell that "they could hang three as easy as they could hang one."[24] Parker reassured the crowd that there would be no appeal made and that they should return home. Estes boarded a train for El Paso that very evening. Later he would go on record stating that he feared for his life on that hot summer afternoon. Parker and Isaacks returned to Johnson's hotel, had a private, "whispered discussion," and decided not to appeal the decision. Both Estes and Parker were ambitious politicians. Further representation of the Mexican boy, they now feared, would damage their reputations. Parker served the county's elite for years. Johnson, among the most vocal of the mob, advised Parker days later to leave Pecos.[25] Meanwhile, Judge Isaacks ordered that Martínez be hanged on September 1, 1911.

THE MARTÍNEZ CASE AND THE MEXICAN REVOLUTION

Leon Martínez Jr. was arrested for the crime of murder, but on the night of his arrest an angry posse demanded his life for the death of Emma Brown. Martínez might have heard stories about attacks on Mexican men such as Antonio Rodríguez, who had been doused with oil and burned alive by a savage mob in Rocksprings. Any Mexican male, regardless of age, who committed a crime against Anglo Texans could be subjected to extralegal violence. As the case of Antonio Gómez demonstrates, Mexican boys as well as men could be victims of such heinous crimes. In this case and others, mobs dispensed vigilante justice within hours of an alleged crime against one of their own. Large mobs removed Mexicans who had been detained in jails. One wounded Mexican man was taken from his hospital bed, hanged, and burned.[26] The public defended these actions by saying they saved the county time and money.

The racial order that existed in Texas stigmatized Mexican migrants as racially inferior, subjugating them as outcasts. Residing far away from their families, these laborers often lived together, creating Mexican barrios in the towns where they settled. To nativists, they lacked moral virtues. Leon Martínez did not find a friendly face in Reeves County, and it would be more than two years before he would return to Pecos for his execution. During his incarceration, his family found Mexicans sympathetic to his case in El Paso, Waco, San Antonio, and cities throughout Mexico. These people and their organizations raised the $50,000 necessary to pay for his legal representation.[27]

Following Martínez's sentencing, the *El Paso Morning Times* reported, "A feeling of general satisfaction prevails throughout the county . . . that justice was meted out to him in a fair and impartial manner."[28] After sentencing on July 29, 1911, Texas Rangers escorted Martínez back to his cell in Midland to await his execution. On Sunday, the day after the trial, Dr. Homer L. Magee, minister of the First Christian Church in Pecos, told his parishioners that he was satisfied that justice had been served. He believed that Martínez's actions would be useful to remind parents to inculcate proper moral virtue in their children. Magee declared that home is where one feeds one's children's bellies and minds: "A crime of this kind is not committed as a result of sudden emotion, but it is the natural outcome of the training, or lack of training, received in the home. . . . Home is God's first ordained institution where the conscience is trained to discern between right and wrong."[29] Many Mexican boys, including Martínez, lived in homes where the father was out all day looking for employment, or where the boy himself was laboring alongside his father. In Magee's eyes, boys living in these kinds of circumstances did not received a proper moral education.

On August 6, 1911, District Attorney Brown received a telegram from Governor Oscar B. Colquitt stating that he would not interfere with the Martínez case.[30] Pecos officials tried to refute the stories printed in newspapers across the state that described Reeves County as a vigilante society. They published an editorial in the *El Paso Morning Times* praising the people of Reeves County for being law-abiding citizens. It read, "Almost anywhere else on the face of the earth a resentful and indignant people would have acted otherwise, and have taken justice into their own hands without the law"; and further, "There is no more peace loving people in the southwest."[31] In truth, however, the citizens of Reeves County had growing fears that Martínez might escape execution. National newspapers were reporting that a child had been sentenced to death in Texas. The people of Reeves County sent letters to Governor Colquitt urging him not to get involved, warning that the citizens of Texas would lose faith in a legal system that should protect them and that any intervention would force them to settle future matters with "Judge Lynch." Attached to one letter was a petition claiming to hold the names of every citizen in Reeves County.[32]

Their concerns that Martínez's life might be spared were legitimate. The story about a boy facing execution made national news. Newspapers in large and small communities around the country, from the *New York Times* on down, reported on the Martínez case. Letters arrived from as far off as New Jersey questioning Colquitt about the Texas legal system and the pending execution of a minor.[33] Concerned Americans and angry Mexicans wrote letters to the governor. The letters expressed outrage that Martínez's trial had occurred in Reeves County, given the hostility of local residents toward the boy. Albert Anders, a father from Canyon Creek, Montana, appealed to the governor to investigate the case, stating, "To prove him innocent after his death will be too late." Ida C. Airhart of Lake Charles, Louisiana, argued that it would be a crime to hang someone so young and asked Colquitt "to investigate and think of the matter in a Christian spirit." J. W. Arrowsmith, president of a surgical supply company with offices in Chicago, San Francisco, and Toronto, was infuriated: "How the great state of Texas can 'string up' an infant is beyond my comprehension."[34]

These kinds of protests impelled Colquitt to delay the execution thirty days pending further investigation into the case.[35] During that time, Martínez's family sought financial support for the boy and furnished a legal team that filed an appeal to the Texas Criminal Court of Appeals. The supporters who came to his aid created as much outrage in the media as the initial murder and actually intensified Martínez's problems with white Texans. His family's association with Mexican radicals connected him with the Mexican Revolution, making him not just a "killer" but an enemy of the state.

One of the most influential and outspoken leaders of the Mexican Revolution was Ricardo Flores Magón. Born in 1873 of working-class parents, Magón became a journalist who opposed the dictatorship of Porfirio Díaz. His open opposition to Díaz led to several arrests and eventually his flight from Mexico to Laredo, Texas, in 1904. A year later he founded the Mexican Liberal Party (PLM), an opposition group that sought reform and a new leadership for the people of Mexico. The group called for open elections in Mexico, land reform for the peasantry, increased wages, and improved conditions for the Mexican working class. In Texas, the PLM attempted to organize Mexican and Mexican American laborers. The response by the Mexican communities in Texas varied. Some ethnic Mexicans supported these efforts and others distanced themselves. PLM supporters criticized US foreign policy, Texas officials for their lack of concern for Mexicans killed along the border, and Wall Street's "domination of Mexican affairs."

Texas became a popular location for exiles of this sort. In San Antonio, Magón reestablished *Regeneración*, a Mexican radical newspaper that emphasized restoring Mexican land to the Mexican working class.[36] In November 1910 Magón declared, "The Liberal Party works for the welfare of the poor classes of the Mexican people. It does not impose a candidate, because it will be up to the will of the people to settle the question: Do the people want a master?" His *Regeneración* article "El Derecho de Propiedad" (The Right of Property) argued that people's right to property is as ancient as their stupidity.[37] In most speeches, Magón condemned wealthy Anglos as thieves and as the exploiters of working-class Mexicans. Supporters of Magón became known as Magónistas.

Anglo Texans became suspicious of Magón's intentions when these words circulated around the state:

> The expropriation of the land possessed by the rich should be realized during the present insurrection. We liberals will not be committing a crime by turning over the land to the working people, because it belongs to them, the people; it is the land that their most distant ancestors lived on and watered with their sweat. . . . That land belongs to all Mexicans by natural law. Some of them [Anglos] might have bought it, but where did they get the money to make the purchase if not from the work of the Mexican unskilled workers and laborers?[38]

The land he desired was Texas, and the thieves were Anglo Texans. Anglo citizens in Texas worried about a hostile attempt to reclaim this land. The Magónistas were only one of several radical factions on both sides of the border to flourish during the Mexican Revolution. As rebels and bandits pillaged southwestern ranches for food, supplies, and weapons, Anglo Texans became suspicious of all revolutionary factions.

Working-class Mexicans in Texas had a negative stigma imposed on them by Anglos. After the 1910 revolution, whites questioned Mexicans about their allegiance to anarchist factions. El Paso had the greatest population of Mexicans in Texas during the 1910s, and by the end of the decade an unprecedented number of Mexican nationals had sought refuge in the United States.[39] Spanish-language newspapers increased their circulation in border towns, some simply reporting the news in Spanish and others fostering radical thought. Papers like *Regeneración* had subscribers in the United States, Mexico, and Cuba, but the largest distribution occurred in Texas. According to one 1915 issue, 42 percent of a given issue of the paper was sent to Texas, 13 percent to California, 12 percent to Mexico, 5 percent to Cuba, and 4 percent to Arizona. The addresses of the remaining 24 percent of subscribers are unknown.[40] Conservative Anglos condemned these papers and the writers and editors who produced them.

W. A. Hudson, an attorney and shareholder of the Citizens Bank of Barstow, located seven miles east of Pecos, reported to the editors of the *El Paso Morning Times* that he knew that Leon Martínez Sr. was a Magónista, and Anglo newspapers subsequently reported it. Hudson wrote that Martínez Sr. was "a well-known socialist—one of the Magonista faction, and it is the socialist party who is exerting its money and influence" to save Martínez's son[41]; he declared that radical groups had provided the funds "to save a guilty wretch."[42] As mentioned above, Martínez Sr. worked for a Toyah, Texas, Spanish-language newspaper that printed articles in support of Magón. Toyah, a railroad town several miles east of Pecos, was also home to two members of the jury in Leon Jr.'s trial: W. M. Hopper and A. J. Hart.[43] Hopper and Hart might have known of Martínez Sr. and of his reputation as a Magónista. The elder Martínez was even rumored to have worked for Magón's paper, *Regeneración*. He might have been an assistant editor, as some Anglo papers speculated, but this cannot be verified. What is clear is that the elder Martínez was known to the editors of this radical newspaper. In one published piece he appealed directly to Mexicans in both Mexico and Texas to help his family pay for legal representation for an appeal for his son. As a result, money began arriving at his El Paso attorney's office.[44]

Martínez Sr. wrote to the editors of Spanish-language newspapers in El Paso, San Antonio, and Waco in search of additional financial support for his son's defense. Lauro Aguirre, the editor of one such El Paso newspaper who knew both father and son, reported that he did not believe that Martínez Jr. was guilty of the crime.[45] Martínez Sr. demonstrated a strong command of English in a letter he wrote to the secretary of the Texas Criminal Court of Appeals regarding payment for a transcript of his son's trial.[46] The signature at the bottom of the letter is elegant and in cursive, showing a flair for penmanship that was uncommon among Mexican working-class men.

Whether a Mexican was lower or middle class was inconsequential to most Anglos by 1912; Mexicans of both classes were suspected of insurrection. According to many Anglos, the working class carried out the crimes, while the middle class created revolutionary literature encouraging such crimes. *The El Paso Morning Times* reported a plot that urged "a call to arms of Mexicans in the United States to fight against Americans." The US Secret Service raided an El Paso printing press and found more than five thousand copies of an alleged insurrectionary document. Newspapers printed front-page headlines such as "Anti-American Plot Exposed."[47] Such stories about Mexicans fueled Anglo resentment.

Residents of El Paso current with national events knew that the US Senate was considering curtailing immigration. An editorial in the *El Paso Morning Times* informed the public that the Root Amendment of the Dillingham Bill, favored by the Senate, would protect Texans against radical immigrant factions who sought to undermine US authorities and threaten the country's safety. If passed, the bill would rid the county of undesirable aliens:

> Members of the Senate Foreign Relations Committee and of the Texas congressional delegation conferred with President Taft and his cabinet with regard to the Mexican situation, and the practice of Mexicans of coming into the United States territory as refugees but really to agitate and promote armed expeditions into a country from which they have fled. . . . [The Root Amendment] provides a more adequate remedy, however, for existing conditions than does the present neutrality law, and is actively supported by Governor Colquitt, of Texas.[48]

The author of this editorial argued that if such a provision were in place, subversive plots would fail because the plotters would not be allowed in the country. This legislation would protect Texans from these radicals.[49] Anglos feared that Mexicans associated with groups like the Magónistas were all radicals and, as such, threatening to Anglos.

THE EXECUTION

On November 3, 1911, in Austin, the Texas Criminal Court of Appeals reviewed the murder trial of Leon Martínez Jr. The majority opinion ruled against a new trial. Three appellate judges reviewed the lower court's documents and issued clashing opinions. Appellate Judge A. J. Harper of El Paso wrote the twenty-page opinion that supported the lower court's ruling. A dissenting opinion came from Judge W. H. Davidson, who argued that Martínez deserved a new trial outside of Reeves County. The seventy-four-year-old Judge Davidson had built a reputation as a crusader against injustice. In another dissenting opinion, he sharply criticized the "necessity" defense for a lynching: "It was *necessity* that prompted Pontius Pilate to appease the cry of the howling Jewish mob to murder the innocent Christ."[50] Davidson chastised those in authority who made examples of individuals to appease the populace. He condemned Judge Harper for an opinion "intended for the admiration of the people." He told the outraged Anglos of Reeves County, "I have made it the rule of my judicial life, and shall continue to do so, to decide questions as I see them after as careful investigation as my capacity affords, without reference to what public opinion may be."[51]

Davidson argued that Martínez's conviction violated the due process provision in the Fourteenth Amendment of the Constitution. The Law of Nations and two treaties between the United States and Mexico should have guaranteed Martínez the rights inherent in the Fourteenth Amendment.[52] Davidson provided the following reasons why the case violated the treaties: undue haste in the trial, denial of the defendant's right to be heard by counsel of his own choosing, and the unjust discrimination against Martínez that prompted the court to seek to satisfy the local citizens.[53] Davidson's concluding statement declared, "The law is not designed to be a swift engine of oppression and vengeance, but it was, and is, designed to try men only after due hearing and fair trial. I cannot concur with my brethren."[54]

Davidson's dissenting opinion drew sharp criticism from Judge Harper. The two judges were polar opposites in their views and they openly clashed, a friction that made national headlines from New York to Los Angeles. Letters to the editors of major Texas newspapers criticized both judges for engaging in such a public debate. The *Dallas Morning News* reported, "The hurt to at least the dignity of the State would have been much less severe than that which results from this public exhibition of their spleen."[55] Glenmore Farm resident Charles Metcalfe voiced his mixed opinion of the situation. His letter to the editor began with an argument to reform the process through which these judges were elected. He went on to say that the people of Texas had lost respect for the courts, and this case damaged the confidence of Texans in the laws designed to protect them from criminals. In conclusion, he stated, "The overshadowing elements of uncertainty as to so-called law drive the people to primal, savage action. The result is individuals commit and avenge bloody wrongs."[56] The public debate continued through the summer. Taylor McRae, a Fort Worth resident, read the case transcripts published in the *Southwestern Reporter* on May 8, 1912. He urged for reform of the courts as a result of this case while maintaining that he was not concerned with the guilt or innocence of Martínez, unlike many others who criticized the case.[57] His comments drew a response from Judge Isaacks that pointed out errors in McRae's timeline, that the door was unlocked during the confession, and that the murder had occurred in Reeves and not Pecos County (the city of Pecos is the location of the Reeves County courthouse).[58] This trivial response sidestepped the question about Martínez's baptismal records, which would have verified that Martínez was fifteen on the day of the murder.

The unusual haste of the original trial denied the Martínez family the six days needed to travel to Durango, Mexico, to retrieve baptismal records, and it violated his right to a fair trial. Davidson's dissent provided Martínez's attorney with the document necessary to take the case to the next level: the US Supreme Court, which set a hearing for October 14, 1913. In Texas, strong feelings about the case divided Anglos and ethnic Mexicans. Texas had become so divided that the state's attorney general, B. F. Looney, petitioned the US Supreme Court to advance the case:

> That the matters involved herein are of great public importance to the State of Texas . . . there has arisen a great disturbance and clash between the citizens of Texas and the citizens of Mexico during the pending and past revolutions in Mexico, and such delay in the final determination of this case has exaggerated the tension existing between the citizens of the border counties of Texas and the citizens of Mexico residing within the borders in Texas from Mexico, and that for these reasons this case should be advanced upon the docket by this honorable court and brought to a speedy termination therein.[59]

The press made connections between the Martínez case and the lynching of Antonio Gómez. In 1912, as three of the Thorndale men were in prison, Thorndale citizens were aware that a delay in the Martínez execution meant that Governor Colquitt was considering a pardon of the convicted Mexican murderer. Thorndale citizens believed that their men who sat in a prison prevented a similar situation in their town. The Thorndale men were revered by some for acting "swiftly" with mob "justice," while the Pecos men in Reeves County were ridiculed for allowing the Texas legal system to "protect" the murderer of a twenty-five-year-old white woman. Journalists editorialized that the citizens of Reeves County mistakenly held back their "race feelings and horror" to prevent a lynching and that they did their "best to behave."[60] The Pecos residents announced frustrations that the alleged murderer would probably escape an execution, which they could have secured that fateful night. Even the press in other western states argued in favor of extralegal punishment. A Muskogee, Oklahoma, daily paper argued as much and included a cartoon that read, "Reeves County wonders if it pays to be law-abiding" underneath a drawing of the murder of Emma Brown. A reporter for the paper, W. G. Shepherd, stated that Reeves County had "passed up an excellent chance for a lynching. . . . [H]undreds of virile citizens were itching to string up a young Mexican." However, Shepherd continued, "the murderer isn't hung yet."[61]

The press reported that Mexican men and boys were equally prone to violence. The Gómez stabbing of a German man in Thorndale was thought to support that notion, as was the Martínez conviction. Further damaging to the image of Mexican boys were the reports of young Mexican boys, ranging in age from eight to fifteen, violently playing out the revolution along the Rio Grande. Police often arrested these children for their reenactments of the revolution. Many were pretending to fight for Pancho Villa. El Paso police claimed that they were regularly rounding up Mexican boys living on the Texas side of the Rio Grande who fought Mexican boys on the other side. The young residents of El Paso's Mexican district, Chihuahuita, threw stones across the river at Juárez boys.[62] The police reported that the Mexican boys of Chihuahuita were engaged in daily battles with their counterparts just across the border. Eventually this combat earned the name "playing Juárez." As the revolution intensified, so did the play. Outside of El Paso, two fifteen-year-old Mexican teens fought the revolution with stones; ultimately, one killed the other with a rifle. Witnesses said that they had been "playing Juárez" and remarked how uncivilized Mexican boys were compared to Anglos.[63] While these boys fought their revolution along the banks of the Rio Grande, Martínez battled the legal forces that were determined to follow through with his execution.

During his time in prison, Martínez entertained himself by taking up music and other hobbies. Waco prison officials allowed family members to give him a guitar to keep in his cell. Martínez had not played before, but he taught himself how and entertained both prisoners and guards.[64] One reporter from the *Dallas Morning News* photographed him with a Mexican warship he had constructed out of materials that included a cigar box. In the picture he appeared clean and well dressed. This photo only circulated in the *Dallas Morning News*. Papers in border towns like El Paso refused to publish images that humanized the murderer.[65] The Mexican images most popular among Texans were from the revolution, and a picture postcard craze "captivated" the state.[66]

One of the most striking images was of Mexican boys who participated in the revolution for real (fig. 3.1). Different revolutionary factions recruited children to work as spies and infiltrate enemy positions. Some insurgents were recruited as orphans, while others volunteered because it was their best opportunity to secure a source of food and shelter.[67] These kinds of images overwhelmed the single photograph of Leon Martínez Jr. that was ever published in the Anglo American press as described above. These two images—Martínez with his cigar-box warship and the revolutionary boys pictured in figure 3.1—show the contrast between the boy prisoner and the young soldiers. The boy soldiers are draped with ammunition, and in their hands are rifles. Martínez, in contrast, is wearing a necktie that complements his coat and pants and is shown holding a toy boat that he created in jail. Citizens of Texas border towns possibly imagined Martínez as one of the disruptive boys playing war games along the river, or as similar to the boys fighting in the revolution.

El Paso residents had justifiable concerns. Ciudad Juárez became a battlefield for many rebel groups. In February 1912 the *El Paso Morning Times* reported that Juárez was under attack and businesses there were being looted. El Paso went on alert, and the *Times* provided news throughout the day. Beyond the morning edition of the paper, four subsequent front-page "extras" warned of the events breaking that very day. Following this event, local business owners voiced their frustrations that the Mexican Revolution was bad for business. Hotel and restaurant owners noticed that the trains entering El Paso carried fewer vacationers and salesmen, and the trains leaving the city were carrying Anglo women and children to northern and western cities. Further damaging the town's image was the yellow journalism appearing in major cities around the country. More concerned with paper sales than accuracy, one San Francisco paper reported, "El Paso in Hands of Villa Troops," alleging that four thousand Mexicans had captured the city.[68] Rumors spread that Pancho Villa would come and avenge Martínez's death if the boy was executed, and destroy the town of Pecos.[69] Once again, the events of the Mexican Revolution were damaging to Martínez.

The US Supreme Court dismissed the boy's case on grounds that it lacked jurisdiction. Martínez's only hope rested with Governor Colquitt, widely known for having pardoned over 1,600 prisoners during his four years in

Figure 3.1. Mexican Boys of the Revolution, courtesy of West Texas Collection, Angelo State University, San Angelo, Texas.

office. Colquitt's pardons were ceremonial. He chose Thanksgiving and Christmas holidays to pardon large groups. Race had never deterred the governor. On June 19, Emancipation Day, he shocked the citizens of Texas by "pardoning thirty aged negro convicts."[70] Women quickly learned of his pardoning reputation. Mothers wrote for their sons, and wives for husbands. They were sure to mention how their dire living situation had pressured others in the community to help them survive their financial strain.[71] The *Dallas Morning News* reported the governor's humane but capricious decisions. One story reported that Colquitt was in his office one Sunday morning reviewing pardon requests when his wife phoned him that he must escort her to church. He responded that he was reviewing the records of Carl Craven, a resident of Kaufman County, when Mrs. Colquitt demanded, "Pardon him by all means and come with me to church." With a pen already in his hand, he signed the pardon to please his wife.[72] Not all of his pardons were so whimsically based.

On Mexican Independence Day, in his first year of office, Colquitt pardoned elderly Mexicans as he did African Americans on Emancipation Day.[73] Both actions aroused the ire of many Anglo Texans. Nevertheless, the next year he pardoned black prisoners on Emancipation Day again. Because of the Mexican Revolution, the opposition to his pardoning of Mexican prisoners had grown. Newspapers began exaggerating the numbers of Mexicans he pardoned from nine to six hundred in just one month. Colquitt responded, "There are not six hundred in the penitentiary."[74] The following year, Mexican Independence Day passed without Mexican pardons, and a pardon for Martínez was highly unlikely.

Border violence intensified in the months prior to Martínez's execution date. Ranchers reported a growing problem with theft of their livestock in locations near the border. In Brownsville, rancher J. R. Axsom wrote to Governor Colquitt that theft was growing worse with each day. He explained that neither "honest nor dishonest" Mexicans can be trusted; "the Mexican who is honest and does not steal, will not divulge anything against a thief of his race."[75] Citizens of Texas began to criticize Colquitt for his inability to protect the state. In an attempt to explain why the governor was not more aggressive with the "Mexican problem," many people alleged that he lacked manliness. Men wrote letters offering their assistance to take up arms and defend Texas from Mexican insurgents. An August 30, 1913, letter signed by "Smarty Alexander" and "Sammy Grandstander" expressed anger over the "Mexican problem" and attacked Colquitt's masculinity and leadership. The salutation began, "Dear Little Oscar." Smarty and Sammy desired action and went to so far as to urge Congress to declare war on Mexico. They notified the governor that they would be ready for service in ten days. These "Red River Bottom" men had a hundred locals ready to take up arms against Mexicans, "every one of which would kill a greaser every time he pulled the trigger." Their closing remarks read, "Yours to lick 'em."[76]

Hundreds of letters arrived in Governor Colquitt's office during his four years in office, from 1911 to 1915, many from Texas men eager to join the ranks of the Texas Rangers and fight Mexican bandits raiding Texas ranches. Fifty-five-year-old Jet Allen of Fort Worth wrote a three-page letter to Colquitt on November 17, 1913, in which he described himself as an "old-timer" who was angry and disgusted with the "Copper Colored Cuss who frowns on the Stars and Stripes or refuses to tip his hat in respect to the Flag."[77] He believed that American leaders balked in dealing with President Victoriano Huerta of Mexico, describing bilateral relations as "Wilson-Bryon [sic] Sissy Diplomacy." Further insulting President Woodrow Wilson and his secretary of state, William Jennings Bryan, Allen declared the Boy Scouts of Texas as a "more fit bunch to deal with the Mexican forces," and he signed his letter, "Sincerely yours for dignified manhood."[78]

Despite this enthusiasm for citizen militias, local law enforcement and the Texas Rangers did not have sufficient numbers to keep the peace. Sheriffs from border towns urged Colquitt to secure federal troops to police the border.[79] Colquitt ordered 2,200 troops from Fort Sam Houston in San Antonio to El Paso for protection.[80] President Wilson sent another 4,000 troops to Galveston. When matters worsened, Colquitt ordered the commander of the Texas Rangers to "shoot straight if necessary."[81] The orders were followed, and violent border clashes increased.

Texas Rangers and US troops mobilized in El Paso and Brownsville, Texas, and Douglas, Arizona. Four companies of the state militia went to Brownsville after two US businessmen in the neighboring Mexican town of Matamoros were kidnapped and held for a $20,000 ransom. Captain Head of the Texas Rangers sent a telegram to Colquitt requesting permission to cross the river in an attempt to retrieve the kidnapped Texans. Colquitt refused the request and was newly criticized for his lack of aggression with the Mexican situation.[82] Two separate fights broke out in Douglas in March 1913. Neither side took responsibility for the initial fire, and six Mexicans were killed.[83] It appeared that a major US-Mexican conflict was imminent. In February 1913 Victoriano Huerta assumed power in Mexico, only two weeks after Woodrow Wilson took office in the United States. Mexico's new leader encountered enemies among Pancho Villa's men as well as among the Magónistas, and he found few allies in the Wilson administration. Wilson denounced Huerta as a dictator and cut diplomatic relations with the self-proclaimed president of Mexico.[84] With Wilson distancing the United States from the Huerta government, and the governor of Texas having to appease a population agitated by Mexicans, Leon Martínez Jr. had little chance of a pardon or even a sentence commutation.

US military efforts to monitor the Mexican port cities began in early 1913 as officials in Washington expressed concerns that weapons from Germany might arrive in the ports of Acapulco, Mazatlán, and Veracruz.[85] Later that spring in Veracruz, a minor misunderstanding broke out between Mexican soldiers and US sailors because of a Mexican officer's decision to arrest some of the sailors. As both sides denied any wrongdoing, Wilson and Huerta sparred in newspapers. The incident became known as the Tampico Affair. Wilson demanded a twenty-one-gun salute to the US flag by Huerta's soldiers. When the deadline passed without such a salute, the US

Atlantic fleet attacked Veracruz and occupied the city. The incident resulted in the death of over fifty Mexican troops, hundreds of citizens, and nineteen US servicemen.[86] The US military occupied the port city for six months. Following the American departure, Mexicans declared Veracruz as *quatro veces heroica* (four times heroic), referring to the defense of the port city against four invasions—by Spain in 1825, France in 1838, and the United States in 1847 and 1914.[87]

The invasion strained diplomatic relations, as Mexican citizens believed that the attack on the port city was unprovoked and unjust. Following the attack, Mexicans mourned the death of José Azueta, who had fought courageously against the Americans at Veracruz. Thousands attended the funeral for Azueta, who had been promoted to captain on his deathbed. Azueta was the son of flamboyant and popular Commodore Manuel Azueta. On the first day of the invasion, the younger Azueta defended the Veracruz Naval Academy entirely on his own and wounded many attacking American soldiers. Azueta was mortally wounded and died days later. Veracruz residents celebrated his heroics with a funeral procession that included thousands of the Mexican faithful. Today, a memorial statue stands in front of the naval academy in his honor.[88]

With the death of American soldiers and devastation in Mexico, the turbulent situation most certainly worsened Martínez's hope for a stay of execution.[89] While the American public mourned the loss of US soldiers, Texans finally got the "justice" they had been demanding for over three years—a hanging for the murder of Emma Brown. On the fateful day of the boy's execution, US newspapers coast to coast recognized the courage of the country's fallen soldiers at Veracruz. President Wilson proclaimed that the efforts in Veracruz had been on behalf of "mankind." One last plea for Martínez came from Juan Raino, Spain's ambassador in Washington. Speaking on behalf of Mexico in an act of humanity, he requested that the governor commute the sentence to life in prison because of Martínez's "tender age."[90] Colquitt denied the request, and Martínez returned to Reeves County for his execution. Martínez wrote a letter to his younger brother Manuel. Trying to instill good virtues in his brother, he warned the younger boy about ills of society. Martínez composed a disquisition on the use of opium, cocaine, morphine, and "other evils that beset the path of the younger generation."[91]

The night before his death, Martínez condemned the court: "My conviction is the result of race prejudice upon the part of the jurors. I feel perfectly well and have absolutely no fears for the future. We all must die, you as well as I."[92] His only request was to wear the Mexican colors when he was hanged.[93] He quoted Saint John in his final statement: "Come unto me, all ye that labor and I will give ye rest. . . . God so loved the world that he gave his only begotten son."[94] On May 11, 1914, standing in view of an Anglo crowd, he announced that he was innocent.[95] As he stood on a scaffold in the center of Pecos, with a Catholic grotto in the distance (fig. 3.2), Martínez never waivered from his innocence, nor did he beg his Anglo executioner for mercy. He maintained the calm demeanor he had become known for over the preceding three years among the reporters who had met him. In an ironic twist, the executioner was the newly elected sheriff, Tom Harrison, and not his predecessor, Sheriff Brown, Martínez's vocal opponent who had urged court officers not to appeal the original case. Harrison is said to have lost thirty pounds in the month leading up to the execution as he struggled with the personal and public ramifications of his court-ordered duty.[96] As several people in Reeves County watched, Harrison sprang the trap at noon, and fourteen minutes later Leon Martínez Jr. was pronounced dead.

CONCLUSION

Leon Martínez Jr. represented the "Mexican problem" to the people of Texas. A member of an ethnic group that had arrived in large numbers in Texas, Martínez suffered from being categorized as racially inferior to Anglo Texans. During the years of the Mexican Revolution, Mexican refugees fleeing to Texas exacerbated Anglo resentment. New developments involving the growing number of Mexican radicals in Texas and allegations of revolutionary plots further damaged Mexicans' reputation and left them even more vulnerable in white Texas communities. This period was damaging to the people of a country that had once ruled what was now the southwestern region of the United States. Many were caught between two worlds: Mexico, embroiled in civil war, and the United States, fostering ethnic hostilities against them.

Leon Martínez Jr. lived in an Anglo world that determined his guilt without closely examining the evidence. If he was guilty, then Martínez indeed paid the ultimate price for taking the life of Emma Brown. But the burden of proof falls on the district attorney, not on the defense, and not on this historian. A forced confession by an intimidating mob on the night

Figure 3.2 Oak Street, downtown Pecos, Texas, 1915, courtesy of West of Pecos Museum.

of his arrest, and the haste to secure a guilty verdict within a week of the crime, offer evidence that Martínez was vulnerable to the Anglo-Mexican social order in West Texas. Violent death threats to his attorneys prevented an appeal and illustrate the power this community had to persuade authorities to acquiesce to their demands. Far worse were the actions of the state's highest judges and politicians, who concerned themselves with elections and pandered to the majority rather than determine what was "just" for a Mexican boy living in Texas. The execution of Leon Martínez Jr. served as a legal lynching.

The years of the Mexican Revolution damaged the image of ethnic Mexicans living in Texas. On the day that President Wilson honored the soldiers who had died at Veracruz, a Mexican boy had his life taken at a public execution, even though the swirl of stories about the crime, his apprehension, and his trial created more questions than answers. For Mexicans living in Mexico and the United States, the decade of the 1910s was one of fear and confusion. In towns along the US-Mexico border, ethnic Mexicans, both American citizens and otherwise, were profiled by a prejudiced society and became targets of unwarranted searches, unjust legal decisions, and one of the most evil acts of violence—lynching. The legal system did not provide Martínez with adequate protection of his rights, and earlier Antonio Gómez had fallen victim to a posse out for vengeance. By mid-decade, the borderland would become a region consumed by chaos and violence. Numerous human rights violations occurred during these years. The Mexican Revolution destabilized the borderland and intensified Anglo fear and suspicion of ethnic Mexicans. The destabilization led to an increase of hostile campaigns directed against ethnic Mexicans, and these crimes often went unpunished. Martínez, Rodríguez, Gómez, and other victims became martyrs and proto–civil rights icons, and, as the final chapter of this book will illustrate, early civil rights activities by ethnic Mexicans emerged in Texas in the wake of the violence.

CHAPTER FOUR

The Devil and the Bandit in the Big Bend

RANCH RAIDS AND MOB VIOLENCE IN WEST TEXAS

I beg to make a report of a fight with Mexicans on the Night of the 28th. Eight Rangers in company with four Ranchmen were scouting on the river and found several Mexicans . . . and when they had gathered several of them [Mexicans] together they were fired upon by other Mexicans, and had a general fight. . . . [F]ifteen dead Mexicans were found there. Several articles were found in their possession belonging to Mr. Brite, taken during the raid, December 25, 1917.

Most respectfully yours, Captain J. M. Fox
—*James Monroe Fox to James A. Harley 1918*[1]

Captain James Monroe Fox of the Texas Rangers detailed the battle between his soldiers and fifteen Mexican men killed on January 28, 1918. His letter to General James A. Harley at the Rangers' headquarters in Austin reported that their "successful" mission concluded with the burial of the suspected "bandits" they had tracked to a refugee village in Texas— El Porvenir. The event that triggered the raid on El Porvenir was the Luke Brite Ranch raid on Christmas Day one month earlier. Fox explained that one of the Mexican suspects wore a pair of boots similar to the boots stolen from the general store at Brite Ranch.

The Mexican men at El Porvenir were not bandits or criminals; rather, some were American-born citizens of Mexican descent while others were refugees who had fled the revolutionary fighting with their wives and children. El Porvenir was not a haven for bandits; it was home to 140 ethnic Mexicans, most of whom were women and children. When the Texas Rangers and ranchmen arrived in the early morning hours of January 28, they searched the village for weapons and stolen goods. The search of El Porvenir revealed two weapons: an antique Winchester of a "special make" belonging to Rosendo Mesa and a pistol belonging to John Baily, the only Anglo man living in the village.[2] Nevertheless, the Anglo posse lynched fifteen Mexican men and boys they suspected of being bandits. Following an investigation ordered by Texas governor William Hobby, the murdered men of El Porvenir were all but cleared of guilt for the Brite Ranch raid. General Harley discharged Captain Fox and his men, but none faced criminal charges. In a letter to Fox, Harley announced, "Officers should know that every man, whether he be white or black, yellow or brown, has the constitutional right to a trial by jury, and that no organized band operating under the laws of this state has the right to constitute itself judge and executioner."[3] These were strong and admirable words, but they did little to change Anglo opinions about Mexican refugees living in camps like El Porvenir. Anglo Texans believed that the poorest class of Mexican refugees who lived in the isolated region of the Big Bend were nothing more than "bandits."

Both Mexicans and Anglo Texans had their own sources of information (and misinformation) through which they formed opinions and created stereotypes of each other. Anglo Texans heard stories about ranch raids by revolutionaries as early as 1911. Additionally, stories about the "savagery" of Mexican-on-Mexican revolutionary violence south of the border arrived in Texas as refugees fled the nation, along with rumors about armed Mexican uprisings against Anglos. Likewise, ethnic Mexicans living in the borderland had reason to believe that they were in danger from Anglo Texans, causing them to live in fear of civilian posses and Texas law enforcement. Mexicans living in Texas heard stories about Texas Rangers kidnapping Mexican men in the middle of the night, the lynching of Mexican men who were taken from county jails, and a criminal justice system that allowed executions, such as that of Leon Martínez Jr., to occur without a fair trial. For decades, Mexicans told stories that Rangers carried old, rusted weapons and planted them on mortally wounded Mexicans shot by the "border cowboys." Such manipulations of crime scenes allowed the Rangers to claim that they had shot "bandits" in acts of self-defense.[4] Mexican fear of the Texas Rangers dated back to the time of the Mexican-American War. US General Zachary Taylor wrote about the atrocities committed by the Ranger force, and "Los Diablos Tejanos," or the Texas Devils, was a moniker that stayed with the Rangers for decades to follow.[5]

This chapter explores the roots of vigilante violence on both sides of the border, which often occurred in response to rumors and false reports by the Anglo press. Mexican refugees were caught in a crossfire: in Mexico they fled from revolutionary violence, and in Texas they were seen as an "enemy other" both because of the stereotypes Anglos held of Mexicans and because of the very real brutality of revolutionary fighting. A challenging situation for Anglo Texans was deteriorating. While ranch raids on American soil escalated, the federal government was inconsistent in its policy about the army's presence in the region. President William Howard Taft initially sent a large deployment to San Antonio, removed them within a year, and then left a scattering of regular army personal in the region. Before leaving office, Taft met with Texas governor Oscar B. Colquitt to discuss the growing violence in the borderland. Taft offered little reassurance that the incoming Woodrow Wilson administration would intervene in Mexico, suggesting that the "Mexican problem" was a "Texas problem" and that the governor should increase recruitment of Texas Rangers and assign them to border duty.[6] President Wilson recalled the remaining regular troops in the state once America's entry into World War I seemed imminent, replacing them with an untrained militia. Anglo Texans, as a consequence of such inconsistency, believed that vigilantism was justified to keep order in their state. Anglo violence intensified as stories of American casualties in Mexico multiplied, and as rumors spread about armed Mexicans seeking to stage an uprising in Texas to reclaim their lost frontier. Moreover, Anglos believed that the numbers of Mexican "bandits" in the borderland had increased.

The term "bandit," which too often is used as a moniker for Mexican criminals in the literature about this period, has complex meanings. If some Mexicans were bandits, then the same is true of some Anglos. Several primary source documents use the term "Jingo Bandit" to describe the Anglo raiders, a term absent from the secondary literature. I define Anglo bandits as those who acted without authority against suspected Mexican criminals, as well as Texas Rangers who abused their authority and acted as judge, jury, and executioner. Mexican "bandits" of the period were "social bandits," a term first expressed by Eric Hobsbawm in his book *Bandits*. In the Southwest, these Mexican outlaws challenged the legal and political power of the Anglo populace with acts of resistance. However, Anglo Texans defined this activity as lawlessness and "banditry."

This chapter also demonstrates how desire for retaliation and revenge transformed innocent men into murderers on both sides of the border and how lawlessness had overtaken civility in the region by 1918. The Antonio

Gómez lynching of 1911 (chapter 2) and the Leon Martínez execution of 1914 (chapter 3) legitimized Anglo-on-Mexican vigilantism in Texas. In this chapter, I first identify the characteristics of Mexican refugees that Anglo Texans disliked and examine the internment of five thousand Mexican refugees at Fort Bliss. Then, I demonstrate how the intensifying violence of the raids in Mexico and the United States further damaged Anglo-Mexican relations in the region. Next, I show that a brief period of stability existed while US National Guardsmen patrolled the region. Finally, I discuss the return to lawlessness and demonstrate how the Big Bend region devolved into chaos, as raids were less about property and more about revenge over earlier disputes between Anglos and Mexicans.

By 1918 escalating violence on both sides of the border had rendered the borderland lawless and violent. Anglo Texans initially believed that the Mexican Revolution threatened to contaminate only their cultural purity by sending masses of foreigners fleeing into their state. By the mid-decade, however, they worried about the threat the revolution posed to their personal property and safety. Indeed, in some cases, Anglos had reason to be fearful of Mexican bands that had become lawless. Mexicans, on the other hand, faced a genuine threat as revenge motivated Anglo-on-Mexican violence, and as public officials and the courts failed to protect ethnic Mexicans in Texas. In the Big Bend of West Texas, the Mexican revolution transformed both Anglos and Mexicans into "devils" and "bandits," and fortified the negative stereotypes that the two groups held of each other.

RUMORS AND MYTHS OF MEXICAN REFUGEES IN WEST TEXAS

Few other places in the world have as many references to the devil in landmarks and on maps as does this 250-square-mile region, which includes "a Devil's River with a Devil's Lake, a Devil's Backbone, a Devil's Ridge, a Sierra Diablo, a Diablo Plateau." Deep within Big Bend National Park lies the Devil's Den.[7] Retaliation and revenge took a more gruesome turn here than in any other region of the border during the decade of the Mexican Revolution.

Border violence was both Mexican and Anglo-American made. Hundreds of innocent victims lost their lives during the years leading up to the El Porvenir raid in 1918. Anglo Texans believed that "bandits" were the root of the Mexican problem along the border. Banditry in the Southwest has a long history, one that precedes the Mexican Revolution. It is a story that includes Anglos, Native Americans, Mexicans, and others involved in criminal acts. Often the term "bandit" is interchangeable with the term "outlaw." Billy the Kid, born William Henry McCarty Jr. in 1859, was a legendary bandit who, in his short twenty-one years of life, thieved and murdered in the West, committing his first crime in Silver City, New Mexico, at the age of fifteen. Some of the most notorious bandits were train robbers such as the Dalton Gang of the late nineteenth century. Men and women of the Southwest and West committed various crimes, including theft, murder, bank and train robberies, and even cannibalistic serial killing.

During the decade of the Mexican Revolution, Anglo men saw Mexican revolutionaries as "bandits." In Mexico, on the other hand, revolutionary leaders such as Pancho Villa were both demonized and lionized—"the social bandit of 1911 became the terrorist of 1917; the social bandit of one valley crossed the mountains and terrorized another."[8]

A more regulated legal system of law and justice came to these western territories as they gained settlers and statehood. However, these changes came more slowly to the Big Bend. Cattle ranchers and cowboys revered the Big Bend as the last of the great frontiers in Texas, still being conquered by Anglos, where rough manliness and vigilante justice still mattered. Many ethnic Mexicans in northern Mexico and parts of the American Southwest saw the Big Bend differently, as lands taken from their ancestors. Animosity among them toward Anglos in this contested space ran deep. Anglo Texans and Mexicans had a long history of contestation in the borderland, and the Mexican Revolution reawakened nationalist feelings on both sides, prompting a level of conflict akin to an unofficial war along this part of the border between 1915 and 1918.

Ranch raids by Mexicans on the US side of the border were not common during the early months of the revolution. Rebels at the time focused on haciendas, foreign-owned businesses, and Mormon colonies in Mexico. That did not prevent the press from falsely reporting about such crimes. The *Galveston Daily News* ran an article about border banditry in early 1911 only a few months after the start of the revolution. The article warned the public that Mexican bandits were a possible threat to their communities. The words "bandit" and "raid" were used fourteen times in the article. However, this article made no mention of any actual contemporary raid, focusing instead on an 1875 raid in Corpus Christi by thirty Mexican criminals. The article's bold font announced only that "AMERICANS WERE TERRORIZED" and that "WOMEN AND CHILDREN SUFFERED," making it seem as though this raid had just happened and thereby creating the myth that the border was swarming with Mexican bandits.[9] The *Galveston Daily News* used anti-Mexican language to spread fear that the Mexican Revolution had led to increased numbers of Mexican nationals in Texas who were poor and prone to violence, disease, and alcoholism. By mid-decade, daily news reports connected rebels and revolutionaries with banditry and warned Texans to monitor the poorer class of Mexicans. The *San Antonio Light* reported that "it would be relatively easy" for two thousand or more Mexican rebels to cross the bridge into Brownsville and take control of the city. A related article on the same page ran the headline "New Raid Feared" and disclosed that "a party of eighty Mexicans" at "Rio Grande City, Mexico," was approaching Laredo.[10] Additionally, the press reported that those responsible for the raids were Mexican "peons" with "inherited ignorance . . . superstition . . . habits of poor housing," and "weakness to . . . diseases." The poorer class of Mexicans should concern Texans the most, the Anglo press warned.[11]

From the onset of the revolution, refugees fled Mexico in large numbers, and Mexican American citizens had to decide whether or not to help them and risk drawing the unwanted attention of Anglo citizens. While welcoming middle- and upper-class refugees into their communities, urban Mexican Americans harbored more negative attitudes toward the poorest of the refugees. The latter thus turned to poor Mexican Americans for help, in the process either overpopulating Mexican districts in the cities or establishing isolated rural communities like El Porvenir on their own, where they could work on nearby Anglo ranches. These poor refuges were caught between a land that did not want them and a home they feared.[12] Thus, many of these families formed communities along the Rio Grande. They remained close to a world familiar to them without venturing too far into the unknown.

One hundred and forty Mexicans lived in El Porvenir. The small village was located in western Presidio County along the Rio Grande in the Big Bend. El Porvenir, "the future," was home to refugees of the Mexican Revolution, many of whom fled after the villages they lived in and haciendas they worked on were raided by revolutionary fighters. In the state of Morelos, one of the largest planters reported that the revolution and chaos had "degenerated into bandit raids. As a result the laborers have quit the fields and taken refuge in the mountains. Neither bandits nor federals can conscript them into service."[13] The planter felt the impact immediately, as his crops were more than 50 percent short that season. The long-term consequences were even greater, as field workers in Mexico began to flee the country for Texas with their families for work and safety.[14]

El Porvenir was a haven for families who fled Mexico, set up to be so by two Mexicans who owned the land and who had spread word that this was a place where Mexican refugees could find safety and enough arable land to support their families. The settlement was organized communally, with individual families contributing to the general welfare without owning the land themselves. This communalism and altruism struck Anglo ranchers as odd and worrying.[15]

Those refugees who could not find their way to El Porvenir had a more harrowing journey. During the winter of 1913–1914, refugees fled into the Big Bend following a Mexican Army defeat at Ojinaga by Pancho Villa's army. The Battle of Ojinaga produced more than a thousand casualties. The *New York Times* reported that "a steady stream of suffering humanity trailing down the Camino del Muerto, 'road of the dead,' arrived daily" in southwestern Texas. Some men carried their comrades across the river, others were seen "crawling to the American side with stumps of arms appealing for aid," and many of the severely wounded remained on the battlefield as a "feast of human flesh" for the buzzards wheeling overhead. A first lieutenant of the federal army crawled through the brush to the feet of an American soldier and begged to be shot in the head—his mortal wounds and loss of upper extremities were too much to bear. Local Presidio officials called out for all available physicians, surgeons, and nurses within a three-hundred-mile radius, and the US Army arrived with tents and cots for the wounded.[16]

Joining the civilian refugees were armed Mexican soldiers, immediately detained by American officials upon crossing the border. The American soldiers in the region were part of President Taft's War Plan Green, implemented in February 1913, which sent the US Army's Second Division to Galveston and ordered an Atlantic fleet to Veracruz to monitor the revolutionary situation there. The troops in Texas escorted the refugees another sixty-seven miles north to Marfa; the journey became known as El Camino Dolores (the Road of Sorrows).[17] The terrain was dangerous; the road was narrow, with sudden turns and an elevation that reached 4,900 feet above sea level. Along the roadside were makeshift graves of stone piles holding wooden crosses that marked the site of a fallen refugee or a victim of revolutionary fighting. As the refugees passed each marker, they solemnly motioned the sign of the cross and whispered, "probrecito" (poor fellow).[18]

The four-day march to Marfa began each day at sunrise and ended upon sunset. The refugee caravan was full of women and children and resembled, according to the American commander, the "migration of some primitive people in the early dawn of history, rather than the orderly procedure of an army of modern times." And he described them to be "nearly all of Indian strain."[19] At the end of this four-day journey to Marfa, the refugees boarded trains to Fort Bliss, near El Paso, where they were corralled behind barbed-wire fences as "guests" of the United States. A timeline for release was not given, and the refugees would remain in internment camps for eight months. Texans did not want the visitors, but they also did not want to release such a large group of poor Mexican refugees in the United States. Texans feared that any of those released would join outlaws known as "river men" along the Rio Grande, become a financial burden on charitable American organizations in the cities, or swell to overcrowded impoverished Mexican neighborhoods in El Paso.

There were more than five thousand Mexican prisoners at Fort Bliss, which cost the army \$719,883 in supplies and aid. The camp had an electrical lighting system, bathing facilities, and tents that resembled barracks. Mexican generals had their own tents where they lived with their families. The adjutant general's office instructed officials at Fort Bliss on the daily operations of the prisoners, who were all to be vaccinated for smallpox and inoculated against typhoid. Officials at Fort Bliss established a school for the numerous Mexican children and put men to work "mixing adobe to build Mexican style huts."[20] A glowing report from El Paso circulated throughout the national press announcing that the conditions were hospitable for America's "guests" and that "those in the camp are glad to be there."[21] Press reports announced that the Mexican children who had made the desert and mountain journey "half-naked" and "barefoot" were now clothed and appeared "happier than it usually befalls a Mexican child to be, even in its own land, under favorable conditions."[22] One political cartoon, "Uncle Sam's Mexican Refugee Restaurant," quipped that the conditions in the camp were so impressive that the creation of more camps similar to the one at Fort Bliss could bring an end to the revolution once news of the camps reached central Mexico.

Articles in the Anglo press reported that hundreds of Mexicans in the El Paso area tried to break into the internment camp because of the good conditions there. However, the official report from the Fort Bliss historical records makes no mention of this, suggesting that the camps were not the coveted destinations that the Anglo press made them out to be.[23] This silence did not deter the propagandists, who portrayed the camps as a worthwhile tourist attraction.

Indeed, El Pasoans now looked upon the compound with pride. Sightseers took photographs of the refugees and told themselves that they were being offered a better life than what they had experienced in Mexico.[24] Inside the camp, the prisoners were at first divided by politics but then united by their anger at the US government for keeping them locked up.[25] Release was problematic. The northern Mexican states bordering Texas and New Mexico were heavily fortified by rebels, and if Mexican federal soldiers were released and sent back they would more than likely be captured and executed. The same fate might have befallen captive soldiers if turned over either to President Victoriano Huerta or to General Venustiano Carranza, for both saw these men as enemy combatants. Nevertheless, Huerta wanted them returned, and diplomatic relations between the two countries worsened as the United States refused to do so.[26]

Anglo Texans believed that refugees who managed to escape from the camp were armed and dangerous. On the night of April 18, two men, Zarco and Pallares, crawled under the barbed-wire fence on the east side of the camp, where they had previously destroyed the lights, and fled on foot. Melvin Switzer and A. T. Flanery were the guards on patrol, and each fired at the escapees. Zarco was struck in the leg and Pallares in the back. The bullet pierced through the latter man and exited his stomach; he died a few days later. Following the incident, escape attempts became more frequent, and many succeeded.[27] Labeled as criminals and hiding in the mountainous terrain of the border region, these men eventually found refuge in small Mexican communities along the Rio Grande. As for the interned, the federal government relocated the camp to Fort Wingate, New Mexico, over 350 miles from the Mexican border. On May 5, 1914, three trains transported 4,825 Mexican people to their new location. As they exited the transport, many pleaded for their release. "We have done no harm, take us back to Mexico" was a cry frequently heard.[28] But authorities would not release any of them until Huerta fell from power, which happened in July 1914, and the US government received assurances from Pancho Villa that their repatriation would not be met with violence.[29]

It is unknown how many refugees fled Mexico during the decade of the Mexican Revolution, or how many were involved in border raids, but it is clear that Anglo Texans were suspicious of ethnic Mexicans who were not kept under the watchful eye of the military or segregated into the Mexican districts of cities like San Antonio and El Paso. In addition to Fort Bliss and Fort Wingate, Mexican nationals were interned at Fort McIntosh, Texas, and Fort Rosecrans, California. A total of 5,379 Mexican citizens were interned during the summer of 1914. By mid-decade, the "Mexican problem" Anglos spoke about referred to the large number of refugees who had entered Texas and escaped to the "river section" of the Big Bend.

TEXAS RANCH RAIDS

Border raids in Texas by Mexicans became more frequent by mid-decade. While the press continued to publish reports about a growing foreign threat along the border, Texas governor Oscar B. Colquitt wrestled with the federal government over who would be physically and fiscally responsible for polic-ing the border. When neither the state nor the federal government responded swiftly to border violence, civilians formed posses to pursue suspected crimi-nals. The question of responsibility began with President Taft and continued with President Wilson: Should the federal government send troops to the border, or was this the responsibility of the state of Texas? In March 1911 Taft sent thirty thousand troops to San Antonio but refused to deploy them along the border or to engage much with Mexican troops. Moreover, the federal government required Texas officials to get Washington's approval before tak-ing action; however, Washington did not have to inform the state of Texas what its plans were. Equally problematic for Colquitt was the fact that may-ors, judges, and sheriffs had the power to call up the Texas Rangers without the governor's approval and charge Ranger expenses to the state. On several occasions, Sheriff Payton J. Edwards of El Paso County assembled Anglo men to fight on behalf of the state, which prompted Colquitt to describe the sheriff as "an excitable person, prone to jump to conclusions."[30] Colquitt walked a fine line: he needed to downplay the border problems locally to prevent civilian posses and talk up the problem with Washington in order to encourage federal involvement.

Following the resignation of Porfirio Díaz in May, US ambassador Henry Lane Wilson prematurely believed that Mexico would return to stability. Thus, by August 1911, Taft had disbanded the troops stationed in San Anto-nio.[31] Wilson inherited the "Mexican problem" from Taft in 1913, as did Gov-ernor James E. Ferguson, who succeeded Colquitt in 1915. The Anglo press kept Texans aware that no official policy was in place and declared that in

sparse regions like the Texas Big Bend, citizens had the right to protect their property at any cost, especially after news broke of a Mexican manifesto to reclaim the Southwest for Mexico. Those who took the pledge allegedly vowed to murder all Anglo men sixteen years of age and older.

In January 1915 immigration authorities arrested Basilio Ramos Jr., a native of Nuevo Laredo, Mexico, on charges of sedition. Ramos had entered the United States in possession of the manifesto—the "Plan de San Diego." The purpose of this plan was to start a revolution in the states of Texas, Oklahoma, New Mexico, Arizona, Colorado, Nevada, and California. In Texas, the plan initially called for an uprising of ethnic Mexicans to reclaim the land between the Nueces River and the Rio Grande, and gradually spreading from there.[32] The federal indictment charged Ramos with attempting to "steal" US property (the targeted states). The charges were ultimately dismissed, with the judge stating that Ramos should not be tried for conspiracy; instead, the judge opined, he "ought to be tried for lunacy."[33] Although the federal court dismissed the case, the court of public opinion in Texas believed that Ramos exemplified the Mexican threat.

The stories of rebel raids on Mexican ranches and haciendas made their way into Texas with the refugees. One man from Santa Rosalía, Mexico, reported that he had witnessed Villa's men capture two women, soak their hair in oil, and light them on fire. These same men declared that they would "kill all Americans and Chinese caught" by their forces.[34] The revolution took a gruesome turn when 224 foreign, mostly Chinese, workers were slain in Torreón. Millionaire business partners Foon Chuck and Sam Wah, living in Ciudad Juárez, received a telegraph from their surviving agent. Wah, the proprietor of the International Hotel in Ciudad Porfirio Díaz (present-day Piedras Negras), and Chuck, the owner of several farms, were businessmen who had profited off Mexican land during the Porfiriato. Mexican revolutionaries were as determined to strike at them as they were at Americans.[35] Chuck and Wah were Chinese immigrants who found themselves trapped in Mexico. Fleeing the revolution and returning to China was not their preferred option, because the businessmen desired to remain close to their investments. Due to the 1882 Chinese Exclusion Act, the men could not seek refuge in the United States. If caught on American soil, they would be deported back to China. However, anti-Chinese rhetoric, fueled by revolutionary leaders, forced Chuck and Wah to abandon their property and return to China. As for the victims and surviving family members of the Torreón massacre, Ambassador Wilson helped negotiate an indemnity case that ordered the Mexican government to pay three million pesos to the Chinese government. By the summer of 1912, more than a year after the Torreón massacre, the Mexican government still had failed to yield to international demands.[36]

Additionally, Pancho Villa promulgated an "expulsion act" in 1914 to rid Torreón of Chinese families.[37] Similar to the US deportation of Chinese workers following the completion of the Southern Pacific Railroad in 1881, Villa wanted to remove the once sought-after Chinese laborers. During the Porfiriato, President Díaz encouraged Chinese migration and went so far as to grant China "most favored nation" status with the 1893 Treaty of Amity and Commerce.[38] Rebel leaders who opposed Díaz supported Chinese exclusion policies and often used racist slurs such as *chinacate* to refer to unwanted Chinese foreigners. Propagandists "depicted Chinese immigration as 'an avalanche that has inundated us.'"[39] Racism against the Chinese was far more common after the ousting of Díaz. Between 1916 and 1918 schoolteacher José María Arana was instrumental in organizing Mexican fraternal organizations that targeted Chinese laborers. These anti-Chinese leagues enrolled more than five thousand members in the northern states of Chihuahua, Sonora, and Baja California. In his weekly tabloid *Pro-Patria*, Arana published the following statement in each issue:

> Improvement of the race is the supreme ideal of all civilized nations, so that if the Chinese are corrupting our race, we ought to restrict them. The Chinese produce on the towns the same effect that the locust has on the crops: they destroy them. The Mexican that defends the Chinese with detriment to the national good, is a traitor to the country.[40]

Mexican violence against Chinese laborers during the 1910s was often racially motivated, and the Torreón massacre demonstrated the brutality.

These were the stories of Mexican-on-foreigner violence that made their way into Texas homes via the American press as thousands of refugees were entering the country. Revolutionary forces were already operating in northern Mexico in part to secure supplies. As the population in northern Mexico thinned, rebels started extending their raids in American territory, provoking Anglo Texans to resort to extralegal punishment for suspected Mexican criminals.

The most notorious raid on American soil was an attack in Columbus, New Mexico. The raid, led by Pancho Villa's men in March 1916, quickly escalated into a battle between US soldiers and Villistas, which resulted in the death of eighty Mexicans and eighteen US soldiers. A fatal prison fire in El Paso might have provoked this raid; nineteen of the prisoners who died in the fire were Villista soldiers. Brigadier General S. L. A. Marshall recalled what happened at the prison. Almost a week before the Columbus raid, jailer Frank Scotten Sr. was delousing the prisoners to prevent the spread of typhus. Nineteen Mexican soldiers had just been incarcerated after crossing the border, and the delousing procedure in the jail involved showering the prisoners with a mixture of gasoline, kerosene, and vinegar. The news reported that one prisoner, unmindful of the contents of the mixture, struck a match to light a cigarette and engulfed the prison in flames. Initial reports indicated that eighteen prisoners perished; the nineteenth died a few days later.[41] Whether the Columbus raid was a response to the prison accident is unknown. There was further speculation that the prison fire might not have been an accident; according to Marshall, "when the raid hit [in Columbus], we in El Paso thought that this was a reprisal for what had happened in the jail."[42] The press reported that in Ciudad Juárez, rumors quickly spread that "200 Mexicans had been thrown in jail in El Paso and deliberately burned to death."[43] Marshall explained how dozens of El Paso Anglo men responded: "The night after the [Columbus] raid I went downtown to San Antonio Street and there were mobs of Anglos . . . going up and down San Antonio Street armed with clubs and pistols and so on. Every time they ran into a Mexican they would beat him up and throw him into an alley. It was one of the most horrible scenes I've ever seen."[44] The Anglo men in El Paso sent a message to ethnic Mexicans that night: Americans would punish them for raids on US soil.

Two months after the Columbus raids, on the night of May 5, 1916, C. G. Compton, who ran both the general store and the post office at Glenn Springs, awoke around 11:00 p.m. to the sound of armed Mexican men outside. Glenn Springs was an isolated community that employed as many as sixty Mexican workers at a candelilla wax factory, some of whom were refugees. There were Anglos and Mexicans living at Glenn Springs, segregated in separate sections of the ranch: the east side housed the Anglo families and the west side was known as "Mexican Glenn Springs." The location was perfect for the business because of the endless flow of "liquid gold" in this desert region—water. Candelilla is a perennial used to make shoe polish, car wax, and chewing gum. Workers were paid a dollar a day to boil the stem, separate the wax, and package it for shipping.[45] The armed men were suspected to be

Venustiano Carranza's soldiers and Mexican outlaws from the "river section" of the Big Bend. The number of attackers is unclear. Some reports say there were sixty-five, while others estimate up to four hundred men. Regardless, only nine soldiers of the Fourteenth US Cavalry were stationed there.[46]

The Mexican raiders located the bunkhouse where the soldiers slept and set it on fire. When Private Cohen tried to escape through a window, the raiders shot him in the face with a shotgun. Private Colock was shot in the back trying to round up the horses. Privates Defeers and Buck were shot in their arms and legs, respectively, and badly burned. Compton took his daughter to a Mexican woman on the Mexican side of Glenn Springs for safety before returning to fight off the invaders. He fired roughly 140 rounds of ammunition before he escaped and fled the village. When he returned, he found his nine-year-old son shot in the leg, stomach, and chest with his head battered in; "the blood stained floor of the room told a pitiful tale of the child's frantic efforts to escape his assassins" before his death. Another Anglo family at Glenn Springs fell under attack. W. K. Ellis and his wife ran toward the nearby mountains and returned after daybreak to find one son dead on the floor lying next to his deaf brother, who somehow had managed to avoid harm.[47]

Mrs. Alice Hart escaped with the help of a Mexican family who smuggled her in their wagon and covered her up while they drove her to safety in McKinney Springs. They were stopped several times by armed Mexicans, who let them pass unharmed. The press reported that Mexicans on the Texas side of the border knew of the planned attack as well as the identity of many of the attackers. Compton's story of the raid also led many to believe that the Mexicans living at Glenn Springs were aware of the raid and even provided necessary information about the layout of the property and where the soldiers were housed. However, Compton's evidence relied on the fact that his dog barked while the Mexican dogs in Glenn Springs did not; he did not have much more evidence than that.[48]

It was later speculated that Rodríguez Ramírez of Torreón, a Villista living in El Paso, launched the raid, marching with seventeen others along the Rio Grande for 250 miles toward Glenn Springs. Along the way, they recruited more "river men" and crossed the river at Teague Ranch, 25 miles from Glenn Springs, with two hundred men.[49] Following the attack at Glenn Springs, President Woodrow Wilson ordered the Texas National Guard to reinforce the troops on the border and to mobilize at Glenn Springs. The brutality that had left American soldiers and an American boy dead at Glenn Springs persuaded terrified Anglos to take up arms against suspicious foreigners. The region was engrossed in its own war, one that did not have a line of division along a border; the line was between two distinct peoples who lived uneasily alongside each other in the Big Bend.

MOBILIZATION OF THE ORGANIZED MILITIA

When the Glenn Springs raid occurred, General John J. Pershing was leading the Punitive Expedition of 4,800 soldiers into Mexico, in a hunt for Pancho Villa because of his raid on Columbus, New Mexico. When news reached this expedition that Villa might have ordered the raid at Glenn Springs, the Eighth Cavalry, led by Lieutenant George S. Patton, took revenge on San Miguelito Ranch in Rubio, Chihuahua. It was here that Patton shot and killed three Villistas, one of whom was Julio Cardeñas, a captain in Villa's ranks. Clashes between Villistas and US troops continued through February 1917.

President Venustiano Carranza of Mexico sent a letter to Washington charging that the United States had invaded Mexico following the Columbus raid to seize northern Mexican territory under the guise that they were hunting Villa. Carranza demanded that the American troops depart immediately.[50] While searching for Villa, the Tenth Cavalry encountered Mexican federal troops at Carrizal, Chihuahua. The official order was to avoid a collision with federal Mexican soldiers, but, if attacked, US troops were to "inflict as much damage as possible, having regard for the safety" of the troops.[51] Francisco Dawl, an eyewitness and resident of Carrizal, explained that an American detachment led by Captain Charles T. Boyd was headed toward Villa Ahumada when they entered Carrizal. Two Mexican cavalry regiments led by General Félix Gómez were stationed at Carrizal, and they ordered Boyd to bypass the town. With "stubborn insistence," however, Boyd marched his men forward. "American troops fired first," according to Dawl, and the battle left eleven Americans and twenty-four Mexicans dead. The Mexican troops took twenty-four US soldiers as prisoners.[52] The Punitive Expedition never captured Villa and strained diplomatic relations with Carranza, already under suspicion in Washington for his alleged pro-German attitudes.

In May 1916, following the raids at Columbus and Glenn Springs, President Wilson called upon the National Guard. On May 9, Secretary of War Newton D. Baker sent a telegram to the governors of Texas, Arizona, and New Mexico, stating:

Having in view the possibility of further aggression upon the territory of the United States from Mexico and the necessity for the proper protection of that frontier, the President has thought proper to exercise the authority vested in him by the Constitution and laws and call out the Organized Militia necessary for that purpose.[53]

In June 1916 Mexican rebels entered Texas near Laredo and clashed with US soldiers. Wilson responded to this action by calling out the National Guard of all forty-eight states. The first National Guard troops to reach the border were the First Illinois Infantry, which departed from Springfield, Illinois, and arrived in San Antonio on June 30, 1916. A week later, 27,160 troops from fourteen states joined the Illinois troops and were positioned all along the two-thousand-mile border with Mexico. By August 1, 112,000 troops were stationed along the border from Brownsville, Texas, to Douglas, Arizona.[54]

Coordinating these groups of men proved to be a major test for the army. None of the troops had seen combat. Complicating matters further, governors were unwilling to send their best-trained soldiers to the border. Once governors received orders to call up units, a problem with the system of dual control became clear. The governors did not always call up their most efficient units for service. The "Mexican problem" was not a pressing issue with the governors of states located hundreds of miles away from the border. Thus, "due to local or political considerations, any but the most efficient units were called out . . . [and] the Federal Government thus failed to get the best the state was able to produce."[55]

Private Roger Batchelder of the Eighth Massachusetts Regiment published a memoir of his experience as a guardsman along the border, *Watching and Waiting on the Border*, in 1917. Batchelder faulted the US military "system" for the "incompetency" of the soldiers along the border:

It was the fault of the system—a system which drills men for two hours a week, neglects their needs for accouterments, asks a few to perform the duty of the many, and expects to institute a first-class fighting machine. Such expectation would be humorous, were it not now so tragic.[56]

Guardsmen like Batchelder were aware of their poor training and soldiering skills and even commented on how inefficient their reserve force was compared to the regular army in the region.

Many of the troops questioned the necessity of their service along the border and wondered if the haste in which they had been called up "was a political move and that they were making sacrifices for nothing."[57] Training officers argued that the troops were not properly trained, and several of the officers making the decisions were men of questionable character. Lieutenant James W. Everington, an inspector and instructor, sent troops to the border without requiring them to complete the usual twelve-mile march; he reported that only one regiment made it as far as three miles. Everington would later go on to become Los Angeles police chief in 1922. However, after serving in that capacity for only three months, Los Angeles mayor George E. Cryer fired Everington for "rank insubordination and disrespect to superior officers." Everington stated that while an honest man could not be the city's police chief, "a crook can be chief, though, if he's clever enough not to get caught."[58] Such individuals were making decisions to send troops to the border poorly trained and lacking the necessary desire to fight.

In June 1916 the Texas National Guard stationed guardsmen in Glenn Springs. The cartoons of soldier Jodie P. Harris chronicled the daily lives of these guardsmen. Harris, of Mineral Wells, Texas, sent postcards on a weekly basis to his family with sketches of daily life patrolling the border at Glenn Springs. The son of a Civil War veteran, Harris had earlier family who had fought in the American Revolutionary War. Harris would later serve in both world wars. He provides a unique picture of the time as well as of national and international events. He penned satirist newspapers of the military efforts on the frontier, writing both the editorials and drawing the cartoons for the *Big Bend* and *La Noria* (fig. 4.1).

Harris's publications were a direct attack on the US press for raising Anglo hysteria about a Mexican threat along the border. The more excited Americans grew about the problems in the region, he alleged, the more papers were sold. He argued that plots for border raids were "hatched on this side of the border by unscrupulous Americans." Moreover, he was critical of the federal government's motives for Mexican intervention. His cartoon diary voiced the frustrations of his fellow soldiers guarding a nearly abandoned factory at Glenn Springs.

Infused with humor and cynicism, Harris's cartoons bordered on insubordination with his criticism of the US military. In one section of his paper, he posted, "Donkeys, $5; Goats, $1; Wax, $0.19; an honorable discharge from the United States Service, Unobtainable." The only satisfied soldier was the company mascot, Chili, the soldiers' dog. In an attempt to keep themselves

Figure 4.1 "Watchful Waiting," *Big Bend*, Jodie P. Harris Collection, Archives of the Big Bend, Bryan Wildenthal Memorial Library, Sul Ross State University, Alpine, Texas.

entertained, the troops played baseball against each other and even played against Mexican boys who lived in the region. Harris claimed in his cartoons that the press exaggerated the frequency of Mexican raids on Texas property. The reality that such raids hardly ever occurred left the men disappointed, and by the winter of 1916 they were cold, lonely, and missing their families (figs. 4.2a and 4.2b).[59]

Private Batchelder's memoir supported Harris's assessment that the border was less volatile than he and other soldiers expected. His memoir further reveals an additional reason troop morale waned as their time along the border continued. Batchelder indulged in stereotypes of Mexicans as having poor hygiene and likened them to "a bloodthirsty animal that inhabits the wilderness beyond the Rio Grande."[60] However, he disliked Texans almost as much. He stated that all of the guardsmen he spoke with shared a similar feeling about Anglo Texans. The bitterness was a result of the poor conduct Texans exhibited toward nonofficer guardsmen. Texans showed respect to their Rangers and to any wearer of "the gold braid," an emblem that distinguished "an officer and a gentleman," but the enlisted men received little respect from Anglo men and women. Batchelder recalled a sign outside of a dancehall in Ysleta, a small town southeast of El Paso, that read: "DANCING FOR LADIES AND GENTLEMEN, SOLDIERS AND DOGS NOT ALLOWED."[61] Such announcements were similar to signs excluding Mexicans and blacks in all-white establishments. Restrictions like these often led to clashes between soldiers and attendees, reported in the press the following day as disturbances by "unruly soldiers." Batchelder declared, "I merely claim that a soldier, or a Guardsman, should at least be treated as a man, and not as the Texans treat a Mexican."[62] Batchelder's memoirs and the Harris cartoons support the argument that banditry was infrequent—leading Harris to argue that reported stories of banditry were fabricated. However, the brief period of stability and the decrease in raids was most likely a result of the large presence of the US military in the region. Batchelder and the Eighth Massachusetts Regiment departed Texas in mid-October and arrived back in Worcester, Massachusetts, on October 21, 1916.[63] He recalled learning that raiding resumed in the region as the military pulled out of the borderland. In the end Batchelder believed that the deployment was a success because border raids on the US side decreased when guardsmen were present.[64] However, Mexicans experienced an increase in disturbances on their side of the border as the US military sought Pancho Villa.

LOCALS

90 MILES FROM A POST OFFICE

CAMP MERCER KNOWN AT THE WAR DEPARTMENT AS STILLWELL CROSSING

Lt. C.K. DAVIS WHO IS IN COMMAND AT CAMP MERCER RECEIVED A BIG CAKE FROM MINERAL WELLS ON LAST TRUCK.

Lt. CAMERON WHO IS IN COMMAND AT LANORIA BROUGHT THE PAY ROLL OVER LAST WEEK.

SGTS. ODELL AND HARRIS HAVE FLOORED THEIR TENTS WITH GRAVEL & OTHER IMPROVEMENTS ARE TAKING PLACE HERE.

CORPS HEATH AND HARRISON AND PRVT'S BREWTON, CRAIN, DOTSON AND HOLLYFIELD WENT HUNTING YESTERDAY. THE RABBIT WAS TOO POOR TO EAT.

CORP BLATHERWICK IS CONFINED TO HIS COT THIS WEEK. HIS ILLNESS BEING DUE TO OVEREATING. WE HAD BISCUITS.

PRIVATES HINES, HIGHSAW AND MARTIN ARE ASSISTING OUR POPULAR COOK SUDBERRY IN MAKING A DUTCH OVEN TODAY.

PRIVATES MORGAN AND ROLLINS ARE ON THE SICK LIST.

ELMO SNIDER IS ON A FURLOUGH.

ATTENTION MEN WHO BE IN LAST NIGHT PLAYING BLACKJACK WITH A MEX.

PRIVATE SCHLESSIER AND WELCH BOUGHT A PIE OF MUTTON AND FISH FROM A MEXICAN. THE DOC SAYS THEY WILL RECOVER.

SLAM-SCHELBURMAN OUR EMERGENCY DOG RECEIVED AN BOTTLE OF CASTOR OIL AND A POUND OF SALTS, HIS MINTEN SUPPLY OF DRUGS.

MEREDITH, ROBERTS, ROSE, RAHEY, HARRIS AND VENFRED ARE SINGING A NEW SONG.

McMAHAN, A TEAMSTER WHO WAS DETACHED FROM THE GREENVILLE COMPANY TO COL. WENT OVER THE HILL. WHICH EXPRESSION IS THE ARMY EQUIVALENT FOR DESERTION. WITH THIS EXCEPTION ALL OF THIS DETACHMENT ARE PRESENT OR ACCOUNTED FOR.

WHICH WAY AM I TURNING?

RED TAPE

WINDING OR UNWINDING IT?

RED TAPE

THE REAL BORDER BANDIT

BOQUILLAS

88 MILES FROM A RAILROAD

BOQUILLAS, IS ANOTHER CROSSING ON THE RIO GRANDE 88 MILES FROM A POST OFFICE.

SOME TIME AGO A MAN BY THE NAME OF DEEMER OPENED A STORE THERE WHICH HIS CUSTOMERS CAME FROM A DISTANCE OF MYSTERY. AS NO ONE KNEW THERE EXCEPT THE MEXICANS. CONSEQUENTLY AN ENTERPRISE HAS LOOKED FOR WITH SUSPICION BY ALL GOOD CITIZENS OF BREWSTER COUNTY.

ON MAY 5TH HIS STORE WAS ROBBED, AND AC CORDING TO MR. DEEMER'S STATEMENT $8000 IN MERCHANDISE AND $400 IN CASH WAS CARRIED AWAY BY BANDITS. MR. DEEMER SENT UP A HOWL FOR TROOPS AND ONE TROOP OF CAVALRY AND A COMPANY OF MILITIA WAS SENT TO PROTECT HIM AND HIS PROPERTY.

HE THEN COMPLAINED TO THE GOVERNMENT THAT THE SOLDIERS NEAR STARVED HIS U.S. PROPERTY AND ALSO THAT THEY ATE NOTHING THAT THEY MADE OUR RATIONS. HE IS NOW ENJOYING THE COMFORTS OF SUNNY CALIFORNIA, WHILE THE TEXAS MILITIA IS LEFT TO GUARD THE UNPROTECTED SAND HILLS OF THE RIO GRANDE. DEEMER IS GONE - BOQUILLAS IS FOR RENT - THAT IS WHY WE HAVE NO NEWS FROM THERE IN THIS ISSUE.

UNDER COVER

ONE OF THE FIRST LESSONS IN WARFARE TAUGHT THE RAW RECRUIT IS TO HUNT COVER WHILE IN ACTION. WE WERE LECTURED EVERY FEW DAYS BY THE COLONEL, THE MAJOR AND THE CAPTAIN, AND THE PARTING ADMONITION OF EACH WAS 'BOYS, REMEMBER TO GET UNDER COVER'

A FEW DAYS AGO A NORTHER CAME AND REMEMBERING THE ADVICE OF OUR COMMANDING OFFICERS, WE APPEALED TO THE QUARTERMASTER FOR MORE BLANKETS.

WE WERE THEN TOLD THAT THE QUARTERMASTER DEPARTMENT WERE WAITING THE OUTCOME OF THE MEXICAN MEDIATION MEETING BEFORE ISSUING MORE BLANKETS.

THE BOYS HAVE SENT IN REQUISITIONS TO THEIR MOTHERS FOR COMFORTS, AND UNTIL THEY ARRIVE WE ARE USING GUNNY SACKS, OLD CLOTHES OR ANYTHING TO KEEP US WARM.

LANORIA ONE NEW

80 MILES FROM A POST OFFICE

A REPORT CAME IN THIS MORNING OF A GREAT DISASTER AT LANORIA. A CLOUD OF 'GLOOM WAS CAST OVER' THE ENTIRE COMPANY WHEN THE NEWS WAS RECEIVED THAT THE SUBWAY HAD CAVED IN AT LANORIA. IT WAS LATER LEARNED HOWEVER THAT THE REPORT WAS PROBABLY UNFOUNDED AS SINKY GULLY WAS THE ORIGIN OF THE STATEMENT

SEVERAL OF THE BOYS ARE AWAY ON A FURLOUGH.

COMPANY I RECEIVED ANOTHER TRUCK LOAD OF WOOD - IT COMES IN MIGHTY HANDY AS IT IS COLD

SOME OF THE BOYS HAVE BEEN KNOCKED OUT, IT MUST BE THE WATER

CAPT. BIGGERS IS AWAY ON A FURLOUGH CAPT. CAMERON STAINED OVER FROM CAMP MERCER SOME TIME NO AND IS NOW IN COMMAND AT LANORIA, AS NEWS IS SCARCE AND NOTHING EVER HAPPENS IN LANORIA WE CLOSE FOR THIS TIME. REPORTER.

TERLINGUA

TERLINGUA WHERE THE FAMOUS CHISOS QUICKSILVER MINES ARE LOCATED, IS ABOUT A HUNDRED MILES FROM A RAIL ROAD AND ABOUT 70 MILES FROM THE RIO GRANDE RIVER

THESE MINES FURNISH ABOUT ONE FOURTH OF THE WORLD'S SUPPLY OF QUICKSILVER AND FURNISHES EMPLOYMENT FOR SEVERAL HUNDRED MEXICANS.

SEVERAL YEARS AGO A LAW WAS PASSED IN TEXAS PROHIBITING AN MILL OWNERS FROM THE PAYING WAGES THE PEONS UNDER THE CHECK SYSTEM IN PAYMENT FOR LABOR, BUT EVIDENTLY THIS LAW IS NOT RECOGNIZED AT THE CHISOS MINES, AS THE PEON IN EXCHANGE FOR HIS LABOR GETS LITTLE MORE THAN FOOD AND CLOTHING FOR HIMSELF AND FAMILY.

ONE TROOP OF THE SIXTH CAVALRY AND ONE COMPANY OF THE TEXAS MILITIA IS STATIONED THERE.

VERY LITTLE IS KNOWN AS NO ONE IS ALLOWED TO ENTER THEM, AND THE OWNERS ARE NOT SEEKING PUBLICITY AND FEW PEOPLE KNOW THAT LOCATED IN ANY OBSCURE PORTION OF BREWSTER COUNTY IS ONE OF THE BIG GIST QUICKSILVER MINES IN THE WORLD

AS YET THIS PAPER HAS BEEN UNABLE TO SECURE A CORRESPONDENT.

WITH THE EXCEPTION OF GLEN SPRINGS, WHERE A. AND B. TROOPS OF THE 6TH CAVALRY ARE STATIONED EVERY POINT IN THE BIG BEND SECTION IS GIVEN MENTION, A DISTANCE OF OVER A HUNDRED MILES.

THESE FACTS ARE NOT EXAGGERATED, NEITHER IS THE IMPORTANCE OF THESE PLACES MINIMIZED, SO THE READER CAN DRAW HIS OWN CONCLUSIONS.

AH! THIS WILL BE A FINE VACATION - THE MILITIA WILL BE BACK HOME IN A MONTH AND I CAN ENJOY MYSELF AT THE EXPENSE OF THE GOVERNMENT

SIX MONTHS AGO AND

FREEZING ON AN OUTPOST GUARDING UNPROTECTED HILL SIDES, IS GETTING OLD

TO-NIGHT

Figure 4.2a and 4.2b "Six Months Ago and Tonight," *Big Bend*, Jodie P. Harris Collection, Archives of the Big Bend, Bryan Wildenthal Memorial Library, Sul Ross State University, Alpine, Texas.

LAWLESSNESS AND VENGEANCE

The literature of the Big Bend is full of stories of bandits and raids. One of history's best-kept secrets is that Americans themselves engaged in a bit of raiding in the Big Bend. In order to understand this claim, one must conceptualize the Big Bend as a region that includes both sides of the border, not exclusively the Texas region, and "bandits" must be understood as any persons who attack a community or a group of people without warrant, and who punish their victims through extralegal measures.

Lajitas, in Brewster County, was home to a small detachment of the Eighth Cavalry of the US Army. Their duty was to patrol the riverbed area. On back-to-back days, a patrolman reported that he had been fired upon from the Mexican side of the river. The lieutenant in charge took all of his men up the river to the little Mexican settlement known as Arroyo Frezno (Ash Creek). Without any proof that the community was involved, without any knowledge of weapons that might be there, and ignoring international law, the US soldiers entered Mexico and searched Mexican homes. Residents fled to the hills as the army approached. A Mexican witness of the raid reported that the only guns fired were by the US soldiers, and the only death was that of a pig shot by one of the raiders "to hear him squeal."[65] The US bandits stole corn, chili, honey, dried meats, and ten gallons of sotol (a liquor distilled from the sotol plant). As the "Jingo Bandits" left, they lit the small village on fire and watched the homes quickly burn to the ground. The Mexican families whose homes had just been burned out walked thirty miles to San Carlos for aid and shelter.[66]

If it wasn't for the sotol, this story might not be known to history. The soldiers consumed the intoxicant and allowed too much time to pass without contacting their captain, who was stationed at the neighboring mining camp of Chisos. When he learned that the lieutenant had left his post unguarded and then returned "lit up with Mexican fire water," the captain relieved him of his duties and gave him a dishonorable discharge. Nevertheless, stories of Mexican bandits in the Big Bend led Anglo Texans to believe that the perpetrators were overwhelmingly Mexican.

Raids continued in the Big Bend as US troops began to leave the region. In the foothills of Capote Mountain in Presidio County, the Luke Brite Ranch, also known as the Bar-Cross Ranch, had uninvited guests arrive on Christmas morning, 1917. Fifty to seventy-five men worked and lived on the ranch with their families. Christmas fell on a Tuesday in 1917, and many of the families had begun leaving over the preceding weekend in order to spend Christmas Day in neighboring towns with relatives. The ranch foreman, Van Neill, planned to spend Christmas on the ranch with his wife, his son, Van Jr., and his two daughters. Joining them would be his father, mother, and two teenage nieces.

A few days earlier on Saturday afternoon, a Mexican boy about fifteen years old arrived at the ranch. He claimed to be meeting friends from Pecos for the holidays. The Neills let the boy stay the weekend in the bunkhouse, and he played with the other ranch children. The youngsters, excited about their visitor's arrival, placed a gift for the boy on the Christmas tree. On Christmas Eve, José Sánchez, the cowhand, dressed up in a bright red Santa Claus suit and handed out gifts to the children anxiously sitting around the Christmas tree. During the festivities, the mysterious young visitor vanished, and he was later seen far away from the house building a fire. He appeared to be waving a torch around in the sky. Those who noticed wondered if it was some traditional Mexican Christmas ceremony, while others just thought that he was a lonely boy playing a game.

As the sun rose over the mountains and Sam Neill, Van's father, was drinking his morning coffee, two dozen strangers on horseback approached from the Southwest. "Bandits!" Neill shouted throughout the house. Sam and Van took their shotguns and guarded the two ends of the house while their wives and daughters lay flat on the floor in the dining room. During the raid, José

Sánchez met with both parties as a messenger in an attempt to end the hostilities. The Mexican raiders demanded the keys to the store. Once at the store, they emptied sacks of corn all over the floor to make room for their loot. Mickey Welch, who delivered the mail in the region, arrived at the store and interrupted the men. The raiders believed that Welch recognized them and took him into the store. The men tied a rope around his neck and hanged him from the beams. While Welch struggled for his life, the men cut his throat.

During the gunfight, Mrs. Neill tried to get to the store, which had a telephone, with the assistance of Crescencia Natividad, a Mexican cook. Natividad would not let Mrs. Neill go alone, and she became known as the Heroine of Brite Ranch because of her bravery. She protected Neill by covering Neill's body with her own as they crossed open ground on the ranch. The Neill men continued to defend the ranch and eventually shot and killed the leader of the bandit group, Placido Villanueva. Villanueva's jacket was examined, and it was rumored that a letter was found on him addressed to rebel leader Venustiano Carranza from the Germans instructing the men to raid the ranch.[67] News of the raid reached neighboring Marfa, where US troops were stationed. These troops followed the retreating raiders into Mexico for two days, killing several Mexican men and claiming to have recovered some of the stolen goods.

There were many competing theories about who had ordered the raid. Were these Carranza's men? Their uniforms would suggest that they were. Were they Villistas dressed as Carranza's men, or were there global implications, with Germany perhaps interested in inciting a war between the United States and Mexico? One thing is certain: the raid united Anglo civilians in the Big Bend with Texas Rangers and US soldiers in an effort to police the region. Fear of another raid quickly spread throughout the Big Bend. Woman and children were sent to the Presidio County courthouse, which was heavily guarded by civilian men and soldiers. Anglo men armed themselves, and those with automobiles patrolled the region. On December 29, 1917, a group of two hundred men made up of ranchers, rangers, and other citizens formed a vigilance committee to protect the region. They met at the Stockman's Club in Marfa and listened to Lieutenant Colonel George T. Langhorne and Texas Ranger Jim Gillette as they outlined a plan to monitor Mexicans in the region and to report any "suspicious Mexicans" to the committee. The committee's top priority was to find the men responsible for the Brite Ranch raid. The Mexican outlaws who escaped capture had taken an estimated $1,500 in cash and merchandise that included hats, overalls, coats, and boots.[68]

One month later, on January 26, 1918, a group of Texas Rangers under the command of Captain James Monroe Fox visited the village of El Porvenir, as described at the beginning of this chapter. The Rangers were joined by a group of Anglo civilians: brothers Buck and John Pool, Raymond Fitzgerald, and Tom Snyder. Snyder had told the Rangers that Mexican men at El Porvenir were responsible for the Brite Ranch raid. Snyder, an opportunist, stole several "mares and colts" from the residents of El Porvenir but used the "Mexican problem" to his advantage by falsely accusing the men of that village of having carried out the Brite Ranch raid. Worried that he would be prosecuted for stealing the horses, it is believed that "he schemed to have the Mexicans killed so there would be no witness against him."[69] During the early morning raid, the soldiers entered the *jacales* (mud homes) and searched boxes and trunks for weapons and stolen goods. In addition to the two firearms mentioned previously, the Rangers noticed that three men were wearing Hamilton Brown boots similar to the ones stolen from the general store during the Brite Ranch raid. For the posse, this was enough evidence to take the three Mexican men wearing the Hamilton Browns away for questioning. Accordingly, the Rangers took Manuel Fierro, Eutimio Gonzáles, and Roman Nieves about ten miles away to their camp, an old railroad tunnel in the hills.[70] After a long day of questioning, the men were set free to return to El Porvenir.

Captain Henry H. Anderson of the Eighth Cavalry joined the posse of Rangers and civilians the next day. The cavalry soldiers and the Texas Rangers had a history of discontent with each other prior to 1918. The cavalry responded to military orders from above and had less personal interest in the Big Bend than the Rangers because they came from states as far away as Maine. The Rangers were much more ruthless; having grown up on the frontier, they had been hardened by the violence of the region. For the Rangers and local ranchers, the border fury was a personal matter, and on the night of January 27, 1918, they returned to El Porvenir with the cavalry, but with two different plans. Several of the Rangers were intoxicated as the midnight hour approached. The posse searched the village a second time, finding two more rifles and several knives. Following the search, the Rangers and civilian men took fifteen Mexican men from their families. The cavalrymen and Anderson stayed behind with the villagers.

The moon lit the night sky, and the air was cool and crisp with cries of the women and children of El Porvenir whistling through the canyon. The villagers knew that they were not going to see the men who had been taken alive again; the mere mention of the word "Ranger" struck as much fear in the hearts of the Mexican women and children as the word "bandit" terrified Anglo families. The sound of the footsteps of the men and horses grew softer and softer as they marched away down the road. The Mexican men ranged in age from sixteen to seventy-two; some were Mexican Americans and others Mexican refugees. Back at the village, the fearful women and children huddled around campfires as Anderson tried to reassure them that the Rangers were only questioning the men. Suddenly, the night air was filled with the distinctive sound of multiple gunshots that ended as quickly as they began—a firing squad.[71]

When Captain Fox and his men returned, Anderson cursed them and in a disgraceful tone replied, "What a nice piece of work you have done tonight!" As the Anglo men left El Porvenir, the only sound that could be heard was that of wailing women and children, fearing what the daylight would uncover. The next day, the families of El Porvenir collected the deceased and took their bodies back to Mexico to be buried on their native soil. They then fled to the desert region of northern Chihuahua without shelter, clothing other than what they were wearing, or food. "The Rangers and the four cowmen made 42 orphans that night."[72] Tom Snyder's plan had worked. Mexicans abandoned the village of El Porvenir, and none were left to bear witness against him.

The men who died that night were most likely innocent of the crimes committed during the Brite Ranch raid. There were no uniforms at El Porvenir that resembled those worn by the Brite Ranch raiders. All "bandits" were known to be "armed to the teeth," yet only a few weapons were found in the village.[73] Only the boots worn by three men matched the description of those sold at the Brite Ranch general store, but these men could have purchased their boots at any other time, since the store was the closest outpost for miles, or they could have purchased them from the actual raiders. In a court of law, this evidence would be circumstantial at best, but following the Brite Ranch raid Anglo men in the Big Bend were suspicious of all Mexican activity and decided that they would constitute themselves as the prevailing legal system—judge, jury, and executioner of the frontier.

Almost all of the Mexican men killed at El Porvenir were married with children and lived with their families in the village. Thirty-year-old Macedonio Huertas left behind a wife, Rita. Rita now had to care for her four children: six-year-old Firomeno, three-year-old Elijio, two-year-old Francisco, and an infant girl. Huertas had fled Mexico with Rita and

Firomeno in 1913. Upon arrival in El Paso he had ten pesos, identified himself as a "laborer," and could not read or write.[74] Alberto García died at the
age of thirty-five and left behind his wife, Victoria, two daughters, and a
nineteen-year-old son, Alfonso, who was absent from the village that evening. The four surviving family members would eventually move to Jim
Wells County in East Texas, where Alfonso would work as a farm hand. His
sisters eventually married, but Alfonso continued to care for his mother
into his thirties.[75] Pedro Herrera had only been in El Porvenir for four days,
arriving with Severiano Herrera and Vivian Herrera, all residents of Pecos
who had left for El Porvenir only ten days earlier to live with their grandmother in the farming community. Eutimio Gonzáles, a longtime resident
of the Big Bend, left behind his wife, Concepción, six girls, and three boys,
all born in the United States. Twenty-seven-year-old Pedro Jiménez was
unmarried, seventy-two-year-old Antonio Castanedo was the oldest of the
men killed that night, and Juan Jiménez was the youngest at sixteen years
old. Longino Flores was about to become a grandfather by his oldest daughter, Rosindo; Roman Nieves had a wife and six children with his seventh
born three months after his death; and Manuel Morales died on the same
night his fifth child, Julia, was born. The surviving families abandoned El
Porvenir, "the future."

The truth about what happened at El Porvenir leaked out when the Rangers and cowmen killed Tiburcio Jaquez. Jaquez's daughter, María, was married to the El Porvenir schoolmaster, Harry Warren. News of the massacre
brought Warren to the scene of the crime the next day. When he arrived, he
described the following:

> All the bodies were found lying together, side by side. Some were partly
> lying upon others, about a hundred or so yards from the road, by a little
> rock bluff. I saw the bodies on the early morning of January 29. The
> assassins spared several old Mexicans: Besareo Huertas, Eulogio Gonza-
> les, Gorgonio Hernandez, old man Jimenez, and one other (name
> forgotten).[76]

Warren got word of this massacre to Adjutant General James Harley of the
Rangers. Under orders from Governor William P. Hobby, who had taken
office the previous year, Harley discharged the Rangers responsible and
forced the resignation of Captain Fox. In a letter to Governor Hobby, Fox
accused the governor of "playing politics" trying to gain the Mexican vote:

Why do you not come clean and say that this is purely politics just to gain some Mexican votes? The five men you have discharged are good men and were the best of officers, and I want to ask you and all State Rangers how you expect to hold up the ranger force under such ruling as in this case. It hurts me to have my men treated in this manner. . . . [A] short while ago you sent a man to investigate me as to whether or not I was for you for Governor or a Ferguson man, so you know that there is no use in trying to have me believe that this action was brought about by anything other than your political reasons. We have stood guard to prevent Mexican bandits from murdering the ranchmen, the women and children along this border while you slept on your feather bed of ease. . . . You may consider this my resignation.[77]

The investigation exonerated the Mexican men of any connection with the Brite Ranch raid and found the actions of the Rangers and civilians to be extralegal. However, no arrests were made in the murders of the men at El Porvenir. As for the political allegations made by Fox: Governors Colquitt, Ferguson, and Hobby had all tried to court the growing Mexican vote in Democratic primaries.

Warren took it upon himself to investigate the massacre at El Porvenir. The testimonies of the victims' wives all told similar tales. The wife of Manuel Morales stated that she had lived in El Porvenir for eight years and that two Anglos wearing masks took her husband around midnight. Librada Montoya Jaquez said that four masked men in "civilian clothes" took her husband around the same time. When she fled to a neighbor's house, she saw four additional men in uniform. Juana Bonilla Flores, who had lived in El Porvenir for four years with her husband, Logino, recognized two of the four masked civilian men who took her husband as Ben Frazer and his brother. Felipa Mendez Castaneda, wife of Antonio Castaneda, had only lived at El Porvenir with her husband for three weeks prior to the midnight massacre. Castaneda and her husband were refugees and had not been in Texas long, and thus she did not recognize any of the men. Estefana Jaso Herrera, the grandmother of three of the murdered men, testified that four civilian men took the men shortly before midnight. Finally, Eulalia González Hernández, wife of Ambrocio Hernández, stated that both she and her husband were US citizens and had lived in the farming community for two years. Hernández believed that her home had been the first attacked. Two Rangers came to her house and stood guard at the door as three civilian men broke down the door, punched her husband in the ribs with a pistol, and took him away. Outside the house, she saw "a large bunch of civilians and soldiers" approaching the community. At sunrise, Hernández was the only one of the aforementioned women to disregard Warren's persistent request that they remain in the community while the men retrieved the bodies of the deceased. At the scene, Hernández found her husband's body mutilated by multiple stab wounds and a bullet wound through his head.[78] The investigation concluded that none of the men murdered that night at El Porvenir were involved in the Christmas morning raid at Brite Ranch, and that "this unlawful deed has enraged the Mexicans on the other side to such an extent that we may hear soon of their retaliating on the whites on this side. It will be productive of the most evil consequences."[79]

Harry Warren continued his quest for the truth and for compensation for the victims' families well into the 1930s. Warren wanted local citizens to know that the men killed at El Porvenir, including his father-in-law, were not criminals but innocent victims. However, immediately following the attack, the surviving men of El Porvenir wanted another form of restitution—revenge.[80] Not far from El Porvenir was the Neville ranch. Ed Neville's ranch was not a large compound such as Glenn Springs; Ed, his son Glen, and a Mexican couple who worked for Neville occupied the ranch. The ranch was located along the Rio Grande; Mexican soldiers could often be seen traveling along the riverbed on the Mexican side. Neville reported that he had had very little trouble on his ranch prior to 1918. On one occasion, Neville and his son along with four US militiamen noticed a large group of Mexican men camping about seventy-five yards from the property. Ed Neville believed that they were neither Villistas nor Carrancistas but, rather, opportunists, refugees, and displaced Mexican citizens who lived along the border. In an exchange of "hot words" between the two groups, Neville heard a man who appeared to be the leader order the group, who numbered about fifty, to "go over there and get those gringos."[81] Neville's group ordered them to stay on the Mexican side of the river. The sight of several cavalrymen with Neville possibly helped diffuse the situation. Later that evening, when Neville was alone, the group broke the unofficial truce and stole seven head of cattle. The rancher could only curse and chase the thieves across the border.[82]

Neville leased the ranch along with John Wyatt, but only Neville lived on the ranch and managed it. Neville moved his wife and two daughters to Van Horn for their safety as news of additional raids began to circulate throughout the ranches of the Big Bend. On March 15, 1918, less than two months after the massacre at El Porvenir, Neville was in Van Horn on one of his monthly visits to pay bills and visit his family. Van Horn was located thirty miles north of the ranch and had the nearest post office. That morning, he encountered a patrol of cavalrymen in Van Horn. The soldiers said that "they had understood there was a bunch of Mexicans in the country somewhere; that they had heard that they were going to raid somebody."[83] That was around ten thirty in the morning. Neville suggested that the troops meet him at his ranch later that evening once he finished his business in Van Horn.[84]

Neville arrived at his ranch shortly after sundown. Rosa Castillo, the Mexican cook who lived on the ranch, had just finished preparing dinner. Rosa and her husband, Adrian Castillo, were loyal employees, living on the ranch with their three young children. Prior to the El Porvenir massacre, Neville employed Mexican workers on his ranch who would return to their families at El Porvenir every Friday following each workweek. After the massacre, most of the families abandoned the village and fled back to Mexico, while the Castillos remained on the ranch with the Nevilles. After dinner, as Ed Neville told his son of the rumors of a possible raid, they both heard horses approaching outside. The Nevilles assumed that it was the soldiers Ed had met earlier that day. Waiting outside, however, were fifty armed Mexican men. Without any warning, the raiders began firing at the ranch house. Both Nevilles grabbed their Winchesters and fired out the door at the Mexican men. Some of the raiders took cover at the henhouse while others were protected by darkness. "Those bullets came in through the walls just like paper," Ed later recalled; he told his son to flee with him to a large ditch about 250 yards behind the house, where they could run for cover. As Ed ran across the property, his hat was shot off his head, and one bullet struck his hand causing him to lose his shotgun. Ed made it to the ditch, but his son was nowhere to be found. He hoped that Glen had managed to escape by another route. From the ditch, he could hear the raiders sacking the house after the gunfire ceased. Ed searched for his son on the hillside and hoped that he was hiding safely in bushes or up in the hills. He stayed clear of the ranch house until he heard the sound of Troop G of the Eighth Cavalry arriving around three thirty in the morning.[85]

The ranch house had become a slaughterhouse. Rosa Castillo was dead on the floor from shots to her head and chest. The killers gruesomely desecrated the young mother by cutting off her breasts and leaving her three children in the house to mourn their mother's death; José, an infant, was lying in a pool of her blood on the kitchen floor. Glen Neville's nearly life-less body was found only a few feet from the door by his father, who described "that he had been shot all to pieces, several times; there was a hole in his forehead; you could drop a hen egg through this hole in his forehead."[86] And, in a clear sign of vengeance, the Mexican raiders had repeatedly beaten Glen's face and head with their rifles and a bloody stick, leaving him "black and blue all over"; Glen Neville died two hours later in his father's arms.[87]

The US troops who arrived at the scene vowed to avenge the Neville boy's death and pursued the Mexican men responsible for the raid across the Rio Grande. Their pursuit covered seventy-five miles of Mexican countryside and left Mexican villages destroyed as they searched for the criminals. In Pilares, Mexico, two days after the Neville ranch raid, US troops searched houses and businesses, and they encountered a group of thirty-five Mexican men they suspected of the Neville ranch raid. As the soldiers fired on them, the men fled to the hills into an area known as "the Gap." There, the soldiers cornered the men, wounding twenty and killing ten others.[88] Anglo men believed that they were policing the border, and protecting Americans and American interests. The newspapers often pitted "soldiers" against "bandits" in a fight to the death. According to most of the newspaper reports, the bat-tles between the two sides resulted in multiple casualties on the Mexican side, with very few American losses. The vicious cycle of vengeance showed no signs of ending.

CONCLUSION

The violence of the region left a legacy with the youth of the frontier. Chil-dren of Anglos and Mexicans were baptized in the blood of the revolution. During the 1910s Anglo children and Mexican children were forced to grow up fast, and both witnessed violence on a daily basis along the border. In towns like Presidio in the Big Bend, residents witnessed "a curtain of fire" when fighting occurred at night.[89] Ciudad Juárez resident Oscar Martínez remembered that he and his Mexican friends would sit on rooftops to watch revolutionary fighting. On one occasion, a seven-year-old friend standing a few feet from him was shot and killed by a stray bullet.[90] Lifelong El Paso resident George Barnhart reflected on being a young boy during the 1910s and desiring to take part in the fighting: "I was just a little kid at the time, of course—a young teenager—but I can remember the raiding up there. I remember one time in particular, they raided up within a few miles of Alpine, and the young federal officer was down trying to raise a posse to go after them. I sure wanted to go, but I was a little kid."[91] General S. L. A. Marshall, a World War I veteran, grew up as a teenager in El Paso during the revolution. Marshall was a young boy only ten years old at the outbreak of the revolution, and he recalled that border boys were much stronger than boys elsewhere in the United States because of what they faced in their daily life during the 1910s: "The boys were much more mature. . . . I think being on the border did that for them. Four or five juicy murders a day in El Paso shocked nobody. That was sort of par for the course."[92] Marshall left the Big Bend to fight in World War I when he was eighteen, and he eventually retired from the military as a brigadier general.

The militaristic milieu of the border matured both the men and the women of the region. High school students were forced to choose whether they believed that ethnic Mexicans entering the United States from war-torn Mexico were criminals, as pumped up by press sensationalism, or were simply like the Mexican American classmates they had grown up with. The only identifier they could accept was that it must be the lowest class of refugees, the "peons," who were most threatening. After the raid in Columbus, New Mexico, and the subsequent US pursuit mission—the Punitive Expedition— to Mexico, teenage boys joined their high school ROTC organizations in an effort to "protect" their communities. In El Paso, following the Columbus raid, the El Paso High School ROTC boys took their plug senders (guns) and guarded their school at night. The school, situated high on a hillside, became their military fortress. These boys emulated what their fathers and other rugged men of the frontier were doing in Texas and Mexico. The Kelly sisters— Anne, Elizabeth, and Mary—remembered the boys years later in a 1973 interview. Elizabeth described them as "heroes protecting the school" and said that "everybody brought them fudge and cookies." Mary thought that "it was divine," remarking that the boys would come to school so tired that "they put their heads down on their desks, and nobody disturbed them." These young men were relieved finally of their unofficial duty when the militia arrived. Yet, almost sixty years later these three women still remembered a tale of manly valor that exemplified the men and boys of the border.[93]

During the combative years of the Mexican Revolution, the raids on ranches, farms, and villages along the Rio Grande took the lives of more innocent victims than guilty. The border press criminalized ethnic Mexicans of the poorest class and reported only the raids on American ranches. The raids by Mexican bandits decreased whenever the US military established a presence in the region. However, when the soldiers departed, the raids increased and grew more violent, up to 1918. Policing the borderland evolved from a complex task to a chaotic one on both sides of the border. The civil war in Mexico led to competing factions of the revolution fighting the federal army, US troops, and each other, while on American soil there was a disorganized formation of National Guardsmen, federal troops, civilian posses, and Texas Rangers. Legal historian Michael Ariens argues that at least 20 percent of the 222 ethnic Mexicans killed during the "Bandit War" (the term he used to describe the period examined in this chapter), were lynched by Texas Rangers, who claimed to be acting legally.[94] They were not.

The violence along the border during the mid- to late 1910s brought two countries—neighbors—close to war. And the people who inhabited these two neighboring countries were easily distinguished by the color of their skin and their cultural characteristics. Men and women on both sides of the border were mostly born without evil in their hearts. But the innocent survivors at El Porvenir sought revenge for the midnight murder of their brethren. Ed Neville never looked at a Mexican man the same after holding his son's lifeless body. The violence along the border hardened the men, women, and children on both sides. Fighting in the borderland made life in the region a living hell for many; it stole the innocence of youth from children. And it made cold-blooded killers out of innocent men.

World War I and the Decline
of Mexican Lynching

A t first, the outbreak of war in Europe seemed to worsen circumstances
for ethnic Mexicans in Texas, both because the government became
more suspicious of all foreigners in the United States and also because
Germany seemed to see Mexico as a possible ally against the United States.
But the war, once the United States became actively involved, actually
calmed the situation on the border, causing a substantial decline in
lynchings of ethnic Mexicans in Texas. Hundreds of ethnic Mexicans lost
their lives to Texas Rangers and civilians during the three-year period
leading up to the January 1918 massacre at El Porvenir. Texas archives
contain photographs of the forgotten dead, hogtied and dragged behind
horses. In the tradition of lynching, the perpetrators collected souvenirs as
trophies. A leather picture album found at an Austin gun show contained
slotted pages for images that might have held pictures of lynching victims
(fig. 5.1). The inscription on the cover indicates that it once belonged to a
US soldier who was called up to serve following the Columbus, New
Mexico, raid by Pancho Villa; the inscription reads, "Cause of Service—
Columbus Raid—March 9, 1916—Burning of Town Killing 21 Citizens."

Only two known lynchings of ethnic Mexicans occurred in Texas during
the remainder of the year and only one occurred in 1919.[1] This significant
change resulted from three major factors: first, America's involvement in
World War I transferred the suspicions and negative stereotypes of the borderland enemy from Mexicans to Germans in Texas; second, emerging political stability within Mexico made the border between Texas and Mexico far
less a site of revolutionary violence; and third, an investigation into Texas
Ranger violence against ethnic Mexicans by the Mexican American lawyer
and politician José T. Canales exposed hitherto hidden crimes by Rangers
against ethnic Mexicans and energized a nascent Mexican American civil
rights movement.

Found at Austin, Tx. at a GUN SHOW. Words on left read:
            CAUSE OF SERVICE
            COLUMBUS RAID
            March 9, 1916
            BURNING OF TOWN
            KILLING 21 CITIZENS

Is a leather picture album, containing(empty) slotted ⓟ black
pages for postcards(or PC size photos).

Figure 5.1 Leather picture album, "U.S. Army on Mexican Border Service," Williwood Meador Collection, box 4, file 3, courtesy of West Texas Collection, Angelo State University, San Angelo, Texas.

Historians who have examined the lynching of ethnic Mexicans in the United States assert that a surge in violence occurred during the 1910s with a subsequent sharp decline during the 1920s. They credit the end of the combative years of the Mexican Revolution in 1920 as the reason why violence subsided when it did. While stability in Mexico was a contributing factor, this chapter focuses on an event of more global significance—World War I. The effects of the war on ethnic Mexicans in Texas were complex. Initially, the war intensified Anglo fear of ethnic Mexicans, who were suspected of being disloyal to America and being allies of the Germans. For a time, the Texas Rangers were given an even freer hand than before to mete out "justice" to them. Such vigilante actions caused tens of thousands to flee the state

and repatriate to Mexico. But the war also created opportunities for Mexican Americans in Texas—to serve in the US military and to find other ways to demonstrate their loyalty to the United States. Ethnic Mexicans also benefited in indirect ways: their flight from the state generated a labor shortage in Texas and impelled Anglos there to adjust their attitudes toward needed Mexican laborers; and, by 1918, Germans had taken their place as the "other" whom Anglo Texans feared the most. These changes created a space in Texas politics for Mexican Americans that had not existed before. They used this space to demand and receive from the state government a formal investigation of Texas Ranger violence against ethnic Mexicans. For the first time, the general atmosphere that had led to the lynching of people of Mexican descent was being given a public airing and an opportunity for redress. Hope spread that a new era for ethnic Mexicans in Texas was dawning. This chapter begins with the state investigation of the Rangers, even though, chronologically, the investigation comes at the end of this story. I do so because the investigation reveals how poor Anglo-Mexican relations had become before they began to improve.

RESISTANCE

The 1915–1918 raids by Rangers and "bandits" discussed in chapter 4 led to the death of hundreds of ethnic Mexicans in the borderland. Many of the dead were the innocent victims of overzealous Rangers determined to eliminate the "Mexican problem." José T. Canales, an Austin lawyer, initiated resistance to these men and the kind of violence they had unleashed. In 1918 Canales launched a year-long investigation into the Ranger force for alleged misconduct and violence against ethnic Mexicans. In January 1919 a joint House-Senate committee of the Texas legislature heard the testimony of dozens of witnesses about the conduct of the Rangers. The investigation highlighted crimes committed by the Rangers against ethnic Mexicans, their violation of American neutrality with Mexico by crossing the border in search of suspected criminals, and their frequent abuse of alcohol while on patrol. Canales was not only targeting the Rangers to defend ethnic Mexican rights. He also wanted the investigation to result in a reduction of the Ranger force in numbers and an increase in their pay, in order to attract the best possible force the state could muster. Prior to the investigation, stories of Mexican raids on ranches in the United States and Mexico dominated the press. But the investigation revealed that violence against ethnic Mexicans was equally common and often perpetrated by Rangers, and that at times Rangers formed posses with Texas citizens to locate and punish suspected Mexican criminals. Stories of Ranger-on-Mexican violence had long circulated throughout ethnic Mexican communities but were rarely printed in the Anglo press, unless reporters took up such a story to frame Ranger actions as necessary to defend the people of the state. The testimony of eyewitnesses in the Canales investigation, including Mexicans, Tejanos, Anglos, and Rangers, gave unprecedented publicity and legitimacy to ethnic Mexican grievances about Ranger violence.

Born in Nueces County, Texas, in 1877, José Canales was the son of Andreas and Tomasa (Covazos) Canales. Andreas was a descendant of José Salvador de la Garza, to whom the Spanish, in 1781, had granted 284,414 acres in south Texas in what is now Cameron County. José was born and raised on the family ranch, which was once part of the land grant. He attended several schools in the area before attending Texas Business College in Austin. In 1899 Canales earned his law degree from the University of Michigan. He returned to Texas following graduation and practiced criminal and civil law. In addition to a legal career, Canales became a public servant, beginning with his election as a state representative in 1904. He represented the Ninety-Fifth District of South Texas, which included Brownsville, where he lived.[2] In addition to spearheading the Ranger investigation, Canales was called to testify about his own grievances with the Rangers. Canales recalled that he had once admired them. He recalled that his family's ranch, La Cabra Ranch, was a Ranger "haven" where these men were often stationed and ate their meals. He argued that it wasn't until hostilities between Anglo Texans and Mexicans intensified because of Mexican Revolution trouble that the Rangers followed a darker course. Specifically, he recalled that the year 1915 marked the moment when the misdeeds perpetrated by the new Ranger force began to overshadow their distinguished history.[3] The Rangers he recalled knowing as a child were not the same men carrying on the group's proud tradition. In 1911, shortly after the outbreak of the Mexican Revolution, the Ranger force was only authorized to have 80 active men. Because the border had been relatively peaceful during the prerevolutionary years, the actual force numbered only 14 when fighting broke out. As border problems related to the fighting increased, so did the Ranger force. Initially, Governor Oscar B. Colquitt increased the force to only 43, but then it mushroomed to beyond 1,200.[4] The new Rangers and their increasing anti-Mexican actions were a direct result of border problems related to the Mexican Revolution, and more often then not the targeted "criminals" were "suspicious" ethnic Mexicans along the border.

Canales's 1918 investigation revealed that the Ranger force had degenerated into a "posse" of men who sought out suspicious ethnic Mexicans. Canales himself admitted that there were some "bandit troubles" in the region, but he also insisted that their significance was magnified by German propaganda. As examples of this propaganda, he entered into the record unsigned letters allegedly from "revolutionaries" but in reality manufactured by Germans, urging Tejanos to join bands of rebels to take up arms against Anglos in Texas. Canales believed that the German propaganda was initiated for the purpose of keeping the United States out of the European war by fomenting war in the US-Mexico borderland. However, the German propaganda actually led to greater suspicion of German American communities in Texas (a topic to be discussed later in this chapter).[5]

The Canales investigation depicted the Rangers as a group of cowboys who ruled the border through swift justice and practiced a policy of "shoot first and investigate later," their actions often requiring a cover-up that involved prominent citizens. The new Rangers carried with them whips, rifles, and, most damaging to their reputation, whiskey. Canales further charged that the adjutant general was either negligent in the selection of unqualified men or that he actually sought out "characters in the Ranger force to terrorize and intimidate the citizens of this State."[6] Canales reported on an incident in Hidalgo County in which Arturo García and Pedro Tamez were taken out of a jail cell by several Rangers and driven out to a sparse region of the county, where they were released only for the purpose of target practice. García was shot in the leg and Tamez escaped unharmed. Once the story leaked, Captain Hanson of the Rangers quickly placed the blame on local law enforcement. Still, no arrests were made.[7]

Rangers defended their actions by arguing that most of the men they pursued were bandits. A significant threat along the border from outlawry did exist. But the Rangers used the term "bandit" to describe not just genuine thieves but any revolutionaries who found their way into Texas and, at times, any ethnic Mexicans living along the border. It is estimated that at least three hundred ethnic Mexicans perished during the height of the skirmishing between the Rangers and Mexican bandits in 1915. Historians now largely agree that most of those killed by Rangers were innocent.[8] Historian Benjamin Johnson described the overreach of the Rangers with examples such as

Captain H. L. Ransom, who boasted about driving "all the Mexicans" from three Texas ranches.[9]

As a result of the anti-Mexican campaign of the Rangers, ethnic Mexicans began an exodus from Texas to Mexico. Thousands of Mexicans fled the lower Rio Grande Valley in the first few weeks of September 1915. Immigration officials reported that more than five hundred families departed for Matamoros: "2500 persons have emigrated, most of them taking all of their worldly possessions, including hogs, chickens, goats, horses, mules, burros, and all, including water barrels and tubs."[10] Those who fled did so without plans to return. The conditions in Texas had proven more dangerous for Mexicans than those in their own country, which was engulfed in a civil war.

During the Canales investigation, Constable Ventura Sánchez testified to what he described as standard behavior by Rangers when they had consumed alcohol in his town of San Diego, Texas. He described one Saturday night in December 1918. Sánchez was getting a haircut when he and his barber heard the sound of gunshots fired in the street. When they looked out, they were relieved to see that it was only drunken Rangers causing a stir in the streets, which was a common occurrence. As he approached one of the men, George Hurst, he was greeted with a belligerent quip: "Now, here, you Ventura, you son of a bitch, I don't like to see you in front of me, and if I ever see you before me [again] I am going to shoot [the] hell out of you, you son of a bitch."[11] Ventura ignored the Ranger but approached the deputy sheriff to have him arrested, only further angering the Ranger. The deputy ignored the plea, thus satisfying Hurst that he was above punishment with his Ranger status. A week later Hurst continued his harassment of Ventura, following him home and once again threatening his life. Several people in the county knew that Hurst was looking for any reason to shoot and kill Ventura. However, Ventura's request for a warrant to arrest Hurst was refused. The county clerk said that there was no warrant for Hurst, that he was just drunk, stating: "You might as will let [it] go."[12]

Anglo citizens generally turned a blind eye to Ranger misconduct. They believed that the Rangers were protecting the border and the safety of residents in border communities. They did not protest the money the Rangers extorted from illicit gambling and prostitution businesses in return for protection. One report noted that the Rangers "collected ten dollars a week from Booze Gows and Pussy joints."[13] Moreover, it was commonly known that the best place to get a drink in dry counties was in a Ranger camp.[14]

The testimony of R. B. Creager, a Brownsville attorney, before the Canales committee identified one of the most atrocious miscarriages of justice—Mexican "evaporation." No Texas newspaper discussed this injustice, but Creager, Canales, and several members of the joint committee involved in the proceedings appeared to have been commonly familiar with the term. "Evaporation" referred to the disappearance of an ethnic Mexican whose name appeared on a blacklist kept by Ranger officials. Creager estimated that from 1915 to 1916 an estimated two hundred ethnic Mexicans were killed by Texas Rangers and civilian posses in his home county of Cameron alone. He believed that 90 percent of those killed were innocent.[15] Many of these victims and countless unknown victims were part of a blacklist system that Rangers and civilians used to monitor suspicious ethnic Mexicans in South Texas. The name of any ethnic Mexican, male or female, suspected of a crime could be placed on the list by "any men of standing in the valley or even half way standing." An accuser could place a suspected "bad Mexican" on the list if he or she suspected that person of having committed a crime. Creager reported, "It was a common rumor and report, and it was true, that in most instances that Mexican would disappear."[16] In one case, five ethnic Mexican men who had been blacklisted were found shot to death, lying on their bellies, with the butts of beer bottles protruding from their mouths. Creager testified that he had actually seen one of these lists. The mere suspicion that their names might be on a blacklist led ethnic Mexicans to flee across the border. Others who were on a list but unaware of it just disappeared. Community members said that these missing Mexicans had simply evaporated; many were never seen or heard from again.[17]

On April 4, 1918, the Mexican consul's office in San Antonio informed Cameron County attorney Oscar C. Dancy that the father of Florencia García had reported his teenage son missing and presumably dead at the hands of Texas Rangers. The elder García made several visits to Dancy's Brownsville office, providing a physical description of the boy including his shoes, the light-colored Stetson cowboy hat he wore, and his reddish-brown jumpsuit. Dancy learned that the boy had been arrested by the county sheriff at a rural farm, but he was never taken to the county jail. It is unknown whether an arrest actually occurred or if the boy was picked up and then handed over to Rangers in the area. However, on May 20, 1918, an unidentifiable body of a boy, mostly only hair, bones, and decomposed flesh, was found near Ray Waits's pasture between Brownsville and Point Isabel. Dancy's testimony during the Canales investigation revealed that the clothes matched those of the missing Mexican boy. The jacket had bullet holes in the back, and a

Stetson hat found with the body had the words "L. Garebo & Sons" stitched on the inside. This was the name of the merchant who had sold García his cowboy hat.[18]

The evidence at the crime scene, and eyewitness testimony that Sheriff Williams of Cameron County had arrested the boy on the day of his disappearance, should have been enough to make some arrests. Attorney Dancy conducted a vigorous investigation at first. He identified three Rangers—named Sadler, Sitter, and Loche—who were known to have been seen with the boy. Captain Stevens of the Rangers explained that the three men had taken García that day but eventually released him, and what happened thereafter was unknown to them. Dancy wrote to Governor William Hobby about the alleged misconduct of the three Rangers and the possible murder they had committed. Dancy's protest got the men reassigned to Marfa, in the Big Bend. But even Dancy himself was reluctant to see them tried for murder.[19] Dancy worried more that the Mexican government would use the trial to drum up pro-German and anti-American sentiment in Mexico. He explained, "I did not think it was to the best interests of the public for that testimony to be put in writing to be spread by German propagandists probably in Mexico, and I maneuvered Judge W. R. Jones, ex–United States District Attorney . . . and [the] examination was waived."[20]

Nevertheless, the Canales investigation had at least brought the existence of these events to public attention. It also brought to light additional stories of Anglo Texan complicity in covering up other suspected Ranger crimes. In Sweetwater, Texas, a man was brought to the local jail by Rangers late one evening while they were transporting him to another county. The jailer agreed to keep the prisoner for the night as the Rangers enjoyed an evening of rest and relaxation that included alcohol. In the morning, the man was found hanging by his belt from the jail cell doors. Dr. S. M. Leach ruled it a suicide. During the Canales investigation, Dr. Leach was called to testify how he had come to that conclusion. Five different members of the investigation questioned Leach, all of whom were skeptical that it was a suicide because of the following details: the forty-five-year-old man's legs were drawn, he was found bruised, and a handkerchief was found lodged deep in his throat past his larynx. Chairman Bledsoe of the investigating committee questioned Leach whether it would be possible for a man of that age to hold himself up on the side of the cell, keep his legs drawn to avoid touching the ground, and, with a handkerchief stuffed down his throat, tie a belt in such a way so as to be able to complete the task. Dr. Leach's response was that, to him, it was a clear case of suicide.[21] Nobody really knows what happened in that cell, but if this was a murder made to look like a suicide, the culprits had the help of a local citizen.

Some of the testimonies presented during the Canales investigation were based on hearsay. In the case of Toribio Rodríguez, however, the testimony was the signed declaration of a dying man. In Tres Puentes, near Brownsville, Rodríguez came upon several men identified as Rangers late at night. The men cursed at him and shot him as he rode away on horseback. Rodríguez went to the house of a Dr. Stell, who cleaned and dressed the wound on his arm and sent him home. Shortly thereafter, the men spotted Rodríguez and fired shots into his back, declaring that they had more if he desired. Rodríguez was not wanted for any crime. On his deathbed, he gave witnesses a description of the Rangers who had attacked him and declared, "I understand and believe I am going to die."[22]

Canales argued that Ranger-on-Mexican violence had begun to increase in 1915. As demonstrated in chapter 4, rampant fear and violence along the border had turned law-abiding men into revenge killers. Canales supported this claim with evidence of a "shoot first, ask questions later" approach by the Rangers that resulted in retaliation by Mexicans living in close proximity to the border who learned of the outrages. Canales argued that banditry had declined in the region due to a new technique of "scouting" initiated by the Rangers. Scouts were Mexicans hired by the Ranger force to scout or spy on revolutionary factions suspected of operating near the border. Rangers were often criticized for violating a US-Mexico neutrality agreement by crossing the border armed and seeking suspected bandits. These Mexican men were paid forty-five dollars per month by the US government as federal scouts. Two scouts were assigned to each camp of Rangers, and their duties included gathering intelligence information, trapping suspected bandits, and watching the camp at night while the soldiers slept. The camps were positioned along a hundred-mile stretch of the border from Brownsville to Rio Grande City, each camp five miles from the next. Their most important discovery, however, was that Mexican revolutionaries fought each other more than they attacked Anglos. Their actions did not justify the "shoot first" attitudes of the Rangers.[23]

Further testimony on banditry by attorney R. B. Creager claimed that bandit problems arose from misconduct by the Rangers and local law enforcement along the border. Creager stated that Rangers, deputy sheriffs, and local peace officers added "fuel to the flame, to make worse the bandit conditions. In fact I believe—I know that the conduct of the officers more than any other one thing caused that bandit trouble to attain the dimensions that it did."[24] Further supporting the argument that the Mexican Revolution hardened men and women on both sides of the border, Creager opined, "Up to the time the Mexican Revolution started there was never a more friendly people on earth than the Mexicans on the Mexican side of the river and the Americans on the American side."[25]

Canales used the evidence to argue that Texas Rangers and their violent campaigns against suspected criminals and innocent Mexicans led to retaliation by ethnic Mexicans. This retaliation, he argued, is what the press saw unfairly as Mexican banditry along the border. Canales told a personal story that involved a friend of his who was a court stenographer. Her father was one of ten men who had been targeted by Texas Rangers seeking a suspected murderer near San Benito, a Texas town that was well within the protective line of the Ranger's hundred-mile-long string of camps. The men were ordered out of their homes and required to relinquish any weapons. After they complied, they were released back to their homes. For unknown reasons, the Rangers returned, entered the homes, and shot all ten men. Canales reported that the men were not given any chance to prove their innocence of any crimes, further saying that the story of the murders quickly made its way to Mexico via relatives and friends of the deceased. The news "aroused a strong feeling between them and the bandits." Instead of minimizing a desire for retaliation, the actions of the Rangers allied law-abiding men with potential criminals. That feeling increased at an alarming rate, to the extent that most civilian Mexicans on the Mexican side of the border came to believe that they were at war with armed men from the United States.[26]

The Canales investigation brought attention to vigilante acts carried out by the Texas Rangers leading up to the lawyer's call for an investigation in January 1918. In addition to the threat posed by Rangers, ethnic Mexicans in Texas believed that they were being unjustly targeted by the state's highest-ranking political figure—Governor James E. Ferguson. In 1916 Ferguson urged ethnic Mexicans in Texas to report "suspicious" Mexicans to authorities, thereby demonstrating their allegiance to Texas and the United States following his Loyalty Proclamation. Ferguson delivered his demands as American involvement in World War I appeared imminent and as rumors of a possible alliance between Germany and Mexico intensified.

GOVERNOR FERGUSON'S LOYALTY PROCLAMATION

The possibility of the United States entering World War I initially worsened the ethnic Mexican experience in Texas. By 1917 the borderland was in greater disarray than it had been in the previous seven years. Law enforcement from the Texas Rangers to the local sheriffs' departments stepped up their recruiting efforts to acquire the manpower to intervene in border hostilities on the Texas side. In Mexico, Venustiano Carranza had declared himself president following the surrender of Victoriano Huerta's soldiers on August 15, 1914, and he sought to bring all the rebels together under his leadership. But the divisions among revolutionary factions in fact increased, as the uneasy alliance of rebels who had defeated Huerta began to fracture, leaving Carranza at odds with Pancho Villa. President Woodrow Wilson and Secretary of State William Jennings Bryan had little confidence by the summer of 1915 that Mexico was anywhere near ending its civil war. Wilson and Bryan made the safety of Americans in Mexico a high priority. Bryan warned that if Americans living in Mexico continued to suffer as a result of revolutionary fighting, or if the Mexican government failed to protect American life and property, "the government of the United States would hold General [Álvaro] Obregón and General Carranza personally responsible."[27]

Conditions in Mexico grew worse along with events in Europe. On May 7, 1915, a German U-boat torpedoed the British ocean liner RMS *Lusitania*. The *Lusitania* carried 1,959 passengers, mostly British and Canadian, and 1,195 of them perished in the sinking. US casualties totaled 123 persons, drawing intense criticism of Germany by the American public. The sinking became an important factor leading Wilson to determine that intervention in World War I was necessary and just. Secretary of State Bryan was a proponent of intervention in Mexico but not in Europe, leading to a fracture in Wilson's administration. Bryan resigned in the summer of 1915; Robert Lansing succeeded him as secretary of state and eventually supported American participation in World War I.

Lansing immediately led an effort to recognize the Carranza government, assembling a pan-American conference of six Latin American countries to do just that in October 1915.[28] This decision, in turn, infuriated Villa, who issued a proclamation in December stating that he "would kill every gringo that fell into his hands if the Washington administration gave further aid to Carranza by permitting his troops to pass through United States territory."[29] Weeks after Villa's proclamation, the US Department of State telegraphed

General Álvaro Obregón and Carranza, giving them permission to pass one thousand Mexican federal troops through US territory from Nogales, Arizona, to El Paso, in their effort to enter Ciudad Juárez and catch Villistas in northern Mexico by surprise. Furthermore, Carranza invited American mine operators who had fled Mexico to return and promised that they would be assured of full protection in Mexico, "armed with passports and personal letters from Carranza authorities."[30]

On January 1, 1916, at a New Year's Day celebration, Obregón was one of the invited guests of El Paso's mayor, Tom Lea. At the banquet, Obregón announced to the crowd,

> I invite all you men to come to Mexico. I want you to come down into our territory and open up you mines and smelters. I give you my word that you will be given full protection. Our government is in complete control of every important center in Chihuahua. Nothing will happen to you, because the Villistas are whipped. Villa is a thing of the past.[31]

Nineteen American men signed on to reopen the Cusi Mine in Cusihuiriachi, Chihuahua. They left ten days after the New Year's Day celebration but were gunned down by Villa's men within forty-eight hours of entering Mexico, all but one dying.

The murder of eighteen American miners enraged Anglos in El Paso, especially as the bodies of the deceased arrived back home and news circulated that they had been mutilated as well as killed. Former president Theodore Roosevelt expressed his anger with Washington, fueling rage among Anglos in El Paso over the massacre:

> President Wilson has permitted these different bandit factions to get from us or with our permission the arms with which they have killed American private citizens, American soldiers, the husbands and fathers of American women whom they have outraged. There is a hundred times the justification for interfering in Mexico that there was for interfering in Cuba. We should have interfered in Mexico years ago.[32]

Large-scale anti-Mexican rioting broke out in the city, led by local Anglo Texans. During the first night of anti-Mexican attacks, over 40 ethnic Mexican men had to be treated at the hospital and more than 150 Anglo Texans were arrested. The mob spontaneously grew out of an "indignation meeting" held in Cleveland Square in the center of town. Witnesses reported that it had happened all at once: "Mexicans were denounced and attacked, and the police wagon had to go out several times to quell fights in the streets and saloons."[33] Cries of "avenge the murdered Americans" and "Remember Cusi" could be heard echoing down alleys. In several hotels, bellboys reportedly attacked Mexican guests in their rooms.[34] The police closed saloons early; crowds formed at Overland Avenue and Santa Fe Street and began to parade through the city. Unsuspecting Mexicans fell victim to the growing mob. The crowd grew to 1,500 men and included civilians as well as army soldiers stationed in El Paso. Mayor Lea and Captain Hall of the El Paso police had only sixty-five members of the police force on hand to suppress the mob.[35]

Ethnic Mexicans in El Paso told stories that Anglo Texans entered their homes while they slept and threw the men out into the streets as their families witnessed the abuse. The violence, and fears of additional violence, drew newspaper headlines across the country. On the second day of rioting, a squad of American soldiers marched through the streets and declared that they would "clean the streets" of Mexicans. Rumors spread throughout the city of plans drawn up by several cattlemen who were friends of the deceased to enter Mexico and kill any Mexican they saw who might be a Villista. An El Paso printing company produced postcards to send to newspapers throughout the country announcing the desire to fight with the slogan, "Remember the Alamo, did we watch and wait? Remember the Cusi, shall we watch and wait?"[36]

Across the river in Ciudad Juárez, anti-American hostilities intensified as news reports alerted ethnic Mexicans in the city of the riots and Anglo assaults on ethnic Mexicans in El Paso. Rumors that Mexicans were killed in the riots complicated the situation further. The riots produced hundreds of injured ethnic Mexicans, but no known fatalities. A US customs officer at the border was approached by a Mexican citizen who asked him, "What do these gringos mean by killing Mexicans over there?"[37] The official denied that killing had occurred, but the man explained that Ciudad Juárez residents believed that three Mexican men had been killed during the rioting and reported that Villa supporters were organizing for retaliation. No such attack was carried out, but El Paso police responded by seeking out suspected Villistas and beginning deportation procedures. An estimated two hundred ethnic Mexicans fled El Paso within forty-eight hours of the riots. Texas cities appeared to be no place for refuge for the thousands of Mexicans who feared for their safety from revolutionary fighting.[38]

By the summer of 1916 Anglo Texans feared that the cities in their state with large Mexican populations living in separate districts had become havens for violent men. Governor James Ferguson now demanded that all ethnic Mexicans living in Texas show complete loyalty to the state. Those who refused were warned that "they will bring trouble on themselves."[39] Ferguson's demand for 100 percent loyalty and cooperation, issued on June 18, 1916, read as follows:

> To Texas Mexicans: At this time I want to say a word to citizens of Mexican parentage residing permanently or temporarily in Texas. The state of Texas demands of all persons while in her borders absolute obedience and respect to her laws and constituted authorities. If Texas Mexicans will aid by words and deeds the various peace officers in Texas to carry out this demand they need have no fear of bodily harm and they will receive the protection of our laws. If they do not in some manner show their loyalty to this state and nation, they will bring trouble upon themselves and many crimes will be committed which cannot be prevented.[40]

That this warning came from the highest-ranking political figure in the state frightened ethnic Mexicans, who, as a result, made their September 1916 independence celebrations much more modest in scale, filling them with tributes to the United States. Ferguson's Loyalty Proclamation deepened the fear among ethnic Mexicans that the state of Texas either could not or would not provide them with protection against anti-Mexican hostilities. Ferguson's proclamation threatened not only their safety but their but livelihood— "employment will continue," he warned, only so long as Mexicans remained loyal to Texas.[41]

Many Mexican Americans in Texas began writing to Ferguson to declare their loyalty to the Lone Star State. Francisco Guerra Morales of Edinburg, Texas, wrote on behalf of his family and friends, declaring their allegiance to the American flag. Ferguson thanked Morales in a return letter and praised the man for the "patriotic attitude" reflected in his communication.[42] In Comal County, Texas, north of San Antonio, J. M. Cordonia wrote on behalf of all ethnic Mexicans living in the county and included the signatures of dozens of ethnic Mexican men. He assured the governor of their loyalty to the United States and their "unwavering fidelity to the laws of the country."[43] Cordonia received a similar reply from the governor, thanking him for his good faith and urging Cordonia to express the governor's gratitude to all the men who had signed the letter. The governor's proclamation appeared only in English and all the letters to Ferguson were written in English, suggesting that the document had reached mostly English-speaking portions of the ethnic Mexican community in Texas.

Francisco A. Chapa of San Antonio led an effort to distribute the proclamation in Spanish to ethnic Mexicans living in and around the city. Chapa belonged to the pro-American Mexican elite living in Texas who believed that the inclusion of Mexicans in the American family came through assimilation. Chapa was considered the most powerful Mexican American politician in Texas during the 1910s. He celebrated his Mexican heritage, but as a member of American society he found newly arriving poor refugees culturally foreign. The previous governor, Oscar Colquitt, considered Chapa a close friend. During the 1910 Democratic primary race in Texas, Chapa mobilized support among Mexican Americans for Colquitt. Prohibition in Texas was a key voter issue, and Colquitt, who was antiprohibition, relied heavily on Chapa to garner support among Mexican Americans in the state.

Anglo Texans saw an assimilation success story in Chapa and admired him for it. Born in Matamoros on October 4, 1870, Chapa immigrated to the United States at the age of seventeen and was naturalized by age twenty. Having been educated in Spanish and English, and having completed primary school and some secondary school in Mexico, he arrived in New Orleans and enrolled at Tulane University, where he studied pharmacy. He worked as a drugstore clerk in Brownsville and eventually as a pharmacist in San Antonio. It was there that he opened his pharmacy, La Botica del León, in 1894, which he operated until his death in 1924.[44] Ethnic Mexicans looked up to Chapa not only for his success but for his commitment to the Mexican American community. Chapa published a San Antonio newspaper, *El Imparcial de Texas*. He provided a political voice for ethnic Mexicans in Texas; with his endorsement, Colquitt carried the Mexican American vote and won the 1910 Democratic primary, which all but guaranteed his election as governor in the fall.[45]

After Colquitt was sworn in as governor of Texas, he appointed Chapa to one of twelve advisory positions with the title "lieutenant colonel," a title and position he would maintain with subsequent governors James E. Ferguson and William P. Hobby. Chapa had gotten himself in trouble with a plan to smuggle weapons into Mexico in the first year after the Porfiriato had come to an end, but his political career survived with the assistance of a pardon from President Taft. Chapa thus remained on the governor's staff and became one of the most powerful Mexican American politicians of the period. Because Anglos in Texas and in Washington had bailed him out, however, he was acutely conscious of his dependence on their goodwill. Thus, he stayed clear of any criticism of US policy toward Mexico. Moreover, he placed emphasis on English-only education in the schools and the Americanization of immigrants as crucial policy issues.[46] This may help explain why Chapa was quick to praise Governor Ferguson for his Loyalty Proclamation and to offer his assistance distributing it among San Antonio's Mexican population. Ferguson replied with a request to have twenty-five thousand copies printed in Spanish on June 21, and fifteen thousand more on July 6, 1916.[47]

Sherriff Antonio Salinas of Webb County, meanwhile, distributed a Spanish translation of the Loyalty Proclamation in the Mexican areas of Laredo. When news of this action reached Ferguson, the governor instructed his secretary to immediately draft a letter cordially thanking Salinas. In the letter, Ferguson said that he "heartily appreciates the interest you have manifested."[48] Salinas's interest in the proclamation was largely tied to the section about banditry along the border. Webb County shared a sixty-mile stretch of the Rio Grande in South Texas with three Mexican states and particularly with the city of Nuevo Laredo, where rumors of Mexican-on-American raids appeared in the press on a weekly basis.

The Loyalty Proclamation addressed banditry by urging ethnic Mexicans to report any suspicious activity and alert authorities of any known Mexican bandits living in Texas. Ferguson stated in the proclamation:

> Unfortunately the prejudice of many Mexicans, who might otherwise remain loyal to Texas, has been aroused by bandit leaders from Mexico[,] and [a] feeling of hatred exists along our Texas border which should not be. In the future when one of these bandit leaders from Mexico comes among you and tries to tell you that Americans want to mistreat you and wants you to join some secret movement, report him at once to the first officer you can get to. Report the names of other Mexicans who are mixed up in the gang. Show that you are loyal to this country.[49]

Like the Big Bend, South Texas was inundated with border violence. The *Laredo Times* published daily reports of suspicious activity by ethnic Mexicans and clashes between "Cowboys and Greasers." On the day that Ferguson made his proclamation, the *Laredo Times* reported that three Mexican bandits were killed and three captured by a posse of ranchers. The report stated that the bandits "took two American cowboys prisoners, but subsequently released them after holding the men in custody throughout the day in Mexico." Two other cowboys, George Conover and Arthur Myers, led an armed posse to apprehend the suspected bandits.[50]

Ferguson appealed to the Mexican press as well, urging it to publish his proclamation to warn Mexicans that if they came to Texas and stirred up trouble, they would worsen the "race hatred and strife" that already existed between the two peoples. Ferguson argued that publishing the proclamation in Mexico would "render a great service to your people and you will be the means of promoting peace and good will."[51] He concluded with a promise to Texas Mexicans who reported reliable information leading to the apprehension of disloyal Mexicans, "a very liberal reward in gold."[52] However, none of the archival records indicate that anyone received such a reward.

Governor Ferguson and his adjutant general, Henry Hutchings, only received a handful of letters warning about "suspicious" Mexicans. The first to arrive was on June 26, 1916, from J. N. Delavan of Lyra, Texas, a mining town of about a thousand people. Delavan warned of Mexican insurrectionists "delivering incendiary speeches to the Mexican population" of Lyra.[53] However, most of the letters were from ethnic Mexicans pledging their allegiance to the United States; they did not report the names of suspected Mexican criminals.

The impact of the Loyalty Proclamation can be seen in a rise of arrests following its release. In San Antonio, Fanstino Reyes was arrested on July 6, 1916, on charges of "inciting rebellion." The following week, eleven Mexican men were arrested as coconspirators. In addition to these arrests, San Antonio police arrested J. Jiménez and Gaspero Ortiz for "carrying a pistol," T. Tostado for breaking "neutrality laws," and T. Louis for "carrying a slingshot." The arrest totals for nonviolent crimes committed by ethnic Mexicans in San Antonio during the month of July were more than four times higher than in the previous month and accounted for 40 percent of the arrests for the entire year.[54] The Loyalty Proclamation fanned Anglo suspicions of ethnic Mexicans and made it more difficult for them to receive the full protection of Texas laws. Additionally, Chapa, who had emerged as a political voice for ethnic Mexicans, supported this measure. Chapa, with his Spanish-language newspaper and influence with Mexican Americans, maintained his position in the governor's office throughout the remainder of the decade, showing more concern for Americanizing ethnic Mexicans than advocating their right to full protection before the laws. Chapa represented a social group of ethnic Mexican elites who were closely allied with Anglo Texans and who believed that inclusion required assimilation—and whatever degree of loyalty the Anglo government demanded.

The Loyalty Proclamation illustrated the complexity of the ethnic Mexican community in Texas. Tejanos like Chapa who had established themselves as social and political elites in the state's ethnic Mexican communities distanced themselves from Mexicans who supported revolutionary causes in Mexico. Mexican refugees who fled to Texas for safety during the 1910s were not as familiar with Anglo society and, thus, found comfort and safety within Mexican neighborhoods—reading Mexican papers, eating Mexican food, and openly celebrating Mexican heritage through festivals. The governor's proclamation unleashed new pressures on ethnic Mexicans in Texas, warning them that their jobs and safety could be jeopardized if they failed to pledge allegiance to the Stars and Stripes.

LOYALTY AND HONOR: WORLD WAR I

American citizens were divided on whether American intervention in World War I was necessary. President Woodrow Wilson initially opposed intervention, but he was also a proponent of securing democracy in America and abroad. By 1917 Wilson had already warned that the United States would not tolerate unrestricted submarine warfare following the sinking of the *Lusitania* in 1915. Thus, when the British intercepted a German telegram intended for the government of Mexico that called for the latter to engage the United States in war, US public opinion tilted in favor of intervention in Europe. The Zimmermann Telegram, authored by Germany's secretary for foreign affairs, Arthur Zimmermann, made the following declaration:

> We intend to begin on the first of February unrestricted submarine warfare. We shall endeavor in spite of this to keep the United States of America neutral. In the event of this not succeeding, we make Mexico a proposal of alliance on the following basis: make war together, make peace together, generous financial support and an understanding on our part that Mexico is to conquer the lost territory in Texas, New Mexico, and Arizona.[55]

As stated in the telegram, Germany did resume unrestricted submarine warfare. Wilson continued to remain neutral, but after the seventh US merchant ship was destroyed by German U-boats, Congress declared war on Germany on April 6, 1917.[56] Surprisingly, two events that appeared unrelated and that were separated by the Atlantic Ocean—the Mexican Revolution and World War I—would both have an impact on lynchings and violent attacks on ethnic Mexicans in Texas. The Mexican Revolution contributed to the increase in violence, and World War I played a role in its decline.

As the world war engulfed more and more of the globe, ethnic Mexicans in Texas began returning to Mexico out of fear of conscription in the US Army as well as in response to Ranger terror. The coroner of Cameron County, Henry J. Kirk, who had examined the body of Florencia García, testified during the Canales investigation that he was regularly called to collect the remains of decomposing bodies—sometimes one or two, other times six—and recounted a time when he was called to a scene where there were twenty dead ethnic Mexicans. Kirk explained that ethnic Mexicans were afraid to search the countryside for their "evaporated" friends or relatives out of fear that they too would disappear. When he asked a man why he didn't go and retrieve or bury the bodies, Kirk explained, the man replied that "he was afraid that the Rangers would shoot them."[57] As a consequence, Kirk feared that ethnic Mexicans would once again flee Texas, as had happened in 1915, and laborers necessary for farming and agricultural work would be in short supply. "We don't want them to leave," declared Kirk; "they have been leaving there for some cause in an alarming way. It was a common occurrence to see team after team loaded with household goods going across into Mexico."[58] In 1917 immigration records show that ninety-three thousand people left the United States for Mexico.[59]

By 1918 Texas Rangers and border agents were claiming that ethnic Mexicans, some of whom were Mexican Americans, were fleeing to Mexico to dodge US military service. Ironically, as Congress passed the 1917 Immigration Act requiring immigrants to be literate and subjecting them to head taxes, making immigration more restrictive, agents were also attempting to prevent ethnic Mexicans from fleeing because they believed that these men were citizens trying to avoid the war. Secretary of Labor William B. Wilson "suspended the literacy test, head tax, and contract labor clause for agricultural workers, effective until March 2, 1921," in an effort to encourage Mexican laborers to return to the United States.[60] Furthermore, if foreign workers could prove that they had not begun the naturalization process, then they were excluded from the military draft. However, this did little to convince ethnic Mexicans to remain in Texas or to encourage laborers who had left to return.[61] Jesús Villareal testified to being tortured on the suspicion he was smuggling two Mexican American teenage boys out of the United States to escape the draft. Driving west from Brownsville to Roma, Texas, with the two boys headed to Villareal's niece's wedding, the most direct path along the Rio Grande required them to cross the river where the waterway snaked around the terrain. When stopped by two Rangers, Villareal was beaten because the officers believed that he was helping the young men avoid "registration day."[62] In fact, one of the young Mexican American boys already had registration papers in his possession.

Intimidation by Rangers and now the fear of being called to serve in World War I led to a considerable decline in the ethnic Mexican labor force. While the number of those who left the United States is uncertain, border agents reported that thousands of ethnic Mexicans crossed into Mexico from Brownsville alone in the month after the American entry in the war. Historians refer to this movement as an "exodus." Ethnic Mexicans left with their families, possessions, and in one case an entire adobe-style home.[63] Moreover, thirty thousand Anglo Americans sought to avoid conscription by traveling to Mexico, and an estimated ten thousand of these draft dodgers remained in Mexico in 1921, three years after the war's end.[64]

Not all ethnic Mexicans tried to avoid conscription. Approximately two hundred thousand people of Hispanic origin served in the US military in World War I, and most of them were of Mexican descent.[65] Those Mexican Americans who willfully enlisted and served in the war wanted to demonstrate their loyalty to the United States. They feared anti-Mexican violence in Texas; to some of them, losing their life abroad hardly seemed a worse alternative. One Mexican American World War I veteran described the intolerable conditions in Texas as being caught "between the Devil and the deep blue sea."[66] Nevertheless, those who enlisted would continue to experience the Jim Crow South during their training days. Even though service was not segregated along white-Mexican lines as it was along white-black lines, military training in the South exposed ethnic Mexicans to a society and culture that was intolerant of men of color, even though they were leaving for Europe to defend the democratic ideals of the nation. What Mexican American soldiers experienced would awaken in some of them a determination to eradicate the culture of hatred in Texas on their return. They believed that their

military service had given them the right to protest the circumstances to which they and other Mexican Americans had been subjected.

Some ethnic Mexicans regarded service in the US military as an opportunity to assimilate into the American mainstream, while others believed that refusal to register for the draft was a protest for being treated like second-class citizens. Those who chose service desired inclusion into the American ranks. If they could speak English, they trained and fought in integrated platoons. As for the Spanish-speaking Mexican Americans, the US military implemented the Camp Gordon plan, under which recruits were organized into units according to "nationality, loyalty, intellect, citizenship, and fitness for military service."[67] Camp Gordon had companies of "Italians, Russians, Greeks, Swedes, and Mexicans." To improve troop morale, the officers in charge of training the men came from northern cities; anti-Mexican officers from the South and the Southwest were avoided as much as possible. According to one report, the Mexican American willingness to fight in World War I increased by 100 percent following the implementation of this plan: "The opportunity to train under and alongside their ethnic peers performed wonders for the soldiers in the so-called Foreign Legion Companies."[68] Proponents of the Camp Gordon plan believed that the soldiers, referred to as a "Foreign Legion," would have a greater opportunity for inclusion in the American mainstream once they returned from the Great War as English-speaking veterans.

Mexican American soldiers who served came from central Texas, the Big Bend, and South Texas. Francisco Ramírez, son of Pedro and Albina Ramírez of Alpine, was twenty-one years old when he left for service with the US Army in 1917 (fig. 5.2). He was born the same year as Antonio Gómez, the Thorndale lynching victim discussed in chapter 2, and he was familiar with the anti-Mexican violence of the decade. Alpine was a neighboring town to Marfa, where 3,500 Mexican refugees had boarded trains to Fort Bliss for internment as discussed in chapter 4. Alpine was also ninety miles south of Pecos; residents there were familiar with the three-year-long legal case of Leon Martínez Jr., ending in Martínez's execution. Ramírez had himself been forced to attend segregated schools. However, when called to duty, he served the United States in Europe.[69] Mexican Americans, through their experiences in World War I as US soldiers, enhanced their sense of inclusion in America. However, it also made them more impatient with the Juan Crow system in Texas that they again experienced upon returning from the war.

Charles V. Porras, born in El Paso on July 13, 1901, was a Mexican

Figure 5.2 Francisco Ramírez, World War I, Casey Collection, Archives of the Big Bend, Bryan Wildenthal Memorial Library, Sul Ross State University, Alpine, Texas.

American World War I veteran whose experience abroad and anger at Anglo mistreatment of ethnic Mexicans in Texas led him to pursue activism. Porras explained that in Texas there was a racial hierarchy: "Negros" were at the bottom, and "paisanos" were considered to be "a couple of degrees above the Negro."[70] A paisano was a Mexican man who had lived most of his life in Mexico but who was now living in the United States, seen near the bottom of the racial hierarchy because he was unlikely to assimilate into Anglo American society given his advanced age. Paisanos were not necessarily the lowest class of Mexicans, and they were not all uneducated; many were middle class as well. They did not feel the need or desire to be accepted by Anglo Texans, and they were disliked in urban areas for their political aspirations, as they often formed fraternal orders and clubs.[71] Porras knew the term from an early age because his father often used it to describe his friends. Porras told a story about how his father and several of his companions from the mutual aid society La Agrupacíon Protectora Mexicana (discussed in chapter 2) were ordered to leave "one of the best cafés in El Paso at the corner of Oregon and Overland Streets." The German American owner, Mr. Zieger, ordered them out even though the Mexican men were properly dressed, because "Mexicans weren't being served there."[72] The younger Porras grew up in El Paso and witnessed the Jim Crow–era segregation laws as a system that targeted ethnic Mexicans as well as blacks. Porras did not question whether he was white; rather, he questioned why white Texans applied laws that targeted blacks to Mexicans as well.

Porras attended El Paso's Mexican school, Juan Jacinto, until the eighth grade. As a teenager, he attended El Paso High School; Anglos didn't encourage Mexican American students to attend, but they were not prohibited. Most Mexican boys of that age did not continue beyond the Mexican primary schools, instead seeking employment to help provide for their families. Porras did not experience much discrimination from his fellow students, but the teachers were less favorable to ethnic Mexicans in the classroom. While in attendance, he recalled having several Anglo friends, but socially outside of school there was less mixing. Anglo parents generally excluded ethnic Mexican teenagers from their social gatherings. Porras recalled only two families that invited him into their homes: an Irish family, the McQuarters, and a Jewish family. He didn't recall at the time feeling excluded, a sentiment that only developed after his experience abroad serving in the US Navy.[73]

In the navy Porras developed a friendship with a black cook from his ship. The young cook was badly beaten by a drunken mob of white men when they left the ship together in Key West, Florida. Porras recalled, "Wherever we went away from Texas, away from the South, we noticed that there was no difference [in their treatment because of their skin color]. When I first went to California—Los Angeles, San Diego—we used to go everywhere and nobody said a thing. Down South, in the southern states, that was different."[74] While stationed at a camp in Gulfport, Mississippi, Porras feared leaving the base at night. The young Mexican American understood the Jim Crow–era rules of the South, that he could not leave the base at night and enjoy a "picture show" or restaurants because "if your skin was just a little dark, brother, that's it . . . trouble."[75]

On his way to Chicago from New Orleans, Porras was excited because the navy transported its sailors in first class, a perk that a young sailor would be eager to experience. Nevertheless, in the dining car of the train, an Anglo man quickly alerted the steward when Porras, who was dressed in uniform, sat at the table next to him. He demanded that Porras be escorted out of first class, shouting, "You think I'm going to sit along side of that black so-and so? That black son-of-a-bitch." Porras later explained that this experience in the South left him with a burning desire to stand up against social and racial injustice: "That left an everlasting memory in my mind that is bitter, very bitter. To think that I was in uniform and I was very well presented; I was a first-class petty officer; clean. And this yokel here—the way he called me 'that Black son-of-a-bitch'—like that."[76] His military experience was an awakening for Porras, one that would forever change him. As a veteran, he would soon fight a war for Mexican American rights—"When I came back, they weren't going to push me around. They weren't going to tell me, 'Well, you can't sit here; you can't come here.' Then is when I woke up."[77]

Historian José Ramírez points out that the Mexican American experience is largely absent from the literature on World War I. He argues that military scholars have struggled to find adequate sources because the military simply classified Mexican Americans as "white."[78] However, the historical anonymity was further complicated by Tejanos who tried to disguise their Mexicanness from army officials. Ramírez discusses the case of David Cantú Barkley, the son of an Anglo man and an ethnic Mexican woman. Barkley, a light-skinned Tejano, "took every precaution to conceal his heritage in order to serve on the front lines." These precautions included only disclosing his Anglo heritage and requesting that his mother not write to him using her Spanish surname.[79] Barkley had witnessed how ethnic Mexicans were treated in Texas during the Jim Crow era, and he feared being segregated like African Americans were during

World War I. His motivation for hiding his Mexican heritage was to avoid possible discrimination, segregation, or assignments to menial tasks forced upon African Americans. Barkley understood that while the military did not have a separate category for ethnic Mexicans, the culture of the South made him fully aware that Anglos did not view ethnic Mexicans as white. On November 9, 1918, Barkley died while on a reconnaissance mission. He was awarded the Medal of Honor (the thirty-eighth Hispanic recipient of the award), along with the Croix de Guerre by France and the Croce al Merito di Guerra by Italy.[80] In general, the ethnic Mexicans from Texas who served in World War I who were lighter skinned, such as Barkley, with an Anglo father who bestowed a non-Spanish family name, distanced themselves from ethnic Mexicans if they could pass as white. Another group of ethnic Mexicans was represented by Porras. Members of this group did not hide their identity and, after the war, would continue to fight for equal protection and equal rights for ethnic Mexicans in Texas.

World War I provided an opportunity for ethnic Mexicans to demonstrate their loyalty to the United States, not only abroad but on the home front as well. Just as Governor Ferguson had appealed to citizens as well as alien residents of Texas to demonstrate their loyalty to the state, President Wilson urged the foreign-born to demonstrate their loyalty by joining Americans in Fourth of July celebrations. The celebration in 1918 became know as "Loyalty Day" in many cities around the country. Wilson declared that nothing had been more gratifying during the war "than the manner in which our foreign-born fellow citizens, and the sons and daughters of the foreign-born, have risen to this greatest of all national emergencies . . . your frequent professions of loyalty . . . your eager response to call for patriotic service, including the supreme service of offering life itself in battle for justice, freedom, and democracy."[81] Wilson believed that Independence Day in 1918 was a time to celebrate a diversified military united to fight in Europe for the greater good of Americans and humankind. As a result, it was, he suggested, the second most significant July Fourth celebration in the country's history: "As July 4, 1776, was the dawn of democracy for this nation," declared Wilson, "let us, on July 4, 1918, celebrate the birth of a new and greater spirit of democracy . . . what the signers of the Declaration of Independence dreamed of for themselves and their fellow-countrymen shall be fulfilled for all mankind."[82]

From coast to coast, Loyalty Day celebrations occurred in cities and neighborhoods that included citizens and the foreign-born. The Polish, Irish, and Jewish communities of northeastern cities pledged to Wilson their commitment to the patriotic celebration. New York Italians, with the help of a national organization known as the Roman Legion of America, planned elaborate celebrations for Loyalty Day and urged the Roman Legion to cooperate with mayors of cities around the country.[83] In Texas Wilson's address reached ethnic Mexicans. Near the border in Kingsville the Loyalty Day celebration included more than one hundred Mexican and Mexican American young men who offered their service to the US military.[84] South, Central, and West Texas communities like San Angelo and El Paso all witnessed a demonstration of loyalty following Wilson's address. José Canales saw this as an opportunity for Mexican Americans to demonstrate their loyalty to the United States. He was selected as one of seventy-five thousand Americans to be a "Four-Minute Man." With this title came the task of rallying support for the war effort among Mexican Americans and giving four-minute speeches in support of the war at churches and movie theaters.[85]

Demonstrating loyalty was important to some ethnic Mexicans in Texas, but not all. Shortly after Congress declared war on Germany in April 1917, thousands of Mexicans unwilling to enlist and fight on behalf of the United States began to flee south into Mexico, a movement that Texans referred to as the "Mexican exodus." Under the Selective Service Act of 1917, all adult males living in the United States were required to register. However, any foreign-born male who had not made a declaration of intention to become a citizen of the United States was not liable for conscription. Upon satisfying draft board officials of their alien status, these men were exempt from US military service. The *Dallas Morning News* reported that "the impression prevails that Mexican citizens are liable for draft in the national army and this impression has caused the exodus to Mexico of many foreign laborers."[86]

By the summer of 1917 Texas farmers became increasingly concerned about a labor shortage. Canales's pro-American speeches to Mexican American communities urged them not to leave Texas for Mexico. Nevertheless, the Mexican flight drained the region of unskilled workers at the same time that northern cities began attracting African American workers because of better wages in factories manufacturing goods for the war effort. The Department of Agriculture sent representatives to Austin to work with state officials to solve the labor shortage in Texas, which had begun several years earlier because of increased Ranger violence and subsequent ethnic Mexican flight.[87] As a result the Department of Labor and the Department of Agriculture organized a summer

youth program that brought northern and eastern boys to the Southwest to fill the labor shortages. The US Boys' Working Reserve brought more than two hundred thousand teenage boys to the region during their summer vacation from school.[88] In Chicago boys from Lane Technical High School volunteered for the Working Reserve, and, like boys from other participating schools, they received medals for their service. Upon their return home they were celebrated with a parade through the streets of Chicago, reinforcing President Wilson's desire to see Americans come together for the war effort abroad and on the home front.

"Boy Power," as it was referred to by the Department of Labor, was a patriotic war initiative encouraging young men to enroll with the understanding that they were doing their part. Representatives from the Department of Agriculture met in St. Louis during the week of November 5–10 to evaluate the success of Boy Power from the previous summer. The representatives opined "that school boys rightly trained and led would make capable farm helpers and would be a potent factor in winning the war against Germany."[89] William E. Hall, the national director of the Boys' Working Reserve, received a letter from former president Theodore Roosevelt expressing his support for the loyalty to the nation the program championed:

> One of the great benefits you confer is that of making a boy realize that he is part of Uncle Sam's team; that he is doing his share in the great war, that he holds his services in trust for the Nation, and that although it is proper to consider the question of material gain and the question of his own desires, yet that what he must most strongly consider at this time is where his services will do most good to our people as a whole. I earnestly wish you every success in your wise and patriotic effort.[90]

The economic situation in Texas by 1918 was dire. The state needed Mexican laborers to return. The "Mexican problem" initially referred to the influx of undesirable aliens fleeing revolutionary Mexico; the "problem" was now redefined as a severe shortage of essential Mexican labor. The labor shortage was exacerbated by the need to fill manufacturing positions related to wartime industries in the North, which also accelerated Mexican migration to Chicago; Gary, Indiana; and other northern cities. Labor shortages would eventually lead to the return of ethnic Mexicans to Texas and elsewhere by the decade's end. In 1919 more than 15,100 Mexican families would resettle in Texas.[91] Anglo-Mexican relations were not necessarily improving by the decade's end, but at least they were not getting any worse. Anglo Texans were encouraging ethnic Mexicans to return to work the fields and mines. More often than any other time during the previous decade, newspapers reported the dire need for "good Mexicans" to return and work the fields. Mexicans were no longer characterized as a threat in the Texas-Mexico borderland. A new threat had emerged—"Huns."

QUESTIONING THE LOYALTY OF GERMAN AMERICANS

A growing suspicion of German activity in South and West Texas led Anglos to focus on a new enemy of the state: Germans. Americans had long suspected that Germany was supporting Mexican revolutionary efforts and possibly Mexican raids on American soil such as Pancho Villa's raid on Columbus, New Mexico. Customs inspector Marcus Hines testified during a Senate investigation of Mexican affairs in 1919 that he removed a German flag from a rancher's house during the height of the Anglo-Mexican border raids of 1916 to 1917. The rancher had several Mexican laborers working for him and was told that if he raised the German flag on his ranch, raiders would bypass his property and he would be left unharmed. The ranch was located along the Rio Grande outside of the South Texas town of Santa Maria.[92] Tom Mayfield of the Texas Ranger force of Hidalgo County reported to the Senate committee that the region was plagued with rumors that bandits were armed with German weapons. These were the rumors that Texans were growing increasingly concerned about prior to the US entry into World War I.

The hunt for pro-German saboteurs and spies in the United States broadened with US entry into the war, and in Texas the negative campaign against Germans led to more favorable conditions for ethnic Mexicans. During the decade of the Mexican Revolution, Texans had convinced themselves that they were practically at war with Mexico, or, at the very least, they were suspicious of Mexicans around the border and elsewhere in the state. Yet when the United States declared war against Germany and the government called upon men to fight, this actual, declared war supplanted the feigned war against Mexico. Moreover, the infamous Zimmermann Telegram was more than a mere rumor about a possible threat; it demonstrated the existence of an actual threat. Nationally, terms like "liberty cabbage" and "liberty dogs" replaced the German words "sauerkraut" and "dachshunds." The National Food Commission debated whether to ban sauerkraut entirely, coming to the decision in May 1918 to only officially change the name.[93] Germans were referred to as "Huns," German schools and churches that primarily operated using the German language were forced to adopt "English only" practices, and in heavily German regions of the United States like the Missouri River Valley, towns "Americanized" their names. President Wilson ordered all German-born males fifteen and older to report to their local US Post Office and file for a registration card. They were then investigated and sometimes interrogated. If they were found to be an enemy of the state, they were interned at one of two camps depending on where they lived in relation to the Mississippi River: Fort Douglas, Utah, or Fort Oglethorpe, Georgia. In Texas this growing suspicion of German Americans mirrored some aspects of the anti-Mexican rhetoric of the decade.

The *Galveston Daily News* reported that the US Treasury Department had uncovered a plan by pro-German agents operating in the country to undermine the liberty loan program. The program encouraged Americans to purchase war bonds to help fund the military and assist US allies. The article suggested that pro-German agents were operating in Texas to discourage subscriptions.[94] Once again, the press was responsible for fueling anti-German rhetoric, and, as with the Mexican Revolution stories, mistreatment of Americans abroad became an important focus. The *San Antonio Light* reported that American POWs would be starving if not for packages delivered by the American Red Cross and the YMCA. An American escapee reported that until the packages arrived their daily food ration consisted of a slice of black sour bread and a cup of cold coffee for breakfast, and for dinner, if they were lucky, a pint and a half of warm soup made of water and boiled turnips.[95]

Anglo paranoia now shifted from Mexican "bandits" to "German agents" operating in Texas. The Newcastle Coal Company in Wichita Falls closed for two days because of a report that a "German agent" was hiding in the mine and was prepared to blow it up once the mine workers arrived.[96] As with suspected banditry, many of the reports were false. A German American woman was accused of attempting to poison soldiers training at Camp Bowie, Fort Worth, even though she was visiting family in New York at the time.[97] The *Corsicana (TX) Daily Sun* took the anti-German rhetoric in a more violent direction. Without literally encouraging mob violence, the paper suggested that anti-Americanism should be punishable by death and argued that German agents were evading treasonous charges because of intellectually ill-equipped juries. The article was titled "Let's Shoot Traitors" and appeared to urge Texans to seek out suspected German agents: "Kill the spies and traitors and they will be where they can do no further damage. Furthermore, the executioners will have a wholesome effect on others who might be tempted."[98] Across Texas mobs organized to physically assault German Americans suspected of being German sympathizers, and in Shamrock, Texas, a Methodist preacher was nearly lynched by a group of men for "allegedly baptizing an infant in the name of Kaiser Wilhelm II."[99]

Anti-German feelings ran high throughout the county. The *New York Herald* printed a cartoon image, "enemy alien menace," looming over the city. In Chicago and cities around the Midwest, signs posted warnings that German Americans were not welcome in public spaces. The *Los Angeles Times* printed an image of a sign warning the "alien enemy" that they were not permitted any closer to the port than the sign's location. This sign, and many like it, were a direct result of federal restrictions prohibiting German Americans from entering ports and warehouses.[100] Across the country Germans were harassed, beaten, and in one known case lynched. Robert Prager of Collinsville, Illinois, was accused by his fellow miners of making seditious remarks. Walter Clark, superintendent of the mine, dismissed rumors that Prager had hoarded gunpowder while employed at the mine. On April 4, 1918, after twice escaping pursuing miners, Prager was apprehended by a mob of over 350 men and hanged from a tree. Before the lynching, he wrote a final statement to his family in German: "Dear Parents [and brother] Carl Henry Prager . . . I must on this, the fourth day of April, 1918, die. Please pray for me, my dear parents. This is my last letter and testament, your dear son and brother, Robert Paul Prager."[101] When the police arrived, only two men remained at the scene, and they tried to prevent the officers from removing Prager's body from the tree. Officials found a loyalty proclamation in his coat pocket that swore his allegiance to the United States. Germans and German Americans who feared for their safety carried such documents and did their best to demonstrate their absolute fealty to the United States, often to no avail. They were now enemies of the state.

As Americans grew more confident that the war in Europe would end with an Allied victory, nativists questioned what would happen with the interned German agents. The *Denton (TX) Record-Chronicle* argued that the internment camps had "cleaned up" Texas and the country. The essay, anonymously authored by "Harriman of the Vigilantes," was a nativist diatribe about foreign-born citizens in the United States. The author argued for swift assimilation of the subjects and encouraged violence against them if they did not submit: "Get to work within the confines of your own country. Build up and purify your land. Purge it of the filth that clogs its spirit. Wash it clean of the evil it has clung to so long." The writer's concern originated with the release of the Germans internees at the war's end. He argued that "rotten masses" would "spew out on our land." The author concluded, "We have no room in America for the man who shouts 'Hurrah for America!' and follows it with a whisper of 'Gott sei dank, Ich bin Deutsch' (Thanks be to God, I am German)."[102]

As tension escalated, the US attorney general, Thomas Watt Gregory, advised by his fellow cabinet members, argued that officers of the law must vigorously enforce the espionage law "with great vigor, and to leave nothing undone to stop German propaganda." He feared that if non-German citizens took the law into their own hands, the lynching of German Americans could become an everyday affair. Gregory believed that "there will be a reign of lynch law, and that German sympathizers will be found adorning lamp posts or suspended from the limbs of trees."[103]

The anti-German hysteria made its way to the state's highest office. Governor Ferguson's hopes for reelection in 1918 were dashed after the Texas House of Representatives prepared twenty-one charges against him for impeachment over a highly publicized dispute with the University of Texas. Of those charges, one questioned a loan of $156,500 from an unknown source. The press suggested that the money came from one of his numerous German American supporters. The Senate convicted Ferguson on ten of the twenty-one charges. On January 18, 1917, William P. Hobby was sworn in as lieutenant governor of Texas. Ferguson's support from the German community came largely from German businessmen who owned breweries, given that Ferguson was an opponent of prohibition. In 1918 Ferguson ran against Hobby in the Democratic primary. Hobby won with help from his supporters, who spread rumors that the loan had come directly from the German kaiser. After the election it was revealed that the loan had come from two brewers in San Antonio and Galveston.[104]

German-language newspapers responded to the anti-German propaganda by printing articles expressing loyalty to the United States. The *Katholische Rundschau, Neu-Braunfelser,* and *Fredericksburger Wochenblatt* urged readers to demonstrate their commitment to the United States. In April 1917 the *Giddings Deutsches Volksblatt* "printed the Star Spangled Banner on the front page and told its readers that the time had come for German Texans to sever their ties with Germany."[105] Across the state, German American associations suspended celebrations of their heritage. During the American involvement in World War I, German Americans became the new "enemy other" in Texas, replacing ethnic Mexicans and creating an opportunity for ethnic Mexican grievances to be heard.

CONCLUSION

The focus on Germans during World War I took a great deal of attention off ethnic Mexicans. Rangers and other border officers became more concerned with hunting down alleged German spies as well as Americans who crossed into Mexico to avoid the draft. Additionally, the depleted male population during the war led Texans to encourage Mexican immigration. Due to pressure from employers in the Southwest, border agents mostly ignored the literacy tests and head taxes implemented by the Immigration Act of 1917.[106] Tejanos like José T. Canales gave patriotic speeches to ethnic Mexicans encouraging unconditional Americanism. Mexican and Anglo tension had not disappeared, but conditions significantly improved from the 1915–1917 period of intense hostility. The overall atmosphere in the state was more favorable than at any other time in the previous ten years for Mexican American demands to be heard.

The Canales investigation received serious attention. In addition to the crimes committed against ethnic Mexicans, Canales introduced into evidence Ranger abuse of German Americans. The evidence told of a group of men who unlawfully acted as judge, jury, and executioner in their misguided efforts to "protect" the state of Texas. Canales intertwined the attacks on ethnic Mexicans with the anti-German abuse, presenting a group of men who distrusted the "others" of Texas society. He also indicated white-on-white violence by the Rangers but pointed out that many of these incidents resulted from drunkenness on the part of some Rangers who were perhaps more morally degenerate than their colleagues. At the conclusion of the investigation, it was clear to the committee that Canales had made a strong case for a reconstitution of the Ranger force, with the dismissal of the men who were most responsible for the atrocities against ethnic Mexicans.

The Canales investigation had a significant impact on the Texas Rangers and on Mexican American rights statewide. The investigation brought attention specifically to Ranger-on-Mexican violence and prevented the stories of vigilante violence such as the El Porvenir massacre, mysterious hangings in

jail cells, and unlawful practices by unscrupulous law enforcers from being buried along with unknown victims in the mesquite-lined valleys of rural Texas. Texas newspapers reported the findings of the investigation and placed the once-revered Rangers in a negative light. Moreover, witnesses who testified were not exclusively ethnic Mexicans. Anglo Texans willing to testify helped bring down the Ranger force as well. The Canales investigation gave Texans an opportunity to demonstrate that civility could win over lawlessness, and 1919 marked the end of the freewheeling Ranger force that had dominated this period of frontier history. On March 31, 1919, the Texas state legislature passed a law that reduced the Ranger force to four companies with a maximum of fifteen soldiers and two officers, and the law required that the adjutant general investigate all complaints filed against any Rangers in the future.[107]

World War I also marked a turning point for ethnic Mexicans in Texas. Mexican American veterans returned from the war with a new hope for civility in Texas and a greater confidence that they deserved to be treated as equals in the United States. Mexican American veterans were at the forefront of the Mexican American civil rights organizations that formed in the early 1920s. These men were returning from Europe while state officials were investigating the Anglo-on-Mexican violence that had occurred during the previous decade. The investigation, along with evolving public opinion about lynching, the growing political stability in Mexico, and the proliferation of war veterans who were ready to fight a battle for equal rights, generated additional and more effective investigations into suspected lynchings during the early 1920s.

During the 1910s there were 124 confirmed lynchings of ethnic Mexicans in the United States.[108] That number is much higher if we include unjust but "legal" executions and the offenses committed by the Texas Rangers. In the end, Anglo-on-Mexican violence resulted in 3,500 to 5,000 casualties.[109] Most occurred between 1910 and 1918. Conditions had in fact improved by the 1920s, when only two confirmed lynchings and three suspected lynchings of ethnic Mexicans occurred in the state. The last confirmed lynching of an ethnic Mexican in the United States was that of Rafael Benavides in Farmington, New Mexico, on November 16, 1928.[110]

A Mexican American civil rights movement emerged out of the violence of the 1910s. In 1922 the Álvaro Obregón government in Mexico demanded that US officials investigate Anglo abuse of Mexican nationals in the United States. These investigations led to the arrest and prosecution of mob participants and even provided reparations for the victims' family. And in Texas, when these charges were made, the Texas Rangers were summoned to protect the foreigners from additional violence—a Ranger force that had only a few years earlier believed ethnic Mexicans to be the sworn enemies of the state now had the duty to protect foreign nationals from Anglo violence. The Mexican Revolution had brought the devastation of war to the borderland, resulting in the loss of Mexican and American lives. Yet civility returned to the region, and a voice could be heard from an emerging Mexican American civil rights movement that would only grow stronger as the twentieth century progressed.

Conclusion

TOWARD A MEXICAN AMERICAN CIVIL RIGHTS MOVEMENT

This study has documented the rise in lynchings of ethnic Mexicans and the emergence of a Mexican American civil rights movement in Texas during the 1910s. Both occurred during a period of great social and political contestation along the US-Mexico border. The legacy of this decade would be the struggle for equal rights and protection in the United States by ethnic Mexican men and women in the 1920s and beyond. World War I diverted negative attention from ethnic Mexicans in Texas as Germans took their place as the "other" whom Anglo Texans feared the most. With the end of the Mexican Revolution, political stability returned to Mexico, further calming the region. During the 1920s the Mexican families of lynching victims in the United States sought support from their new government to pressure US leaders to pursue legal measures against the perpetrators of the violence. Additionally, defenders of Anglo-on-Mexican lynching could no longer cite the violence of the Mexican Revolution to rationalize their actions, leading to a change in public opinion about whether these acts were necessary and justified.

This is not to suggest, however, that the same public opinion shifted fully toward the acceptance of ethnic Mexicans in the United States. In 1921 the term "wetback" was introduced by the American press, eventually becoming as common as the term "greaser" as a derogatory term used to describe Mexican immigrants. The term "wetback," with its sociopolitical references to Mexicans who avoided the immigration requirements for literacy tests and head taxes, referred to those Mexicans who crossed the Rio Grande at unregulated locations. In Texas the legacy of racism continued with segregated schools until the 1945 *Mendez v. Westminster* decision in California, in which Judge Paul McCormick ruled that the segregation of Mexican children "found no justification in the Laws of California and furthermore was a clear denial of the 'equal protection' clause of the Fourteenth Amendment." This decision desegregated the non-Mexican, all-white public schools in California and accelerated the fight of Mexican American rights organizations for desegregation in Texas. At that time, in border towns as well as in major cities like Dallas and Fort Worth, business associations were still implementing Jim Crow restrictions on ethnic Mexicans with signs that read, "No Dogs, Negros, and Mexicans."[1]

The José Canales investigation brought attention to the unjust acts carried out by the Texas Rangers, which, along with evolving public opinion regarding lynching and the political stabilization of Mexico, led to successful campaigns to arrest and prosecute mob participants and even to provide reparations for victims' families. Moreover, in 1922, when the Álvaro Obregón government in Mexico demanded that US officials investigate Anglo abuse of Mexican nationals in Texas, the Texas Rangers were summoned to protect foreigners from additional violence—a Ranger force that had gone through a complete overhaul immediately following the Canales investigation. On November 11, 1922, Elias Villareal Zarate, a Mexican man incarcerated for fighting with an Anglo man, was taken from his Weslaco, Texas, jail and lynched. When an ethnic Mexican protest broke out in neighboring Breckenridge, three hundred Anglo men paraded through the streets threatening the lives of every Mexican in town if they did not leave by the following day. Ethnic Mexicans in Breckenridge contacted the Mexican consul in San Antonio, Don Manuel Téllez, who then urged the US State Department and Texas governor Pat Morris Neff to protect Mexicans living in Breckenridge.

In 1923 the Mexican embassy investigated allegations that suspected Mexican criminals in Dallas County had been sent to jail and unofficially sentenced to ten-day work details before being released—without ever having seen their day in court. Octaviano Escutia, arrested in Denison, Texas, for example, was placed on a road gang detail. Escutia stated that when he became thirsty and asked the Anglo foreman for a drink, the man began kicking him and threw him in a ditch, calling him a "dirty, low-down Mexican."[2] Manuel Zamora, another prisoner held without trial in Denison, described similar abuse: "I was forced to work from seven o'clock in the morning until five o'clock at night, and during that time I was not permitted to leave my work to go to the toilet. . . . I became weak and exhausted and on the 20th day of February AD 1923, I fell to the ground. . . . The man in charge refused to give me any assistance, but gathered about and laughed at me and abused me in bad language."[3] With political stability in Mexico and US leaders optimistic about improving foreign relations, Téllez was successful in getting these cases investigated.

In addition to investigations, improved foreign relations led to reparations for family members of Mexican victims. In February 1921 an Anglo American girl, Maria Schroeder, disappeared after school near Rio Hondo, Texas. Community members searched for the girl and eventually found her body in a dense thicket in Cameron County; investigators determined that she had been raped and murdered. When the press published accounts of the crime, it was said that the entire population of Cameron Country became aroused, "and immediately thereafter it became evident that the perpetrator of the crime, when apprehended, would be lynched."[4] When Salvador Saucedo's name was mentioned as a possible suspect, he immediately knew that lynching without trial was sure to be his punishment. A posse that included law enforcement officials apprehended Saucedo and took him out to a deserted field. When the opportunity presented itself, Saucedo fled on foot, only to be gunned down by the men. It was later discovered that two Anglo men had been responsible for the girl's death, and Mexican officials demanded justice: "In view of the facts herein above-mentioned, the Embassy of Mexico very respectfully again asks of the Department of State that due justice be done, through the proper channel, and that those who may be found guilty of the murder of Salvador Saucedo be punished, and also that a becoming indemnity be granted to Saucedo's widow and orphan."[5] The American press reported the Mexican embassy's grievances with the United States, as well as Washington's response:

Prompt action has been taken by Secretary [of State Charles Evans] Hughes on the protests made to the American Government yesterday by the Mexican Embassy, acting for the Obregon Government, against the alleged indiscriminant killing of Mexican citizens in the country, especially in Texas and along the international border.[6]

Unlike the mob leaders who carried out the Gómez lynching discussed in chapter 2, perpetrators of anti-Mexican violence in the 1920s were beginning to be brought to justice. International pressure forced the federal government to weigh in on anti-Mexican crimes in Texas, and Mexican American activists seized the opportunity to advocate for the rights of ethnic Mexicans in Texas in the 1920s.

Prior to the Mexican Revolution, the various Mexican protective associations were mostly concerned about employee grievances and better educational facilities, as documented in chapter 1. Arturo Robles, a printer from

Caldwell, Texas, and one of the pioneers of Mexican rights in the United States, wrote letters to the Mexican consul in San Antonio describing the "peonage conditions" that Mexican field workers were subjected to. He was responsible for getting Texas governor James Ferguson to send investigators to probe these accusations; however, the investigation ended on January 17, 1911, when Ferguson left office and a new governor, Oscar Colquitt, took over. Robles then received threats "for his activity on behalf of the Mexican field workers of that region."[7]

In 1911, shortly after the formation of La Agrupacíon Protectora Mexicana, members attended the first Mexican Congress—el primer Congreso Mexicanista. Mexican American activists believed that violence and injustice against ethnic Mexicans should be given more exposure. The lynching of Antonio Rodríguez and Antonio Gómez convinced the organization to shift its focus from labor rights to protecting ethnic Mexicans "whenever they faced Anglo-perpetuated violence or illegal dispossession of their property."[8] Activists who opposed these atrocities organized the group's first annual congress in the summer of 1911. The principal organizer, Nicasio Idár, was the editor of Laredo's Spanish-language newspaper, *La Crónica*.[9] In fact, Idár's family might be considered the most politically successful Mexican American family of the early twentieth century. His daughter, Jovita, was a schoolteacher, turned journalist, turned activist, who organized La Liga Feminil Mexicanista. Idár's brother, Eduardo, was an influential labor rights activist in the 1920s.[10]

Discrimination against Mexican Americans intensified during the years of the Mexican Revolution, generating effects that lasted long after the revolution had ended. Jim Crow laws continued to prohibit Mexicans from entering public swimming pools, and Anglo business owners continued to display signs that read "No Mexicans or Dogs Allowed." Drinking fountains were clearly marked "white only," and local ordinances barring Mexicans from using them were strictly enforced; on one occasion, a young Mexican girl choked to death on a tortilla because her friends were unable to get water for her from a "whites only" fountain.[11]

In 1929, when the three largest Mexican American rights organizations (the Knights of America, the Sons of America, and the League of Latin American Citizens) met in Corpus Christi, group leaders were skeptical about a successful merger of the groups. After four hours of deliberation, however, they agreed to combine their constitutions and form the League of United Latin American Citizens (LULAC), accepting not only Mexican

Americans but all American citizens of Latin American origin. The key ingredient was "American."[12] LULAC members united to protest ethnic violence, and to advocate improved working conditions and educational facilities for their children. Urging assimilation into Anglo American society, LULAC's founders wanted the organization to be a "safe haven" for its members and sought to avoid being perceived as "un-American." Accordingly, LULAC members "adopted the American Flag as its official flag, 'America the Beautiful' as its official song, and 'The George Washington Prayer' as its official prayer."[13] Utilizing whiteness, or becoming culturally white by US citizens' standards of the time, Mexican Americans considered assimilation to be a defense mechanism.[14] LULAC became a successful Mexican American rights organization, widely accepted by Anglo Americans because of its pro-American rhetoric. However, some ethnic Mexicans opposed what LULAC appeared to represent—assimilation. These ethnic Mexicans wanted a more aggressive plan for ethnic Mexican inclusion in Texas. They labeled LULAC members "a bunch of *vendidos*" (sellouts) and favored more confrontation and militancy in pushing civil rights demands.[15]

Despite this divide, LULAC has grown to become the largest civil rights organization for Latinos in the United States. The Mexican Revolution and the Anglo-on-Mexican violence of the 1910s were the catalysts for such organizations to move forward into an ongoing Mexican American civil rights movement lasting throughout the twentieth century. For Mexicans living in Mexico and the United States, the decade of the 1910s was one of fear and confusion. In towns along the US-Mexican border, ethnic Mexicans were profiled by a prejudiced society and became targets of unwarranted searches, unjust legal decisions, and one of the most evil acts of violence ever carried out by people—lynching.

The lynching of ethnic Mexicans in the United States is a story that is largely absent from history books. It is generally agreed by scholars that the last known lynching of an ethnic Mexican in the United States occurred in 1928, as mentioned above. This, too, could be debated by challenging the parameters necessary to define a lynching. Furthermore, anti-Mexican prejudice and violence continued in a series of ebbs and flows throughout the twentieth century and into the twenty-first. The historical memory of the lynching of ethnic Mexicans is skewed as well. In 2010 a civil rights museum in Cincinnati, the Freedom Center, displayed the exhibit *Without Sanctuary: Photographs and Postcards of Lynching in America*. Absent from this display were the stories of the hundreds of ethnic Mexicans who were very much part of this dark chapter in American history. Their exclusion is ironic, because as visitors walked toward the entrance of the Freedom Center, a forty-by-forty-foot sign displays the words of W. E. B. Du Bois: "We must remember, because if the world forgets evil, evil is reborn." Evil was not born during the decade of the Mexican Revolution, nor did it disappear thereafter. But it certainly intensified during that time. It is important that we know about this intensification and its effects on Mexicans in the United States. And it is important, too, that we understand those events not, in the final analysis, in terms of good versus evil, but through careful historical analysis of the forces that unleashed and tolerated racial violence, as well as the forces that sought to, and over the long term succeeded, in restraining it. This book has attempted to provide such a historical analysis and to locate it in the longer history of the Mexican American struggle for freedom in Texas and throughout the nation.

Notes

INTRODUCTION

1. "The Wages of a Hate Crime," *Newsweek*, July 4, 2007.
2. "Death on the Border: Shocking Video Shows Mexican Immigrant Beaten and Tased by Border Patrol Agents," *Democracy Now!*, April 24, 2012, http://www.democracynow.org/2012/4/24/death_on_the_border_shocking_video.
3. Elise Foley, "DOJ: No Civil Rights Charges for Border Agents over Death of Anastasio Hernandez-Rojas," *Huffington Post*, November 6, 2015, http://www.huffingtonpost.com/entry/anastasio-hernandez-rojas-doj-border-patrol_us_563d2bf7e4b0411d307131a3, accessed May 1, 2016.
4. Amber Phillips, "Here Are 12 Other Times Donald Trump Vilified Illegal Immigrants," *Washington Post*, July 1, 2015.
5. Christopher Sherman, "U.S., Mexico Open Anzalduas Bridge," *Brownsville Herald*, January 12, 2010, A2.
6. "Taft and Díaz Meet; Talk of Friendship," *New York Times*, October 17, 1909, 1–2.
7. Ibid., 2.
8. The Treaty of Guadalupe Hidalgo is the peace treaty between the United States and Mexico that ended the Mexican-American War of 1845–1848. Negotiated by Nicholas Trist, the treaty required the Mexican cession of 525,000 square miles of land to the United States in exchange for $15 million. The Mexican cession included land that is part of present-day California, Arizona, New Mexico, Utah, Nevada, and Colorado; most significant to the origin of the conflict that led to war, Mexico relinquished all future claims to Texas and formally recognized the Rio Grande as the US-Mexican border. While the Mexican government agreed to these terms, many Mexicans in the coming decades would urge their fellow citizens to seek the restoration of this territory for Mexico.
9. Villanueva, "Sincerely Yours for Dignified Manhood," 44.
10. Cha-Jua, "The Cry of the Negro," 166.
11. Carrigan and Webb, "*Muerto Por Unos Desconcidos.*"
12. Ibid., 423.
13. Carrigan and Webb, *Forgotten Dead*, 65.
14. Berg, *Popular Justice*, 122.
15. Carrigan and Webb, "The Rise and Fall of Mob Violence," 111.
16. Cha-Jua, "The Cry of the Negro," 170.

17. Waldrep, *The Many Faces of Judge Lynch*, 4.
18. Levario, *Militarizing the Border*, 12.
19. Gordon, *The Great Arizona Orphan Abduction*, 268.
20. Foley, *The White Scourge*, 40–41.
21. I use the term "American" only to represent people from the United States when such usage falls within the context of the historical period or when I am quoting a primary source. I avoid a US American exceptional narrative, but I want that language to come through as used by Anglo Americans of the 1910s.

CHAPTER ONE

1. University of Texas at El Paso, Institute of Oral History, interviewee: Mollie Gossett (McCallick); interviewer: Sarah E. John, December 2, 1975, tape no. 216, transcript no. 216.
2. Ibid.
3. On the Porfiriato, see Hart, *Revolutionary Mexico*; Hart, *Empire and Revolution*; and Knight, *The Mexican Revolution*, vol. 1: *Porfirians, Liberals, and Peasants*.
4. Neeno, "The Mexican Revolution and US Intervention."
5. University of Texas at El Paso, Institute of Oral History, interviewee: Mollie Gossett (McCallick); interviewer: Sarah E. John, December 2, 1975, tape no. 216, transcript no. 216.
6. S. Lee, *Mexico and the United States*, 466.
7. University of Texas at El Paso, Institute of Oral History, interviewee: Mollie Gossett (McCallick); interviewer: Sarah E. John, December 2, 1975, tape no. 216, transcript no. 216.
8. S. Lee, *Mexico and the United States*, 466.
9. United States Senate, Investigation of Mexican Affairs, Preliminary Report and Hearing of the Committee on Foreign Relations, United States Senate, pursuant to Senate Resolution 106, testimony of Dr. Bruce Maker Corbin, 1458.
10. United States Senate, Investigation of Mexican Affairs, Preliminary Report and Hearing of the Committee on Foreign Relations, United States Senate, pursuant to Senate Resolution 106, testimony of William Frank Buckley, 767–77.
11. United States Senate, Investigation of Mexican Affairs, Preliminary Report and Hearing of the Committee on Foreign Relations, United States Senate, pursuant to Senate Resolution 106, testimony of James M. Taylor, 1405.
12. Castellanos, "Cancún and the Campo," 242–43.
13. "Twenty Days in Mexico," Russ Todd Collection, box 3, file 13, Mexico Central Railway, Angelo State University archives.
14. "The Paris of America," Russ Todd Collection, box 3, file 13, Mexico Central Railway, Angelo State University archives.
15. "Summer in Mexico Highlands," Russ Todd Collection, box 3, file 13, Mexico Central Railway, Angelo State University archives.

16. *La Crónica*, June 29, 1911. The Laredo, Texas, Spanish-language publication criticized President Díaz for his discriminatory actions that put a higher degree of importance on skin color.

17. "The Highway to Mexico," Russ Todd Collection, box 3, file 13, Mexico Central Railway, Angelo State University archives.

18. University of Texas at El Paso, Institute of Oral History, interviewees: Howard and Mary K. Quinn; interviewers: David Salazar and Mildred Torok, March 8 and 15, 1973, tape no. 68, transcript no. 68, 19–25.

19. Russ Todd Collection, box 1, Mexican Postcards, Angelo State University archives.

20. Cott, *Public Vow*, 112.

21. Ibid.

22. Arrington and Bitton, *The Mormon Experience*, 180–81.

23. Ibid., 138–39.

24. *Late Corporation of the Church of Jesus Christ of Latter-day Saints v. United States*, 136 US 1 (1890).

25. Hirshson, *The Lion of the Lord*, 36.

26. Ibid.

27. "The Mormons: Life Among the Mormons; Salt Lake City, Its Appearance and Inhabitants," *New York Times*, September 21, 1857.

28. Hirshson, *The Lion of the Lord*, 129–30.

29. Ibid., 129.

30. "The Mormons: Life Among the Mormons; Salt Lake City, Its Appearance and Inhabitants," *New York Times*, September 21, 1857.

31. "Amongst the Mormons," *Lloyds Weekly News* (London), August 5, 1888, 2.

32. "Mormon Lure: English to Stop White Slave Traffic," *Kingston Gleaner* (London), March 15, 1911, 17; and "Girls Lured to Mormon City: Great Britain Supplies More Than a Thousand Converts a Year," *Lloyd's Weekly News* (London), April 23, 1911, 10.

33. "The Mandate and Mormonism," *Salt Lake Tribune*, December 8, 1890, 4.

34. Ibid., 4.

35. Jones, *Forty Years Among the Indians*, 370–71.

36. Tullis, *Mormons in Mexico*, 91; and S. Lee, *Mexico and the United States*, 842.

37. For personal accounts dealing with Mormon missionaries in Mexico, see Utah State Historical Society and California State University, Fullerton, Oral History Program; Jones, *Forty Years Among the Indians*; Romney, *A Divinity Shapes Our Ends*; Jesse N. Smith Family Association, *Journal of Jesse Nathaniel Smith*; and Hatch, *Colonia Juárez*.

38. Utah State Historical Society and California State University, Fullerton, Oral History Program, Southeastern Utah Project, interviewee: Mary Ann Black; interviewer: Louise Lyne, July 10, 1972, subject: Recollections of Mexico.

39. Romney, *A Divinity Shapes Our Ends*, 46.

40. Ibid., 49–51.

41. Utah State Historical Society and California State University, Fullerton, Oral History Program, Southeastern Utah Project, interviewee: Irene Hatch Redd; interviewer: Gary L. Shumway and Scott Blickenstaff, October 18, 1970, subject: Recollections of Mexico.

42. University of Texas at El Paso, Institute of Oral History, interviewee: Nelle S. Hatch; interviewer: Richard Estrada, November 7 and 9, 1977, tape no. 422, transcript no. 422.

43. Ibid.

44. University of Texas at El Paso, Institute of Oral History, interviewee: Nelle S. Hatch; interviewer: Richard Estrada, November 7 and 9, 1977, tape no. 422, transcript no. 422.

45. Ibid.

46. De León, *They Called Them Greasers*, 16.

47. Cumberland, *Mexican Revolution*, 3–5.

48. Gamio, *Mexican Immigration to the United States*, 53.

49. Ibid., 53.

50. Gamio, *The Mexican Immigrant: His Life-Story*, 226–28.

51. Ibid., 229.

52. University of Texas at El Paso, Institute of Oral History, interviewee: Brigadier General S. L. A. Marshall; interviewer: Richard Estrada, July 5, 7, 9, 11, and 19, 1975, tape no. 181, transcript no. 181, 53.

53. US Bureau of the Census, Thirteenth Census of the United States, 1910.

54. City of San Angelo, TX, at www.sanangelotexas.us, accessed June 26, 2012; and Clemens, *Concho County*, 91.

55. Noelke, *Early San Angelo*, 7–8; and Duke, "San Angelo, TX."

56. Padilla Family Collection, Porter Henderson Library, Angelo State University. The Padilla family donated these records, which they had found in their attic; they are the records kept by Manuel Trevino, secretary of Juntá Patriotica.

57. Ibid.

58. Ibid. The names listed included the amount pledged and an "X" indicating whether the money had been collected.

59. US Bureau of the Census, Year: 1900, Census Place: Justice Precinct 1,Val Verde, Texas, Roll: 1675, Page: 22B, Enumeration District: 74, FHL microfilm: 1241675.

60. US Bureau of the Census, Tenth Census of the United States, 1880 (NARA microfilm publication T9, 1,454 rolls); Texas State Library and Archives Commission; Austin, Texas; Confederate Pension Applications, 1899–1975; Collection: CPA16526; Roll: 447; Roll Description: Pension File nos. 03296–08825, Application Years 1899–1902; Records of the Bureau of the Census, Record Group 29, National Archives, Washington, DC; National Park Service, Civil War Soldiers and Sailors System, at http://www.itd.nps.gov/cwss/, accessed June 22, 2012.

61. Padilla Family Collection, Porter Henderson Library, Angelo State University.

62. "The Mexican Opera," *San Angelo Standard*, January 18, 1896, 2.

63. Ibid.

64. Ibid.

65. "Club Latino Americano," *San Angelo Standard*, March 24, 1906, 6.

66. "A Spanish Weekly," *San Angelo Standard*, March 24, 1906, 6.

67. "The San Angelo Mexican School," *San Angelo Standard*, February 29, 1886, 3.

68. Ibid.

69. Sánchez, *Becoming Mexican American*, 19.

70. Ibid., 20.

71. "Importation of Mexicans," *San Antonio Light*, September 23, 1905, 6.

72. City of San Angelo, TX, at www.sanangelotexas.us, accessed June 26, 2012.

73. Ibid.

74. Linda Cuellar, prod., *The Artistic Legacy of the Mexican Revolution*, Films for the Humanities and Sciences, Princeton, New Jersey, 2003.

75. "LULAC History: All for One and One for All," League of United Latin American Citizens, at http://lulac.org/about/history/, accessed January 4, 2011.

76. López, *White by Law*, 27–28.

77. Ariens, *Lone Star Law*, 244.

78. Blanton, *The Strange Career of Bilingual Education*, 61–62.

79. Ariens, *Lone Star Law*, 244.

80. Blanton, *The Strange Career of Bilingual Education*, 36.

81. "Lockhart School Notes," *Galveston Daily News*, August 25, 1909, 4.

82. "Schools," *Galveston Daily News*, November 19, 1908, 9.

83. Historian Carlos Kevin Blanton examined the *Salvatierra v. Del Rio Independent School District* case in which the League of United Latin American Citizens (LULAC) and the parents of Mexican children in Del Rio challenged the segregation of Del Rio schools in 1928. Blanton acknowledged that the victorious decision deemed that de jure racial segregation was illegal, but he described it as a "hollow" victory because "the court ordained English-Only pedagogy already a common subterfuge for racial segregation, as a legal loophole to continue de facto racial segregation." Blanton, *The Strange Career of Bilingual Education*, 95–96. Vicki Ruiz credited the 1945 *Mendez v. Westminster* decision in California in which Judge Paul McCormick ruled that the segregation of Mexican children "found no justification in the Laws of California and furthermore was a clear denial of the 'equal protection' clause of the Fourteenth Amendment" (Ruiz, "South by Southwest," 23). Incidentally, this decision was a precursor for the *Brown v. Board of Education* decision in 1954, and was a precedent used in the desegregation of Mexican schools in Texas and Arizona. The focus on successful desegregation campaigns in the literature needs to shift to include those instances that were less successful as well.

84. "Mexicans Seeking to Enter White Schools," *San Angelo Standard*, June 8, 1910, 1.

85. Ibid.

86. "Mexican Census of City Will Be Retaken," *San Angelo Standard*, June 15, 1910, 1–2.

87. US Bureau of the Census, Thirteenth Census of the United States, 1910 (NARA microfilm publication T624, 1,178 rolls); US Bureau of the Census, Year: 1910,

Census Place: San Angelo, Tom Green, Texas, Roll: T624 1592, Page: 2A, Enumeration District: 0283, Image: 1087, FHL microfilm: 1375605.

88. "Trustees Elect Five More Teachers," *San Angelo Standard*, June 18, 1910.

89. "Refuse Trustees Offer," *San Angelo Standard*, June 20, 1910, 6.

90. "Stirring Speeches," *San Angelo Standard*, June 20, 1910, 6.

91. "Attorneys for Mexicans Determined," *San Angelo Standard*, June 21, 1910, 2.

92. Ibid.

93. F. Johnson, *A History of Texas and Texans*, 3:1458.

94. "Mexicans Determined," *San Angelo Standard*, June 20, 1910, 3.

95. "Attend the Mass Meeting," *San Angelo Standard*, June 28, 1910, 1.

96. "Talk of Mass Meeting," *San Angelo Standard*, June 21, 1910, 3.

97. "Mexicans Refuse to Enter Own Schools," *San Angelo Standard*, September 20, 1910, 1.

98. "Catholics Refuse to Grant Request Made by Mexicans, Will Not Mix Whites and Mexicans," *San Angelo Standard*, September 22, 1910, 1.

99. "Local Mexicans Appeal to the Mexican Consul at San Antonio," *San Angelo Standard*, September 21, 1910, 1.

100. Gerstle, *American Crucible*, 60–61.

101. "Serious," *San Antonio Light*, October 1, 1910, 2.

102. Ibid.

103. "Mexican Committee Says Members Are American Citizens," *San Angelo Standard*, September 23, 1910, 1.

104. "Mexicans in White Schools," *El Paso Morning Times*, September 22, 1911, 6.

105. "Split in Mexican Population of San Angelo Now Seems Certain," *San Angelo Standard*, September 25, 1910, 1.

106. William Howard Taft Papers, series 2, box 48, Manuscript Division, Library of Congress, President William Howard Taft, letter to his wife, October 17, 1909.

107. S. Lee, *Mexico and the United States*, 301, 723–24.

108. Letter from Mexican Embassy, Washington DC, November 19, 1910, in Hanrahan, *Documents on the Mexican Revolution*, 1:65–66.

109. "The Outcasts!," *Monitor Democratico* (San Antonio), September 4, 1910.

110. "A Fighter in the Mexican Revolution Recalls the Bloody Struggle," *Los Angeles Times*, December 12, 1985, 6.

111. Ibid.

112. Utah State Historical Society and California State University, Fullerton, Oral History Program, Southeastern Utah Project, interviewee: Mary Ann Black; interviewer: Louise Lyne, July 10, 1972, subject: Recollections of Mexico.

113. Tullis, *Mormons in Mexico*, 92.

114. Utah State Historical Society and California State University, Fullerton, Oral History Program, Southeastern Utah Project, interviewee: Irene Hatch Redd; interviewer: Gary L. Shumway and Scott Blickenstaff, October 18, 1970, subject: Recollections of Mexico.

115. Romney, *The Mormon Colonies in Mexico*, 152.

116. "Story of Murder at Colonia Díaz," *El Paso Morning Times*, May 10, 1912, 8.
117. Hatch, *Colonia Juárez*, 208.
118. "Rebels May Attack," *Washington Post*, December 3, 1910, 1.
119. "Mormons Beat Back Invaders," *Coshocton (OH) Daily Tribune*, November 11, 1910, 3.
120. Hatch, *Colonia Juárez*, 210.
121. "Ogden Sends Arms to Mexico," *Standard* (Ogden, UT), November 29, 1910, 8.
122. Romney, *The Mormon Colonies in Mexico*, 195.
123. Hardy, "Cultural 'Encystment,'" 446.
124. Romney, *The Mormon Colonies in Mexico*, 195.
125. United States Senate, Investigation of Mexican Affairs, Preliminary Report and Hearing of the Committee on Foreign Relations, United States Senate, pursuant to Senate Resolution 106, testimony of Captain S. H. Veater, pt. 10, 1480.
126. Tullis, *Mormons in Mexico*, 95.
127. "Americans Were Hooted," *San Antonio Light*, April 19, 1911, 5.
128. "American Women Being Insulted," *El Paso Morning Times*, February 18, 1912, 1, 7.
129. Ibid., 1.
130. "Show Hatred for Americans," *El Paso Morning Times*, September 14, 1911, 1.
131. University of Texas at El Paso, Institute of Oral History, interviewee: Mollie Gossett (McCallick); interviewer: Sarah E. John, December 2, 1975, tape no. 216, transcript no. 216.
132. Williwood Meador Collection, Pancho Villa, box 7, file 3, Porter Henderson Library, Angelo State University.
133. University of Texas at El Paso, Institute of Oral History, interviewee: Mollie Gossett (McCallick); interviewer: Sarah E. John, December 2, 1975, tape no. 216, transcript no. 216.
134. National Archives and Records Administration, Washington, DC, *Passenger Lists of Vessels Arriving at Galveston, Texas, 1896–1951*, National Archives Microfilm Publication M1359; Record Group title "Records of the Immigration and Naturalization Service"; Record Group no. 85.
135. Ibid.
136. United States Senate, Investigation of Mexican Affairs, Preliminary Report and Hearing of the Committee on Foreign Relations, United States Senate, pursuant to Senate Resolution 106, "Foreigners Other Than Americans Killed in Mexico," 3396. As for the Chinese, 303 were killed in the Torreón massacre, to be discussed in chapter 4.
137. Menchaca, *Naturalizing Mexican Immigrants*, 216. The actual number of Mexican refugees who entered Texas was much higher, but many returned when the United States entered World War I. Young Mexican males feared that they would be conscripted into service for the US military. This is discussed in chapter 5.
138. "Mexican Town Deserted," *Dallas Morning News*, October 10, 1913, 2.
139. "Deport 6000 Refugees," *El Paso Morning Times*, October 10, 1913, 1.

140. "Alien Labor Hits: El Paso Hard Blow," *El Paso Morning Times*, November 24, 1911, 1.

141. "Show Hatred for Americans: Peon Class Worked Up to Threatening Attitude," *El Paso Morning Times*, September 14, 1911, 1.

142. "American Women Being Insulted," *El Paso Morning Times*, February 18, 1912, 1; and "Red Flag Rebels Violate Woman: Wife of American Ranchman Criminally Assaulted Five Times in Succession," *El Paso Morning Times*, March 12, 1912, 1.

CHAPTER TWO

1. "La Pezuna de Dollaria," *El Debate* (Mexico City), November 5, 1910, 1.

2. "Why Rodríguez Was Burned," *New York Times*, November 11, 1910, 2.

3. Pfeifer, *The Roots of Rough Justice*, 46.

4. "A Dark Epoch for Mexican America," League of United Latin American Citizens, at http://lulac.org/about/history/past_presidents/, accessed October 31, 2016.

5. Carrigan and Webb, *Forgotten Dead*, 1.

6. Ibid., 65.

7. Carrigan and Webb, "The Lynching of Persons of Mexican Origin," 412.

8. Ibid., 2.

9. "Armed Men Hunting for Mexican," *Waco Times Herald*, November 3, 1910, 8.

10. "Mexican Crazy or a Fugitive," *Waco Times Herald*, November 18, 1910, 2.

11. "Mexican Murdered Woman: State Probably Will Not Investigate Lynching at Rocksprings," *Waco Times Herald*, November 10, 1910, 1; and "Armed Men Hunting for Mexican," *Waco Times Herald*, November 3, 1910, 8.

12. "Why Rodríguez Was Burned," *New York Times*, November 11, 1910, 2.

13. "The Mexican Riots," *New York Times*, November 11, 1910, 8.

14. "Mexico Prevents Further Rioting," *New York Times*, November 11, 1910, 1; and "Refugees Pour out of Mexico," *Waco Times Herald*, November 23, 1910, 8.

15. Letter from an anonymous American in Guadalajara, November 23, 1919, in Hanrahan, *Documents on the Mexican Revolution*, 1:81–82.

16. "Another Riot in Mexico," *New York Times*, November 15, 1910, 1.

17. "Hard Fighting in Pueblo," *New York Times*, May 8, 1911, 2.

18. Letter from an anonymous American in Guadalajara, November 23, 1919, in Hanrahan, *Documents on the Mexican Revolution*, 1:81–82.

19. "Refugees Pour out of Mexico," *Waco Times Herald*, November 23, 1910, 8.

20. "More Mexican Rumors," *New York Times*, November 12, 1910, 1.

21. "Los Estados Unidos y Rodríguez," *El Diario del Hogar* (Mexico City), November 9, 1910, 1.

22. Texas State Archives, box 141, folder 1–31, 1913, "M," December 2–14, folder 4.

23. Governor James Ferguson's 1916 Loyalty Proclamation is detailed in chapter 5.

24. Sánchez, *Becoming Mexican American*, 27.

25. Texas State Archives, box 140, folder 1–31, 1911, "M," June 26–30, folder 8.

26. Letter from Starr County judge J. R. Monroe, Texas State Archives, box 140, folder 1–31, 1911, "M," June 16–26, folder 7.

27. Texas State Archives, box 139, folder 1–31, 1910, "M," July 26–August 10, folder 2.

28. Petition from Starr County judge J. R. Monroe, Texas State Archives, box 140, folder 1–31, 1911, "M," June 16–26, folder 7.

29. "Deport 6000 Refugees," *El Paso Morning Times*, October 10, 1913, 1.

30. Levario, *Militarizing the Border*, 88.

31. "Commendation for Colquitt," *Dallas Morning News*, June 26, 1911, 5; "Colquitt Pardons Negros," *Dallas Morning News*, June 18, 1912, 7; "Governor Issues Pardon," *Dallas Morning News*, March 28, 1911, 13.

32. Texas State Archives, box 141, folder 1–31, 1914, "C," May 2–16, folder 4.

33. Texas State Archives, box 140, folder 1–31, 1911, "M," June 16–26, folder 7.

34. Texas State Archives, box 141, folder 1–31, 1914, "C," April 2–14, folder 4.

35. Ibid.

36. "Azcona Will Stay in Jail as Courtesy," *San Antonio Light and Gazette*, December 15, 1910, 3.

37. "Mexican Sentence Enrages Americans," *New York Times*, March 2, 1911, 1.

38. US Department of State, *Foreign Relations of the United States: Diplomatic Papers, 1911* (Washington, DC: Government Printing Office, 1919), 843.

39. F. W. Meyers to President William H. Taft, November 10, 1910, National Archives, RG 59, 311.122 R61.

40. "Criticism of 'Message of President Taft' by El Paso, Texas, *Herald*," in Hanrahan, *Documents on the Mexican Revolution*, 1:65–66.

41. "Mexican Lynched in Texas: Shouted 'Viva Díaz!' While Others Celebrated Madero's Victory," *New York Times*, May 31, 1911; very little is known about this event.

42. Vivian Elizabeth Smyrl, "Thorndale, TX," Texas State Historical Association, *Handbook of Texas Online*, June 5, 2010, https://www.tshaonline.org/handbook/online/articles/hjt04.

43. Batte, *History of Milam County*, 175.

44. Ibid.; Smyrl, "Thorndale, TX."

45. US Bureau of the Census, Year: 1910, Census Place: Justice Precinct 8, Milam, Texas, Roll: T624 1578. For the purpose of distinguishing between adults and children, I determined that those fifteen years old and above would be considered adults. The US Census for 1910 recorded one female married at the age of fifteen and one fifteen-year-old male working in the county.

46. US Bureau of the Census, Year: 1910, Census Place: Justice Precinct 8, Milam, Texas, Roll: T624 1578, Page: 8A, Enumeration District: 72, Image: 301.

47. Milam County Historical Commission, http://www.milamcountyhistoricalcommission.org/.

48. Ibid.

49. Ibid.

50. Nielsen, *Vengeance in a Small Town*, 102–3.

51. Gabriel Gómez is listed as "Gamez" in some primary and secondary documents. Overwhelmingly, the name appears as "Gómez," and on the 1910 federal census the name is listed as "Gomez"; thus, for purposes of clarity and consistency, "Gómez" will be used in this text.

52. US Bureau of the Census, Year: 1910, Census Place: Justice Precinct 5, Caldwell, Texas, Roll: T624 1536, Page: 14B, Enumeration District: 0033, Image: 495, FHL microfilm: 1375549.

53. Information about local residents is from articles in the *Thorndale Thorn* and the *Rockdale Reporter and Messenger*.

54. The events of the stabbing are an accumulation of newspaper reports and trial records, all of which have glaring inconsistencies. The two local papers, the *Thorndale Thorn* and the *Rockdale Reporter and Messenger*, provided some of the most detailed early reports, but as time passed their reporting focused less on justice for the Mexican boy and more on the innocence of the Thorndale men responsible for the lynching. The *San Antonio Light* provided a more balanced report of the events, but the paper's reporters were based too far from Thorndale to conduct interviews with witnesses. The Laredo paper *La Crónica*, which catered to the Mexican American community in Texas, favored the boy in its reporting. There are also inconstancies in the records provided to the initial court of inquiry. *San Antonio Light*, June 22, 1911, 1–2.

55. *Rockdale Reporter and Messenger*, November 7, 1907.

56. "The Most Infamous of All Our Crimes," *Dallas Morning News*, June 21, 1911, 1.

57. *San Antonio Light*, June 22, 1911, 1–2.

58. "The Most Infamous of All Our Crimes," *Dallas Morning News*, June 21, 1911, 1.

59. "Lynching Angers Mexico, Washington to Take Up the Hanging of a Mexican Boy in Texas," *New York Times*, June 26, 1911, 4.

60. "The Most Infamous of All Our Crimes," *Dallas Morning News*, June 21, 1911, 1.

61. Ibid., 1–2.

62. "The Thorndale Mob," *Rockdale Reporter and Messenger*, June 29, 1911, 2.

63. *San Antonio Light*, June 22, 1911, 1–2.

64. *San Antonio Light*, March 20, 1915, 5.

65. University of Texas at El Paso, Institute of Oral History, interview with Symposium on International Relations and Human Rights, sponsored by the El Paso Council on the Arts and Humanities, 1979, "Interview no. 335."

66. "Mexican Protective Society," *Laredo Times*, July 2, 1911, 4.

67. Texas State Library, Archives Division 301–301, Governor's Records, Oscar B. Colquitt, May 10, 1911–October 19, 1911, letter to Donaciano R. Davilo, president of La Agrupacíon Protectora Mexicana, July 7, 1911.

68. "To Condemn Lynching of Boy in Resolutions," *San Antonio Light*, June 25, 1911, 1; and "Governor Is Thanked," *Galveston Daily News*, July 7, 1911, 9.

69. Ibid.; and Texas State Library, Archives Division 301–301, Governor's Records, Oscar B. Colquitt, May 10, 1911–October 19, 1911, letter to Miguel E. Diebold, consul of Mexico in San Antonio.

70. "That Thorndale Lynching," *San Antonio Light*, June 28, 1911, 4.

71. Milam County Historical Commission, http://www.milamcountyhistoricalcommission.org/.

72. US Bureau of the Census, Year: 1900, Census Place: Justice Precinct 6, Williamson, Texas, Roll: T623 1679, Page: 7A, Enumeration District: 132.

73. Land ownership listed as "free" on the 1910 US Census indicates that the head of household owned the property free of a bank mortgage.

74. US Bureau of the Census, Year: 1900, Census Place: Justice Precinct 6, Williamson, Texas, Roll: T623 1679, Page: 7A, Enumeration District: 132; and US Bureau of the Census, Year: 1910, Census Place: Justice Precinct 6, Williamson, Texas, Roll: T624 1598, Page: 4B, Enumeration District: 139, Image: 437.

75. US Bureau of the Census, Year: 1910, Census Place: Justice Precinct 8, Milam, Texas, Roll: T624 1578, Page: 7A, Enumeration District: 72, Image: 299; and US Bureau of the Census, Year: 1910, Census Place: Justice Precinct 8, Milam, Texas, Roll: T624 1578, Page: 10A, Enumeration District: 72, Image: 305.

76. US Bureau of the Census, Year: 1910, Census Place: Justice Precinct 8, Milam, Texas, Roll: T624 1578, Page: 10A, Enumeration District: 72, Image: 305.

77. Burnett and Luebbering, *German Settlement in Missouri*, 6–7; and Parrish, *A History of Missouri*, 38–39.

78. Nielsen, *Vengeance in a Small Town*, 33–35.

79. US Bureau of the Census, Year: 1910, Census Place: Justice Precinct 8, Milam, Texas, Roll: T624_1578.

80. Higham, *Strangers in the Land*, 196.

81. University of Texas at El Paso, Institute of Oral History, interview with Symposium on International Relations and Human Rights, sponsored by the El Paso Council on the Arts and Humanities, 1979, "Interview no. 335."

82. Milam County Historical Commission, at http://www.milamcountyhistoricalcommission.org/; and US Bureau of the Census, Census Place: Justice Precinct 8, Milam, Texas, Roll: T624 1578, Page: 8A, Enumeration District: 72, Image: 301.

83. US Bureau of the Census, Year: 1910, Census Place: Justice Precinct 8, Milam, Texas, Roll: T624 1578, Page: 8A, Enumeration District: 72, Image: 301; and Texas Department of Health, State Vital Statistics Unit, Texas Death Indexes, 1903–2000, Austin.

84. University of Texas at El Paso, Institute of Oral History, interview with Symposium on International Relations and Human Rights, sponsored by the El Paso Council on the Arts and Humanities, 1979, "Interview no. 335."

85. Milam County Historical Commission, http://www.milamcountyhistoricalcommission.org/.

86. "Gore Allowed Bail," *Galveston Daily News*, August 2, 1911, 1; and *Thorndale Thorn*, October 20, 1911.

87. *State of Texas v. E. T. Gore Jr.*, Milam County District Court, Criminal Minutes no. 7616 (November 13, 1911).

88. "G. P. Noack Not Guilty," *Galveston Daily News*, March 3, 1912, 6.

89. "Spoke Ill of Texas: Mexican Consul, Once Active Against Madero, Is Now Recalled," *New York Times*, October 8, 1911.

90. *Anaconda (MT) Standard*, March 3, 1912, 10.

91. "Hunt Mexican Murderers," *San Antonio Express*, September 12, 1913, 1.

92. "Crowd Seeks Slayers of Hulen and Sitters," *Dallas Morning News*, May 28, 1915, 1.

CHAPTER THREE

1. "Honor Navy's Dead," *Washington Post*, May 12, 1914, 2.

2. Ibid., 2.

3. Hughes, *Pecos: A History of the Pioneer West*, 94.

4. "Miss Emma Brown Slain in Pecos," *Laredo Times*, July 30, 1911, 1.

5. "Martinez to Hang Today," *El Paso Morning Times*, May 11, 1914, 1–2.

6. Ibid., 1–2.

7. Ex Parte Martinez, no. 1457, "Opinion," 1.

8. Ibid., "Dissenting Opinion," 14.

9. Ibid., 29.

10. Ibid., "Opinion," 3.

11. Ibid., "Dissenting Opinion," 30.

12. Ibid., "Opinion," 14.

13. Vanderwood, *Juan Soldado*, 48.

14. "Father of Murderer Asks for Justice," *El Paso Morning Times*, July 27, 1911, 1.

15. "Leon Martinez Now in Abilene," *Abilene Daily Reporter*, August 29, 1911, 1.

16. "Irrigation Hope of Trans-Pecos Section," *Galveston Daily News*, January 7, 1912, 12.

17. Ex Parte Martinez, no. 1457, "Dissenting Opinion," 1.

18. Ibid., 5.

19. Ibid., 4.

20. Ibid.

21. Ibid., 6–7.

22. Hughes, *Pecos: A History of the Pioneer West*, 340–41.

23. Ex Parte Martinez, no. 1457, "Dissenting Opinion," 8.

24. Ibid., 5.

25. Ibid., 7.

26. "Mexican Murder Removed," *El Paso Morning Times*, August 1, 1911, 4.

27. Ex Parte Martinez, no. 1457, "Dissenting Opinion," 68.

28. "Mexican Murder Removed," *El Paso Morning Times*, August 1, 1911, 4.

29. Ibid.

30. "Governor Colquitt Will Not Interfere," *El Paso Morning Times*, August 7, 1911, 2.

31. "People of Reeves County," *El Paso Morning Times*, August 2, 1911, 5.

32. Ex Parte Martinez, no. 1457, "Dissenting Opinion," 9.

33. Texas State Archives, box 140, folder 1–31, 1912.

34. Texas State Archives, box 140, folder 1–31, 1912, "A," October 16–November 8, 1911, folder 12; and Texas State Archives, box 140, folder 1–31, 1912, "A" August 5–September 20, 1911, folder 10.

35. "Oppose Commutation of Sentence," *Dallas Morning News*, September 3, 1911, 15.

36. Hall and Coerver, *Revolution on the Border*, 17.

37. Ricardo Flores Magón, "El Derecho de Propiedad," *Regeneración*, March 18, 1911, 1.

38. Ibid., 1.

39. Hall and Coerver, *Revolution on the Border*, 130.

40. Sandos, *Rebellion in the Borderlands*, 59.

41. "Father Is Mexican Liberal," *El Paso Morning Times*, September 12, 1911, 2.

42. "Pecos Attorney on the Martinez Case," *El Paso Morning Times*, September 12, 1911, 1.

43. "Father of Murderer Asks for Justice," *El Paso Morning Times*, July 27, 1911, 1.

44. "Martinez to Hang Today," *El Paso Morning Times*, May 11, 1914, 2.

45. "Mexican Given Death Sentence," *El Paso Morning Times*, July 30, 1911, 1.

46. It's also possible that the English-language letter was translated and typed for Martínez; it's clear, however, that he was literate in Spanish.

47. "Anti-American Plot Exposed," *El Paso Morning Times*, February 25, 1912, 1.

48. "Rid Country of Undesirable Aliens," *El Paso Morning Times*, May 8, 1912, 6.

49. Ibid., 6.

50. *Virginia Law Register*, "Tyranny or Necessity," 72–73.

51. "Clash of Opinions in Martinez Case," *Dallas Morning News*, March 28, 1912, 1.

52. The two treaties referred to guaranteeing Mexican citizens rights under the Due Process of Law provision of the Fourteenth Amendment of the US Constitution are: March 24, 1908, Article III (US Document no. 5, 61st Congress, Second Session, 1909–1910, vol. 47, the same being vol. 1, p. 1205 of Treaties and Conventions); and the Treaty of Guadalupe Hidalgo (id. p. 1107, Articles I and XXVI).

53. Ex Parte Martinez, no. 1457, "Dissenting Opinion," 52.

54. Ibid., 63.

55. *Dallas Morning News*, March 29, 1912, 8.

56. "Martinez Case and Recall of Judges," *Dallas Morning News*, April 14, 1912, 6.

57. "Should Make Slow Haste About Courts," *Dallas Morning News*, June 18, 1912, 13.

58. "Judge S. J. Isaacks Replies to M'Rae," *Dallas Morning News*, June 23, 1912, 5.

59. "Supreme Court Will Hear Martinez Case," *Dallas Morning News*, May 13, 1913, 11.

60. "Texans Didn't Lynch Youth Who Murdered Defenseless School Teacher; No, They Are Wondering if It Pays to Be Law-Abiding," *Muskogee (OK) Times Democrat*, November 25, 1911, 4.

61. Ibid.

62. "Mexican Juveniles in War," *El Paso Morning Times*, August 20, 1911, 4.

63. "Mexican Boy Held for Killing Another," *El Paso Morning Times*, April 26, 1912, 4.

64. "Condemned Mexican Boy Learning to Play Guitar," *Wichita Falls Daily Times*, February 26, 1914, 1.

65. "Mexican Boy Who Is Under Death Sentence," *Dallas Morning News*, April 7, 1912, 5.

66. Vanderwood and Samponaro, *Border Fury*, vii.

67. Ibid., 164–65.

68. "El Paso in Hands of Villa Troops," *El Paso Morning Times*, April 24, 1914, 2.

69. Hughes, *Pecos: A History of the Pioneer West*, 195.

70. "Commendation for Colquitt," *Dallas Morning News*, June 26, 1911, 5.

71. "Colquitt Pardons Negros," *Dallas Morning News*, June 18, 1912, 7.

72. "Governor Issues Pardon," *Dallas Morning News*, March 28, 1911, 13.

73. "Colquitt Pardons Negros," *Dallas Morning News*, June 18, 1912, 7.

74. "Colquitt Answers Ramsey's Challenge," *Dallas Morning News*, July 21, 1912, 10.

75. Texas State Archives, box 141, folder 1–10, 1914.

76. Texas State Archives, box 140, folder 1–31, 1912.

77. Texas State Archives, box 141, folder 1–31, 1913, "A," November 3–29, folder 17.

78. Ibid.

79. Ibid.

80. "2200 Troops Are Now in El Paso," *El Paso Morning Times*, February 28, 1912, 1.

81. "Texas Governor Wires Ranger Captain to Shoot Straight if It Is Necessary," *El Paso Morning Times*, January 31, 1913, 1.

82. "Clash Possible at Brownsville," *El Paso Morning Times*, February 25, 1913, 1.

83. "American and Mexican Troops Clash on Border Near Douglas," *El Paso Morning Times*, March 3, 1913, 1; and "Another Fight Near Douglas," *El Paso Morning Times*, March 5, 1913, 1.

84. "Breach Has Come Between the United States and Mexico," *El Paso Morning Times*, April 20, 1914, 1.

85. "U.S. Warships to Mexican Waters Result of Washington Conference," *El Paso Morning Times*, February 11, 1913, 1.

86. "Mexican Loss Two Hundred," *El Paso Morning Times*, April 22, 1914, 1.

87. Wood, "Birth of the Modern Festival."

88. "Mexicans Honor Hero at Vera Cruz as Americans Did Dead at New York," *Washington Post*, Sunday May 24, 1914, 7.

89. "Una Gloria de Abril," *Tiempo Laredo*, April 25, 1914, 1.

90. "Ask Leniency for Martinez," *Dallas Morning News*, May 10, 1914, 11.

91. "Martinez to Hang Today," *El Paso Morning Times*, May 11, 1914, 2.

92. Ibid., 1.

93. "Martinez Case Before Court," *El Paso Morning Times*, November 4, 1911, 2.

94. "Martinez to Hang Today," *El Paso Morning Times*, May 11, 1914, 1.

95. Ibid., 1.

96. Hughes, *Pecos: A History of the Pioneer West*, 195.

CHAPTER FOUR

1. Casey Collection, box 380, Brite Ranch Raid folder, Archives of the Big Bend, Sul Ross State University, Alpine, Texas. Fox sent this letter to General James A. Harley of the Texas Rangers reporting the death of fifteen Mexican men suspected of raiding Brite Ranch on December 25, 1918.

2. Harry Warren Collection, folder 88, "The Porvenir Massacre in Presidio County, Texas, January 28, 1918," Archives of the Big Bend, Sul Ross State University, San Angelo, Texas.

3. Harry Warren Collection, folder 88, Archives of the Big Bend, Sul Ross State University, Alpine, Texas, letter from General James A. Harley to Captain J. M. Fox, July 12, 1918.

4. Utley, *Lone Star Justice*, 293.

5. Clayton and Chance, *The March to Monterrey*, 93.

6. "Conditions on Both Sides of the Line Separating America from Mexico," in Hanrahan, *Documents on the Mexican Revolution*, 1:64–66.

7. Ibid., 17.

8. Frazer, *Bandit Nation*, 4–5. Frazer referenced Alan Knight's argument that "banditry and rebellion are mutable over time and geography" in Frazer's analysis of revolutionary leaders such as Pancho Villa. See also Knight, *The Mexican Revolution*.

9. "Story of Raids by Mexican Bandits," *Galveston Daily News*, February 4, 1911, 25.

10. "Artillery and Aeroplane to Be Requested," *San Antonio Light*, August 14, 1915, 1; and "New Raid Feared," *San Antonio Light*, August 14, 1915, 1.

11. McLean, *That Mexican As He Really Is*, 126.

12. Whittington, "The Road of Sorrow," 1.

13. "Raids in the South," *Galveston Daily News*, April 1, 1911, 1.

14. Ibid., 1.

15. Harry Warren Collection, folder 88, "The Porvenir Massacre in Presidio County, Texas, January 28, 1918," Archives of the Big Bend, Sul Ross State University, Alpine, Texas; and Williwood Meador Collection, box 4, file 11, "Porvenir," Angelo State University, San Angelo, Texas.

16. "1,000 Men Slain in Ojinaga Fight," *New York Times*, January 2, 1914, 1; "Fort Bliss Is Promised Land for Refugees," *San Antonio Light*, January 25, 1914, 13; "Refugees Start Trek to Marfa," *El Paso Herald*, January 14, 1914, 1; "Federals Fortify Ojinaga; Refugees Crossing the Line," *El Paso Herald*, December 9, 1913, 1; and "Vanguard of Refugees Is in Marfa Ready to Board Trains for Fort Bliss," *El Paso Herald*, January 19, 1914, 1.

17. Whittington, "The Road of Sorrow," 1.

18. "Vanguard of Refugees Is in Marfa Ready to Board Trains for Fort Bliss," *El Paso Herald*, January 19, 1914, 1.

19. "Hegira to El Paso Is Underway," *El Paso Herald*, January 16, 1914, 1.

20. Jamieson, "A Survey History of Fort Bliss."

21. *San Antonio Light*, January 25, 1914, 18.

22. "Hegira to El Paso Is Underway," *El Paso Herald*, January 16, 1914, 1.

23. Jamieson, "A Survey History of Fort Bliss."

24. *San Antonio Light*, January 25, 1914, 18.

25. Jamieson, "A Survey History of Fort Bliss"; and *San Antonio Light*, January 25, 1914, 18.

26. "Mexican Refugees Won't Be Sent Back," *New York Times*, January 13, 1914, 1.

27. "Two Mexicans Shot by U.S. Sentries," *New York Times*, April 19, 1914, 1.

28. US Congress, Hearing before Subcommittee of the House Committee on Appropriations, Deficiency Appropriations for 1915 and Prior Years, Sixty-Third Congress, Third Session, 82–90; and "Refugees Reach Fort Wingate Under Guard of U.S. Troops," *Belen (NM) News*, May 7, 1914, 1.

29. National Archives and Records Administration I, Record Group 393, Fort Wingate, New Mexico, Box 11.

30. Coerver, "Wire Me Before Shooting"; Neeno, "The Mexican Revolution and US Intervention"; and "Colquitt Wants Hundred Rangers to Guard Border," *Daily Bulletin* (Brownwood, TX), March 13, 1914, 1.

31. Neeno, "The Mexican Revolution and US Intervention."

32. US Department of State, *Foreign Relations of the United States: Diplomatic Papers*, address of the president to Congress, December 5, 1916, Mexico (Washington, DC: Government Printing Office, 1919), 463–799 (570–72); and *United States v. Basilio Ramos Jr. et al.*, District Court, Brownsville, Texas, Federal Records Center, Fort Worth, Texas, no. 2152.

33. B. H. Johnson, *Revolution in Texas*, 74.

34. "Women Reported Burned," *Galveston Daily News*, November 8, 1916, 1.

35. "Report Rebels Kill Hundreds of Chinamen," *San Antonio Light*, May 22, 1911, 1.

36. Telegram to President William Taft from Ambassador Henry Lane Wilson in Mexico City, Mexico, in Hanrahan, *Documents on the Mexican Revolution*, 1:379.

37. Romo, *Ringside Seat to a Revolution*, 201.

38. Ibid., 199–200.

39. Hu-DeHart, "Immigrants to a Developing Society," 56–60.

40. Ibid.

41. "Death List Is Eighteen," *Corsicana (TX) Daily Sun*, March 7, 1916, 1.

42. University of Texas at El Paso, Institute of Oral History, interviewee: Brigadier General S. L. A. Marshall; interviewer: Richard Estrada, July 5, 7, 9, 11, and 19, 1975, tape no. 181, transcript no. 181, 15–16.

43. "Death List Is Eighteen," *Corsicana (TX) Daily Sun*, March 7, 1916, 1.

44. Ibid., 16.

45. "Glenn Springs: A Little Desert Village in the Big Bend Born Overnight, Raided by Mexican Bandits, and Abandoned When It Was Only Five Years Old," Casey

Collection, box 423, Glenn Springs Raid folder, Archives of the Big Bend, Sul Ross State University, Alpine, Texas.

46. "Glenn Springs Raided," *Alpine (TX) Avalanche*, May 11, 1916, 1.

47. Ibid.

48. Ibid.

49. "Story of Glenn Springs Raid Is Told from Eye Witnesses of Border Murders," Casey Collection, box 423, Glenn Springs Raid folder, Archives of the Big Bend, Sul Ross State University, Alpine, Texas.

50. US Department of State, *Foreign Relations of the United States: Diplomatic Papers, 1916* (Washington, DC: Government Printing Office, 1919), 577.

51. War Diary, Fifth Cavalry, Punitive Expedition Records, National Archives, R.G. 120, box 60.

52. Vilanova, "American Troops Fired First at El Carrizal."

53. US National Guard Bureau, *Report on Mobilization of the Organized Militia and National Guard of the United States* (Washington, DC: Government Printing Office, 1916), 10.

54. Ibid., 12; Neeno, "The Mexican Revolution and US Intervention."

55. US National Guard Bureau, *Report on Mobilization of the Organized Militia and National Guard of the United States* (Washington, DC: Government Printing Office, 1916), 11.

56. Batchelder, *Watching and Waiting*, x–xi.

57. Ibid., 152.

58. Ibid., 113–19; and "Mayor Fires L.A. Police Chief by Three-Line Note," *Oakland Tribune*, April 21, 1922, 18.

59. Jodie P. Harris Collection, folders AVF, 1–10, Archives of the Big Bend, Sul Ross State University, Alpine, Texas.

60. Batchelder, *Watching and Waiting*, vii.

61. Ibid., 65.

62. Ibid., xii.

63. Ibid., 205.

64. Ibid., 206.

65. Casey Collection, Mexican American Border Region folder, Archives of the Big Bend, Sul Ross State University, Alpine, Texas; and Eugenia Chandley, "Soldiers Tire of Quiet Life on River and Raid Homes for Amusement While Friends Fought in World War," *Sul Ross Skyline*, October 26, 1938.

66. Ibid.

67. Casey Collection, box 380, Brite Ranch Raid folder, Archives of the Big Bend, Sul Ross State University, Alpine, Texas; *Big Bend Sentinel*, Archives of the Big Bend, Sul Ross State University, Alpine, Texas; and "Bandits on the Border," Williwood Meador Collection, box 4, file 3, West Texas Collection, Angelo State University, San Angelo, Texas.

68. *El Paso Morning Times*, December 27, 1917, 1.

69. Harry Warren Collection, folder 88, "The Porvenir Massacre in Presidio County, Texas, January 28, 1918," Archives of the Big Bend, Sul Ross State University, Alpine, Texas; and Williwood Meador Collection, box 4, file 11, "Porvenir," Angelo State University, San Angelo, Texas.

70. Williwood Meador Collection, box 4, file 11, "Porvenir," Angelo State University, San Angelo, Texas.

71. Harry Warren Collection, folder 88, "The Porvenir Massacre in Presidio County, Texas, January 28, 1918," Archives of the Big Bend, Sul Ross State University, Alpine, Texas; and Williwood Meador Collection, box 4, file 11, "Porvenir," Angelo State University, San Angelo, Texas.

72. Harry Warren Collection, folder 88, "The Porvenir Massacre in Presidio County, Texas, January 28, 1918," Archives of the Big Bend, Sul Ross State University, Alpine, Texas.

73. "Mexicans Raid Brewster County Ranches," *Alpine (TX) Avalanche*, February 20, 1913, 1.

74. National Archives and Records Administration, Washington, DC, *Non-Statistical Manifests and Statistical Index Cards of Aliens Arriving at El Paso, Texas, 1905–1927*, Record Group: 85, Records of the Immigration and Naturalization Service, Microfilm Serial: A3406, Microfilm Roll: 57, processed in El Paso on March 25, 1913.

75. US Bureau of the Census, Year: 1920, Census Place: Jim Alice, Wells, Texas, Roll: T625 1821, Page: 10B, Enumeration District: 109, Image: 366.

76. Harry Warren Collection, folder 88, "The Porvenir Massacre in Presidio County, Texas, January 28, 1918," Archives of the Big Bend, Sul Ross State University, Alpine, Texas; and Williwood Meador Collection, box 4, file 11, "Porvenir," Angelo State University, San Angelo, Texas.

77. Proceedings of the Joint Committee of the Senate and the House in the Investigation of the Texas State Ranger Force, 839–40.

78. Ibid., 843–48.

79. Ibid., 850.

80. Harry Warren Collection, folder 88, "The Porvenir Massacre in Presidio County, Texas, January 28, 1918," Archives of the Big Bend, Sul Ross State University, Alpine, Texas; and Williwood Meador Collection, box 4, file 11, "Porvenir," Angelo State University, San Angelo, Texas.

81. United States Senate, Investigation of Mexican Affairs, Preliminary Report and Hearing of the Committee on Foreign Relations, United States Senate, pursuant to Senate Resolution 106, testimony of Ed Neville, part 10, 1510–15; Casey Collection, box 468, Neville Ranch Raid folder, Archives of the Big Bend, Sul Ross State University, Alpine, Texas; and *Big Bend Sentinel*, Archives of the Big Bend, Sul Ross State University, Alpine, Texas.

82. Casey Collection, box 468, Neville Ranch Raid folder, Archives of the Big Bend, Sul Ross State University, Alpine, Texas.

83. Ibid.

84. Ibid.

85. Ibid

86. Ibid.

87. Ibid.

88. "American Troops Cross Border and Fight with Bandits," *San Antonio Light*, March 29, 1918, 1.

89. Sul Ross State University, Oral History Archives, Archives of the Big Bend, interviewee: Pedro Armendarez; interviewer: Theresa Whittington, 1976, OH A728WH.

90. University of Texas at El Paso, Institute of Oral History, interviewee: Pete Leyva; interviewer: Oscar J. Martínez, July 22, 1976, tape no. 312, transcript no. 312, 25.

91. University of Texas at El Paso, Institute of Oral History, interviewee: George Barnhart; interviewer: Carlos Tapia, December 1976, tape no. 282, transcript no. 282, 4.

92. University of Texas at El Paso, Institute of Oral History, interviewee: Brigadier General S. L. A. Marshall; interviewer: Richard Estrada, July 5, 7, 9, 11, and 19, 1975, tape no. 181, transcript no. 181, 18.

93. University of Texas at El Paso, Institute of Oral History, interviewees: Anne and Elizabeth Kelly and Mary Kelly Quinn; interviewers: David Salazar and Mildred Torok, March 26, 1973, tape no. 87A, transcript no. 87A, 13–14, project: El Paso History.

94. Ariens, *Lone Star Law*, 68.

CHAPTER FIVE

1. Carrigan and Webb, *Forgotten Dead*, app. A, B.

2. Anders, "Canales, José Tomas."

3. Proceedings of the Joint Committee of the Senate and the House in the Investigation of the Texas State Ranger Force, 856–57.

4. Harris and Sadler, "The 1911 Reyes Conspiracy," 329; and Harris and Sadler, *The Texas Rangers and the Mexican Revolution*, 427. Harris and Sadler list Regular Rangers to number 150, Special Rangers to number 400, and Loyalty Rangers to number anywhere from 427 to 800.

5. Proceedings of the Joint Committee of the Senate and the House in the Investigation of the Texas State Ranger Force, 856–57.

6. Ibid., 146–48.

7. Ibid., 146–47.

8. Coerver and Hall, *Texas and the Mexican Revolution*, 106–7; and B. H. Johnson, *Revolution in Texas*, 122–23.

9. B. H. Johnson, *Revolution in Texas*, 123.

10. "Exodus Is Continued," *Brownsville Herald*, September 15, 1915, 1.

11. Proceedings of the Joint Committee of the Senate and the House in the Investigation of the Texas State Ranger Force, 335–41.

12. Ibid.

13. Ibid., 87.

14. Ibid., 338.

15. Ibid., 354–55.

16. Ibid., 355.

17. Ibid., 354–55.

18. Ibid., 545–47.

19. Ibid., 543–46.

20. Ibid.

21. Ibid., 291–93.

22. Ibid., 375–76.

23. Ibid., 859–61.

24. Ibid., 354.

25. Ibid.

26. Ibid., 864–66.

27. US Department of State, *Foreign Relations of the United States: Diplomatic Papers*, March 16, 1915 (Washington, DC: Government Printing Office, 1919), 660.

28. World Peace Foundation, "The New Pan Americanism: First Pan American Financial Conference, 1915, Pan American Action Regarding Mexico, President Wilson's Annual Address to Congress, December 7, 1915," World Peace Foundation Pamphlet Series, Column 7, 1917.

29. "Mining Men Stripped Naked and Ruthlessly Shot Down by Band of Villa Savages," *El Paso Morning Times*, January 12, 1916, 1.

30. Ibid.

31. Ibid.

32. Wheeler, "The Mexican Situation," 74.

33. "Mining Men Stripped Naked and Ruthlessly Shot Down by Band of Villa Savages," *El Paso Morning Times*, January 12, 1916, 1.

34. "Americans Enraged over Massacre," *La Crosse(WI) Tribune*, January 14, 1916, 6.

35. "Mining Men Stripped Naked and Ruthlessly Shot Down by Band of Villa Savages," *El Paso Morning Times*, January 12, 1916, 1.

36. "El Paso Quiet After Night of Fighting," *Boston Globe*, January 14, 1916, 2.

37. "Mexicans Hate Americans," *Standard* (Ogden, UT), January 14, 1916, 1.

38. "More Arrests Made," *Salt Lake Tribune*, January 16, 1916, 1.

39. "Texas Mexicans Told They Will Not Be Harmed," *San Antonio Light*, June 19, 1916, 1.

40. Ibid.

41. Ibid.

42. Archives Division, Texas State Library, Governors' Papers, James E. Ferguson, Letter Press Books, box 301–78, vol. 30, letter dated July 13, 1916.

43. Archives Division, Texas State Library, Governors' Papers, James E. Ferguson, Letter Press Books, box 301–78, vol. 29, letter dated July 6, 1916.

44. Acosta, "Chapa, Francisco A."

45. Ibid.; Harris and Sadler, "The 1911 Reyes Conspiracy," 325–48; and Nielsen, *Vengeance in a Small Town*, 82–83.

46. Acosta, "Chapa, Francisco A."; and Harris and Sadler, "The 1911 Reyes Conspiracy," 325–48.

47. Archives Division, Texas State Library, Governors' Papers, James E. Ferguson, Letter Press Books, box 301–78, vol. 28, letters dated June 21, 1916, and July 6, 1916.

48. Archives Division, Texas State Library, Governors' Papers, James E. Ferguson, Letter Press Books, box 301–78, vol. 29, letters dated June 28, 1916.

49. "Texas Mexicans Told They Will Not Be Harmed," *San Antonio Light*, June 19, 1916, 1.

50. "Three Mexican Bandits Killed and Three Captured by Posse," *Laredo Times*, June 18, 1916, 6.

51. Archives Division, Texas State Library, Governors' Papers, James E. Ferguson.

52. "Texas Mexicans Told They Will Not Be Harmed," *San Antonio Light*, June 19, 1916, 1.

53. Archives Division, Texas State Library, Governors' Papers, James E. Ferguson, Letter Press Books, box 301–78, vol. 28, letter dated June 26, 1916.

54. Bexar County Arrest Records, San Antonio, 1910–1920, Archives Division, Texas State Library.

55. Boghardt, *The Zimmermann Telegram*, 123.

56. Haley, *Revolution and Intervention*, 248–53.

57. Proceedings of the Joint Committee of the Senate and the House in the Investigation of the Texas State Ranger Force, 595–600.

58. Ibid., 603–4.

59. Orozco, *No Mexicans, Women, or Dogs Allowed*, 51.

60. Ramírez, *To the Line of Fire!*, 35.

61. B. H. Johnson, *Revolution in Texas*, 151.

62. Proceedings of the Joint Committee of the Senate and the House in the Investigation of the Texas State Ranger Force, 465–70.

63. B. H. Johnson, *Revolution in Texas*, 150–54.

64. La Botz, "American 'Slackers' in the Mexican Revolution," 563.

65. Villahermosa, "America's Hispanics in America's Wars."

66. University of Texas at El Paso, Institute of Oral History, interviewee: Charles V. Porras; interviewer: Oscar J. Martínez, November 18, 1975, tape no. 212, transcript no. 212.

67. "Making Americans of Alien Soldiers," *New York Times*, September 22, 1918, 40.

68. Ramírez, *To the Line of Fire!*, 80.

69. Archives of the Big Bend, Sul Ross State University, Alpine, Texas, Collection ATTCCPC, image no. 509, Francisco Ramírez, World War I, roll no. 65493, neg. H31–32.

70. University of Texas at El Paso, Institute of Oral History, interviewee: Charles V. Porras; interviewer: Oscar J. Martínez, November 18, 1975, tape no. 212, transcript no. 212.

71. Ibid.

72. Ibid.

73. Ibid.

74. Ibid.

75. Ibid.

76. Ibid.

77. Ibid.

78. Ramírez, *To the Line of Fire!*, xiv.

79. Ibid., xiii.

80. "Texan Who Concealed His Origin Is 38th Hispanic Medal of Honor Recipient," *Santa Fe New Mexican*, January 6, 1992, 41.

81. "President Calls for July 4 Celebration," *New York Times*, May 25, 1918.

82. Ibid.

83. "Italians to Take Big Part," *New York Times*, June 9, 1918.

84. Ramírez, *To the Line of Fire!*, 19.

85. B. H. Johnson, *Revolution in Texas*, 159.

86. "Mexicans Not Liable for Service Under Draft Law," *Dallas Morning News*, October 12, 1917, 13.

87. "Federal Government to Aid Texas Solve Labor Problem," *Dallas Morning News*, June 8, 1917, 4.

88. Ibid., 4; US Department of Labor, *Boy Power*.

89. US Department of Labor, *Boy Power*, 1.

90. Ibid., 5.

91. "15,100 Mexican Families Came to Texas Last Year," *Dallas Morning News*, July 15, 1920, 3.

92. United States Senate, Investigation of Mexican Affairs, Preliminary Report and Hearing of the Committee on Foreign Relations, United States Senate, pursuant to Senate Resolution 106, testimony of Marcus Hines, 1311.

93. "Liberty Cabbage," *Indianapolis Star*, May 3, 1918, 6.

94. "Organized Effort to Defeat Liberty Loan," *Galveston Daily News*, October 18, 1917, 1.

95. "American Prisoners Starved by Germans," *San Antonio Light*, October 18, 1917, 2.

96. "Scared of German Agent," *Laredo Times*, January 27, 1918, 9.

97. "Efforts Being Made to Crush Lies of German Propagandists," *Denton (TX) Record-Chronicle*, September 25, 1918, 3.

98. "Let's Shoot Traitors," *Corsicana (TX) Daily Sun*, February 23, 1918, 2.

99. Tippens, *Turning Germans into Texans*, 14.

100. Hormann, "When Patriotic Fevers Ran High"; *Los Angeles Times*, April 7, 1917; and *New York Herald*, March 28, 1918.

101. "German Miner Is Hanged by Illinois Mob," *San Antonio Light*, April 5, 1918, 1.

102. "What Are We Going to Do About It?," *Denton (TX) Record-Chronicle*, September 25, 1918, 3.

103. "Gregory Advised to Crush Spying," *City Times* (Galveston, TX), April 20, 1918, 2.

104. Tippens, *Turning Germans into Texans*, 20–24.

105. Ibid., 21.

106. David G. Gutiérrez, *Walls and Mirrors: Mexican Americans, Mexican Immigrants, and the Politics of Ethnicity* (Berkeley: University of California Press, 1995), 19.

107. General Laws of Texas, Thirty-Sixth Legislature, National Archives and Records Administration, Washington, DC, 263–66; and Webb, *The Texas Rangers*, 516.

108. Carrigan and Webb, "The Lynching of Persons of Mexican Origin," 412.

109. This estimation is based on the following research: Webb, *The Texas Rangers*; Coerver and Hall, *Texas and the Mexican Revolution*; Rosales, *¡Pobre Raza!*; B. H. Johnson, *Revolution in Texas*; Levario, *Militarizing the Border*; and Carrigan and Webb, *Forgotten Dead*.

110. Carrigan and Webb, "A Dangerous Experiment," 265–92.

CONCLUSION

1. League of United Latin American Citizens, at http://lulac.org/about/history/.

2. US Department of State, Record Group 59, Decimal File 311.1221m36–311.1221, letter from the Mexican Consulate in Dallas, Texas, regarding Octaviano Escutia.

3. Ibid.

4. US Department of State, Record Group 59, Decimal File 311.1221m36–311.1221, letter from the Mexican Embassy to the United States regarding the death of Salvador Saucedo.

5. Ibid. The Saucedo family received an indemnity from the US government.

6. "Protect Mexicans, Hughes Tells Neff," *New York Times*, November 17, 1922.

7. *San Antonio Light*, March 20, 1915, 5.

8. Rosales, *Dictionary of Latino Civil Rights History*, 4.

9. Rosales, *Chicano!*, 62.

10. Ibid, 226; League of United Latin American Citizens, at http://lulac.org/about/history/.

11. League of United Latin American Citizens, at http://lulac.org/about/history/.

12. Ibid.

13. Ibid.

14. For more on "whiteness" as a defense mechanism, see Gómez, *Manifest Destinies*; and Morán González, *Border Renaissance*.

15. League of United Latin American Citizens, at http://lulac.org/about/history/.

Bibliography

ARCHIVAL AND OTHER PRIMARY SOURCES

Archivo Histórico de la Secretaría de Relaciones Exteriores, Consular Records, Mexico City.

Arnoldo De León Collection. Porter Henderson Library, Angelo State University, San Angelo, Texas.

Border Heritage Center, Southwest Collection, El Paso Public Library, El Paso, Texas.

Border Patrol Vertical Files. Border Heritage Center, Southwest Collection, El Paso Public Library, El Paso, Texas.

Casey Collection. Archives of the Big Bend, Bryan Wildenthal Memorial Library, Sul Ross State University, Alpine, Texas.

Center for American History, University of Texas at Austin.

Dolph Briscoe Center for American History, University of Texas at Austin.

Harry Warren Collection. Archives of the Big Bend, Bryan Wildenthal Memorial Library, Sul Ross State University, Alpine, Texas.

Hemeroteca de la Biblioteca Estatal de Jalisco, Guadalajara, Jalisco.

Institute of Texan Cultures, San Antonio, Texas.

Institute of Oral History, University of Texas at El Paso.

Jodie P. Harris, Collection. Archives of the Big Bend, Bryan Wildenthal Memorial Library, Sul Ross State University, Alpine, Texas.

National Archives and Records Administration, College Park, Maryland, and Washington, DC.

Padilla Family Collection. Porter Henderson Library, Angelo State University, San Angelo, Texas.

Russ Todd Collection. Porter Henderson Library, Angelo State University, San Angelo, Texas.

Smithers Collection. Dolph Briscoe Center for American History, University of Texas at Austin.

South Texas Archives. Texas A&M University, College Station, Texas.

Southwest Collections, Texas Tech University, Lubbock, Texas.

Texas State Archives, Texas State Library, Austin, Texas.

West Texas Collection. Angelo State University, San Angelo, Texas.

Williwood Meador Collection. Porter Henderson Library, Angelo State University, San Angelo, Texas.

ORAL HISTORIES

Institute of Oral History, University of Texas at El Paso

Aranda, Catalina. Transcript no. 269.

Arredondo, Cecilio A. Transcript no. 59.

Barnhart, George. Transcript no. 282.

Escobedo, José V. Ávila. Transcript no. 179.

Hatch, Nelle S. Transcript no. 422.

Galván, Josephina. Transcript no. 547.

Gossett, Mollie (McCallick). Transcript no. 216.

Kelly, Anne. Transcript no. 87A.

Kelly, Elizabeth. Transcript no. 87A.

Leyva, Pete. Transcript no. 312.

Marshall, Brigadier General S. L. A. Transcript no. 181.

Martínez, Miguel. Transcript no. 760.

Ortiz, Severiano Torres. Transcript no. 254.

Padilla, Edmundo. Transcript no. 262.

Pérez, Jesús. Transcript no. 249.

Porras, Charles V. Transcript no. 212.

Quinn, Howard and Mary K. Transcript no. 68.

Quinn, Mary Kelly. Transcript no. 87A.

Rodríguez, José R. Transcript no. 281.

Rojas de Romero, María Teresa. Transcript no. 729.

Symposium on International Relations and Human Rights, sponsored by the El Paso Council on the Arts and Humanities, 1979, interview no. 335.

Villegas, Hortencia. Transcript no. 235.

Zuñiga, Juana B. Transcript no. 253.

Oral History Archives, Archives of the Big Bend, Bryan Wildenthal Memorial Library, Sul Ross State University, Alpine, Texas

Alvarado, Petra. Record no. OH A472WH.

Armendarez, Pedro. Record no. OH A728WH 16976.

Hinojos, Severiana. Record no. OH H663WH 1976.

Jordan, Ruperto. Record no. OH J82WH 1976.

Payne, Blas. Record no. OH P346WH 1976.

Utah State Historical Society and California State University, Fullerton, Oral History Program

Black, Mary Ann. Interview, July 10, 1972.

Redd, Irene Hatch. Interview, October 18, 1970.

PERIODICALS

Abilene Daily Reporter
Alpine (TX) Avalanche
Anaconda (MT) Standard
Beaumont Journal
Belen (NM) News
Boston Globe
Brownsville Herald
City Times (Galveston, TX)
Corsicana (TX) Daily Sun
Coshocton (OH) Daily Tribune
Daily Bulletin (Brownwood, TX)
Dallas Morning News
Dallas Dispatch
Denton (TX) Record-Chronicle
El Debate (Mexico City)
El Diario del Hogar (Mexico City)
El Mundo (Mexico City)
El Paso Herald
El Paso Morning Times
Galveston Daily News
Houston Chronicle
Indianapolis Star
La Crónica (Laredo, TX)
La Crosse (WI) Tribune
La Patria
Laredo Times
Lloyds Weekly News (London)
Los Angeles Times
Monitor Democrático
Muskogee (OK) Times Democrat
New York Herald
New York Times
Oakland Tribune
Regeneración (San Antonio)
Rockdale (TX) Reporter and Messenger
Santa Fe New Mexican
Salt Lake Tribune
San Angelo (TX) Standard
San Antonio Express
San Antonio Light

San Antonio Light and Gazette
Standard (Ogden, UT)
Sul Ross (TX) Skyline
Thorndale (TX) Thorn
Tiempo Laredo
Waco Times Herald
Washington Post
Wichita Falls Daily Times

GOVERNMENT PUBLICATIONS

Bexar County Arrest Records. San Antonio, 1910–1920. Texas State Library and Archives Commission, Austin.

Ex Parte Martinez, 66 Texas Criminal 1 (Court of Criminal Appeals, March 27, 1912). Texas State Library and Archives Commission, Austin.

Ex Parte Martinez. "Dissenting Opinion." Texas State Library and Archives Commission, Austin.

General Laws of Texas, Thirty-Sixth Legislature. National Archives and Records Administration, Washington, DC.

Jamieson, Perry. "A Survey History of Fort Bliss, 1890–1940." Report no. 5, Cultural Resources Management Program, Directorate of Environment, US Army Air Defense Artillery Center, Fort Bliss, Texas, 1993.

State of Texas v. E. T. Gore Jr. Milam County District Court, Criminal Minutes. Texas Adjutant General Department.

Texas Governor James Edward Ferguson. Papers. Records, Archives and Information Services Division, Texas State Library and Archives Commission, Austin, Texas.

Texas Governor Oscar B. Colquitt. Papers. Records, Archives and Information Services Division, Texas State Library and Archives Commission, Austin, Texas.

Texas Governor William P. Hobby. Papers. Records, Archives and Information Services Division, Texas State Library and Archives Commission, Austin, Texas.

Texas State Legislature. *Proceedings of the Joint Committee of the Senate and House Investigation of the Texas Ranger Force.* 36th Legislature, Regular Session, 1919 Legislative Papers, Texas State Library and Archives Commission, Austin Texas.

US Bureau of the Census. Twelfth Census of the United States Taken in the Year 1900, General Report of Statistics by Subjects. Washington, DC: Government Printing Office.

———. Thirteenth Census of the United States Taken in the Year 1910, General Report of Statistics by Subjects. Washington, DC: Government Printing Office.

———. Fourteenth Census of the United States Taken in the Year 1920, General Report of Statistics by Subjects. Washington, DC: Government Printing Office.

US Department of Labor. *Boy Power: Official Bulletin of the United States Boys' Working Reserve* 1, no. 2 (December 15, 1917).

US Department of State. *Papers Relating to the Foreign Relations of the United States.* Washington, DC: Government Printing Office, 1919.

———. *Records of the Department of State Relating to Internal Affairs of Mexico, 1910–1929.* National Archives Microfilm, National Archives and Records Service, Washington, DC.

US National Guard Bureau. *Report on Mobilization of the Organized Militia and National Guard of the United States, 1916.* Washington, DC: Government Printing Office, 1916.

US Senate. Investigation of Mexican Affairs. Preliminary Report and Hearing of the Committee on Foreign Relations, United States Senate, pursuant to Senate Resolution 106.

War Diary, Fifth Cavalry. Punitive Expedition Records. National Archives.

William Howard Taft Papers. Manuscript Division, Library of Congress.

World Peace Foundation. "The New Pan Americanism: First Pan American Financial Conference, 1915, Pan American Action Regarding Mexico." World Peace Foundation Pamphlet Series, Column 7, 1917.

SECONDARY BOOKS, ARTICLES, AND MANUSCRIPTS

Acuña, Rodolfo. *Occupied America: A History of Chicanos.* New York: Harper and Row, 1988.

Ahmad, Diana L. *Opium Debate and Chinese Exclusion Laws in the Nineteenth-Century American West.* Reno: University of Nevada Press, 2011.

Alonzo, Armando C. *Tejano Legacy: Rancheros and Settlers in South Texas, 1734–1900.* Albuquerque: University of New Mexico Press, 1998.

Anders, Evan. *Boss Rule in South Texas: The Progressive Era.* Austin: University of Texas Press, 1982.

Anderson, Mark Cronlund. *Pancho Villa's Revolution by Headlines.* Norman: University of Oklahoma Press, 2000.

Andreas, Peter. *Border Games: Policing the U.S.-Mexico Divide.* Ithaca, NY: Cornell University Press, 2000.

Ariens, Michael. *Lone Star Law: A Legal History of Texas.* Lubbock: Texas Tech University Press, 2011.

Arrington, Leonard J., and Davis Bitton. *The Mormon Experience: A History of the Latter-day Saints.* Urbana: University of Illinois Press, 1992.

Baker, T. Lindsay. *Ghost Towns of Texas.* Norman: University of Oklahoma Press, 1986.

Batchelder, Roger. *Watching and Waiting on the Border.* Boston, MA: Houghton Mifflin, 1917.

Batte, Lelia M. *History of Milam County, Texas.* San Antonio, TX: Naylor Company, 1956.

Beezley, William H. *Insurgent Governor: Abraham González and the Mexican Revolution in Chihuahua.* Lincoln: University of Nebraska Press, 1973.

Beezley, William H., and Colin M. MacLachlan. *Mexicans in Revolution, 1910–1946: An Introduction.* Lincoln: University of Nebraska Press, 2009.

Bender, Thomas. *A Nation Among Nations: America's Place in World History.* New York: Hill and Wang, 2006.

Berg, Manfred. *Popular Justice: A History of Lynching in America.* Lanham, MD: Ivan R. Dee Publishing, 2011.

Blanton, Carlos Kevin. *The Strange Career of Bilingual Education in Texas, 1836–1981.* College Station: Texas A&M University Press, 2004.

Boghardt, Thomas. *The Zimmermann Telegram: Intelligence, Diplomacy, and America's Entry into World War I.* Annapolis, MD: Naval Institute Press, 2012.

Brenner, Anita. *The Wind That Swept Mexico: The History of the Mexican Revolution, 1910–1942.* Austin: University of Texas Press, 1984.

Brooks, James F. *Captives and Cousins: Slavery, Kinship, and Community in the Southwest Borderlands.* Chapel Hill: University of North Carolina Press, 2001.

Burnett, Robyn, and Ken Luebbering. *German Settlement in Missouri: New Land, Old Ways.* Columbia: University of Missouri Press, 1996.

Bush, Ira Jefferson. *Gringo Doctor.* Caldwell, ID: Caxton Printers, 1939.

Calderón, Roberto R. *Mexican Coal Mining Labor in Texas and Coahuila, 1880–1930.* College Station: Texas A&M University Press, 2000.

Carrigan, William D. *The Making of a Lynching Culture: Violence and Vigilantism in Central Texas, 1836–1916.* Urbana: University of Illinois Press, 2006.

Carrigan, William D., and Clive Webb. "'A Dangerous Experiment': The Lynching of Rafael Benavides." *New Mexico Historical Review* 80, no. 3 (Summer 2005): 265–92.

——. *Forgotten Dead: Mob Violence Against Mexicans in the United States, 1848–1928.* New York: Oxford University Press, 2013.

——. "The Lynching of Persons of Mexican Origin or Descent in the United States, 1848 to 1928." *Journal of Social History* 37 (Winter 2003): 411–38.

——. "*Muerto Por Unos Desconcidos* (Killed by Persons Unknown): Mob Violence Against African Americans and Mexican Americans." In *Beyond Black and White: Race, Ethnicity, and Gender in the US South and Southwest,* edited by Stephanie Cole and Alison Parker, 35–74. College Station: Texas A&M University Press, 2004.

——. "The Rise and Fall of Mob Violence Against Mexicans in Arizona, 1859–1919." In *Lynching Beyond Dixie: American Mob Violence Outside the South,* edited by Michael J. Pfeifer. Urbana: University of Illinois Press, 2013.

Castellanos, M. Bianet. "Cancún and the Campo: Indigenous Migration and Tourism Development in the Yucatán Peninsula." In *Holiday in Mexico: Critical Reflections on Tourism and Tourist Encounters,* edited by Dina Berger and Andrew Grant Wood, 242–43. Durham, NC: Duke University Press, 2010.

Castillo, Pedro, and Albert Camarillo, eds. *Furia y Muerte: Los Bandidos Chicanos.* Los Angeles, CA: Aztlán Publications, 1973.

Cha-Jua, Sundiata Keita. "'The Cry of the Negro Should Not Be Remember the Maine, but Remember the Hanging of Bush': African American Responses to Lynching in Decatur, Illinois, 1893." In *Lynching Beyond Dixie: American Mob Violence Outside the South*, edited by Michael J. Pfeifer. Urbana: University of Illinois Press, 2013.

Clayton, Lawrence R., and Joseph E. Chance. *The March to Monterrey: The Diary of Lt. Rankin Dilworth*. El Paso: Texas Western Press, 1996.

Clemens, Gus. *Concho County*. San Antonio, TX: Mulberry Avenue Books, 1980.

Clendenen, Clarence C. *Blood on the Border: The United States Army and the Mexican Irregulars*. London: Macmillan, 1969.

Coerver, Don M. "'Wire Me Before Shooting': Federalism in Action; The Texas-Mexico Border During the Revolution." Paper presented at the annual Walter Prescott Webb Memorial Lecture Series, University of Texas at Arlington, March 10–11, 2010.

Coerver, Don M., and Linda B. Hall. *Texas and the Mexican Revolution: A Study in State and National Border Policy, 1910–1920*. San Antonio: Trinity University Press, 1984.

Cott, Nancy. *Public Vows: A History of Marriage and the Nation*. Cambridge, MA: Harvard University Press, 2000.

Cumberland, Charles Curtis. *Mexican Revolution: Genesis Under Madero*. Austin: University of Texas Press, 1952.

De León, Arnoldo. *Mexican Americans in Texas: A Brief History*. 3rd ed. Wheeling, IL: Harlan Davidson, 2009.

———. *They Called Them Greasers: Anglo Attitudes Toward Mexicans in Texas, 1821–1900*. Austin: University of Texas Press, 1983.

———. *War Along the Border*. College Station: Texas A&M University Press, 2012.

Foley, Neil. *The White Scourge: Mexicans, Blacks, and Poor Whites in Texas Cotton Culture*. Berkeley: University of California Press, 1997.

Frazer, Chris. *Bandit Nation: A History of Outlaws and Cultural Struggle in Mexico, 1810–1920*. Lincoln: University of Nebraska Press, 2006.

Gamio, Manuel. *The Mexican Immigrant: His Life-Story*. Chicago, IL: University of Chicago Press, 1931.

———. *Mexican Immigration to the United States: A Study of Human Migration and Adjustment*. Chicago, IL: University of Chicago Press, 1930.

García, Mario. *Desert Immigrants: The Mexicans of El Paso, 1880–1920*. New Haven, CT: Yale University Press, 1981.

Gerstle, Gary. *American Crucible: Race and Nation in the Twentieth Century*. Princeton, NJ: Princeton University Press, 2001.

Gilly, Adolfo. *The Mexican Revolution: A People's History*. New York: New Press, 2006.

Goldsby, Jacqueline. *A Spectacular Secret: Lynching in American Life and Literature*. Chicago, IL: University of Chicago Press, 2006.

Gómez, Laura E. *Manifest Destinies: The Making of the Mexican American Race*. New York: New York University Press, 2007.

Gonzales-Day, Ken. *Lynching in the West, 1850–1935*. Durham, NC: Duke University Press, 2006.

Gordon, Linda. *The Great Arizona Orphan Abduction*. Cambridge, MA: Harvard University Press, 1999.

Griswold del Castillo, Richard. *The Treaty of Guadalupe Hidalgo: A Legacy of Conflict*. Norman: University of Oklahoma Press, 1990.

Gutiérrez, David G. *Walls and Mirrors: Mexican Americans, Mexican Immigrants, and the Politics of Ethnicity*. Berkeley: University of California Press, 1995.

Haley, P. Edward. *Revolution and Intervention: The Diplomacy of Taft and Wilson with Mexico, 1910–1917*. Cambridge, MA: MIT Press, 1970.

Hall, Linda B., and Don M. Coerver. *Revolution on the Border: The United States and Mexico, 1910–1920*. Albuquerque: University of New Mexico Press, 1988.

Hanrahan, Gene Z. *Documents on the Mexican Revolution*. Salisbury, NC: Documentary Publications, 1976.

Hardy, B. Carmon. "Cultural 'Encystment' as a Cause of the Mormon Exodus from Mexico in 1912." *Pacific Historical Review* 34, no. 4 (November 1965): 430–46.

Harris, Charles H., III, and Louis R. Sadler. *The Border Revolution: Clandestine Activities of the Mexican Revolution, 1910–1920*. Silver City, NM: High-Lonesome Books, 1988.

———. "The 1911 Reyes Conspiracy: The Texas Side." *Southwestern Historical Quarterly* 83, no. 4 (April 1980): 325–48.

———. *The Secret War in El Paso: Mexican Revolutionary Intrigue, 1906–1920*. Albuquerque: University of New Mexico Press, 2009.

———. *The Texas Rangers and the Mexican Revolution: The Bloodiest Decade, 1910–1920*. Albuquerque: University of New Mexico Press, 2004.

Hart, John Mason. *Empire and Revolution: The Americans in Mexico since the Civil War*. Berkeley: University of California Press, 2006.

———. *Revolutionary Mexico: The Coming and Process of the Mexican Revolution*. Tenth Anniversary Edition. Berkeley: University of California Press, 1997.

Hatch, Nelle S. *Colonia Juárez: An Intimate Account of a Mormon Village*. Salt Lake City, UT: Deseret Book Company, 1954.

Hernández, Kelly Lytle. *Migra! A History of the U.S. Border Patrol*. Berkeley: University of California Press, 2010.

Higham, John. *Strangers in the Land: Patterns of American Nativism, 1860–1925*. New York: Atheneum, 1973.

Hirshson, Stanley P. *The Lion of the Lord: A Biography of Brigham Young*. New York: Alfred A. Knopf, 1969.

Hobsbawm, Eric J. *Bandits*. London: Weidenfeld and Nicolson, 1969.

Hoganson, Kristin L. *Fighting for American Manhood: How Gender Politics Provoked the Spanish-American and Philippine-American Wars*. New Haven, CT: Yale University Press, 1998.

Hu-DeHart, Evelyn. "Immigrants to a Developing Society: The Chinese in Northern Mexico, 1875–1932." *Journal of Arizona History* 21 (Fall 1980): 56–60.

Hughes, Alton. *Pecos: A History of the Pioneer West.* Seagraves, TX: Pioneer Book Publishers, 1978.

Hurst, James W. *Pancho Villa and Black Jack Pershing: The Punitive Expedition in Mexico.* Santa Barbara, CA: Praeger, 2007.

Johnson, Benjamin Heber. *Revolution in Texas: How a Forgotten Rebellion and Its Bloody Suppression Turned Mexicans into Americans.* New Haven, CT: Yale University Press, 2003.

———. "Sedition and Citizenship in South Texas, 1900–1930." PhD diss., Yale University, 2000.

Johnson, Frank W. *A History of Texas and Texans.* Vol. 3. Chicago, IL: American Historical Society, 1914.

Jones, Daniel W. *Forty Years Among the Indians.* Springville, UT: Council Press, 1890.

Knight, Alan. *The Mexican Revolution.* Vol. 1, *Porfirians, Liberals, and Peasants.* Lincoln: University of Nebraska Press, 1990.

———. *The Mexican Revolution.* Vol. 2, *Counter-revolution and Reconstruction.* Lincoln: University of Nebraska Press, 1990.

La Botz, Dan. "American 'Slackers' in the Mexican Revolution: International Proletarian Politics in the Midst of a National Revolution." *The Americas* 62, no. 4 (April 2006): 563–90.

Lee, Erika. *At America's Gates: Chinese Immigration During the Exclusion Era, 1882–1943.* Chapel Hill: University of North Carolina Press, 2003.

Lee, Stacey. *Mexico and the United States.* Tarrytown, NY: Marshall Cavendish, 2003.

Leonard, Stephen J. *Lynching in Colorado, 1859–1919.* Boulder: University of Colorado Press, 2002.

Levario, Miguel Antonio. *Militarizing the Border: When Mexicans Became the Enemy.* College Station: Texas A&M University Press, 2012.

Limerick, Patricia Nelson. *The Legacy of Conquest: The Unbroken Past of the American West.* New York: W. W. Norton, 1987.

López, Ian F. *White by Law: The Legal Construction of Race.* New York: New York University Press, 1996.

Martínez, Oscar J. *Border Boom Town: Ciudad Juárez Since 1848.* Austin: University of Texas Press, 1975.

———. *Troublesome Border.* Tucson: University of Arizona Press, 1988.

McLean, Robert N. *That Mexican As He Really Is, North and South of the Rio Grande.* New York: Fleming H. Revell, 1928.

McWilliams, Carey. *North from Mexico: The Spanish-Speaking People of the United States.* Westport, CT: Greenwood Press, 1948.

Menchaca, Martha. *Naturalizing Mexican Immigrants.* Austin: University of Texas Press, 2011.

Miles, Elton. *Stray Tales of the Big Bend.* College Station: Texas A&M University Press, 1993.

Montejano, David. *Anglos and Mexicans in the Making of Texas, 1836–1986.* Austin: University of Texas Press, 1987.

Morán González, John. *Border Renaissance: The Texas Centennial and the Emergence of Mexican American Literature.* Austin: University of Texas Press, 2010.

Ngai, Mae M. *Impossible Subjects: Illegal Aliens and the Making of Modern America.* Princeton, NJ: Princeton University Press, 2004.

Nevels, Cynthia Skove. *Lynching to Belong: Claiming Whiteness through Racial Violence.* College Station: Texas A&M University Press, 2007.

Nielsen, George R. *Vengeance in a Small Town: The Thorndale Lynching of 1911.* Bloomington, IN: iUniverse, 2011.

Noelke, Virginia. *Early San Angelo.* Charleston, SC: Arcadia Publishing, 2011.

Orozco, Cynthia E. *No Mexicans, Women, or Dogs Allowed.* Austin: University of Texas Press, 2009.

——. "The Origins of the League of United Latin American Citizens (LULAC) and the Mexican American Civil Rights Movement in Texas with an Analysis of Women's Political Participation in a Gendered Context, 1910–1929." PhD diss., University of California, Los Angeles, 1992.

Parrish, William Earl. *A History of Missouri, 1820–1860.* Columbia: University of Missouri Press, 2000.

Pfeifer, Michael J., ed. *Lynching Beyond Dixie: American Mob Violence Outside the South.* Urbana: University of Illinois Press, 2013.

——. *The Roots of Rough Justice: Origins of American Lynching.* Urbana: University of Illinois Press, 2011.

——. *Rough Justice: Lynching and American Society, 1874–1947.* Urbana: University of Illinois Press, 2004.

Ramírez, José. *To the Line of Fire! Mexican Texans and World War I.* College Station: Texas A&M University Press, 2009.

Rice, Harvey F. "The Lynching of Antonio Rodríguez." Master's thesis, University of Texas at Austin, 1990.

Richmond, Douglas W., and Sam W. Haynes. *The Mexican Revolution: Conflict and Consolidation, 1910–1940.* College Station: Texas A&M University Press, 2013.

Romero, Robert Chao. *The Chinese in Mexico, 1882–1940.* Tucson: University of Arizona Press, 2010.

Romney, Thomas Cottam. *A Divinity Shapes Our Ends, as Seen in My Life Story.* Salt Lake City, UT: n.p., 1953.

——. *The Mormon Colonies in Mexico.* 1935; Salt Lake City: University of Utah Press, 2005.

Romo, David Dorando. *Ringside Seat to a Revolution: An Underground Cultural History of El Paso and Juárez, 1893–1923.* El Paso, TX: Cinco Punto Press, 2005.

Rosales, Francisco Arturo. *Chicano! The History of the Mexican American Civil Rights Movement.* Houston, TX: Arte Público Press, 1996.

——. *Dictionary of Latino Civil Rights History.* Houston, TX: Arte Público Press, 2006.

——. *¡Pobre Raza! Violence, Justice, and Mobilization Among México Lindo Immigrants, 1900–1936.* Austin: University of Texas Press, 1999.

Ruiz, Vicki L. "South by Southwest: Mexican Americans and Segregated Schooling, 1900–1950." *OAH Magazine of History* 15, no. 2 (Winter 2001): 23–27.

Sánchez, George J. *Becoming Mexican American: Ethnicity, Culture, and Identity in Chicano Los Angeles, 1900–1945.* New York: Oxford University Press, 1993.

Sandos, James A. *Rebellion in the Borderlands: Anarchism and the Plan of San Diego,1904–1923.* Norman: University of Oklahoma Press, 1992.

Schrag, Peter. *Not Fit for Our Society: Nativism and Immigration.* Berkeley: University of California Press, 2010.

Smith, Jesse N., Family Association. *Journal of Jesse Nathaniel Smith: The Story of a Mormon Pioneer, 1834–1906.* Salt Lake City, UT: n.p., 1953.

Stout, Joseph. *Border Conflict: Villistas, Carrancistas, and the Punitive Expedition, 1915–1920.* Fort Worth: Texas Christian University Press, 1999.

Tippens, Matthew D. *Turning Germans into Texans: World War I and the Assimilation and Survival of German Culture in Texas, 1900–1930.* Austin, TX: Kleingarten Press, 2010.

Tompkins, Frank. *Chasing Villa: The Last Campaign of the U.S. Cavalry.* Silver City, NM: High-Lonesome Books, 1934.

Tullis, F. LaMond. *Mormons in Mexico: The Dynamic of Faith and Culture.* Logan: Utah State University Press, 1987.

Tyler, Ron C. *The Big Bend: A History of the Last Texas Frontier.* Washington, DC: National Park Service, 1975.

Utley, Robert M. *Lone Star Justice: The First Century of the Texas Rangers.* New York: Oxford University Press, 2002.

Vanderwood, Paul J. *Juan Soldado: Rapist, Murderer, Martyr, Saint.* Durham, NC: Duke University Press, 2004.

Vanderwood Paul J., and Frank N. Samponaro. *Border Fury: A Picture Postcard Record of Mexico's Revolution and U.S. War Preparedness, 1910–1917.* Albuquerque: University of New Mexico Press, 1988.

Vilanova, Antonio. "American Troops Fired First at El Carrizal, Says Writer." *Southwesterner,* February 1967.

Villanueva, Nicholas, Jr. "Sincerely Yours for Dignified Manhood: Lynching, Violence, and American Manhood during the Early Years of the Mexican Revolution, 1910–1914." *Journal of the West* 49, no. 1 (Winter 2010): 41–48.

Virginia Law Register. "Tyranny or Necessity." *Virginia Law Register* 18, no. 1 (May 1912): 72–73.

Waldrep, Christopher, ed. *Lynching in America: A History in Documents.* New York: New York University Press, 2006.

———. *The Many Faces of Judge Lynch: Extralegal Violence and Punishment in America.* New York: Palgrave Macmillan, 2002.

Webb, Walter Prescott. *The Texas Rangers: A Century of Frontier Defense.* Austin: University of Texas Press, 1935.

Weber, David J. *New Spain's Far Northern Frontier: Essays on Spain in the American West, 1540–1821.* Albuquerque: University of New Mexico Press, 1979.

Welsome, Eileen. *The General and the Jaguar: Pershing's Hunt for Pancho Villa; A True Story of Revolution and Revenge*. New York: Little, Brown, 2006.

Wheeler, Edward J. "The Mexican Situation Again Becomes Acute." *Current Opinion* 60 (January–June 1915).

White, Walter. *Rope and Faggot: A Biography of Judge Lynch*. Notre Dame, IN: University of Notre Dame Press, 1929.

Whittington, Lona Teresa O'Neal. "The Road of Sorrow: Mexican Refugees Who Fled Pancho Villa through Presidio, Texas, 1913–1914." Master's thesis, Sul Ross State University, Alpine, Texas, 1976.

Winders, Richard B. *Mr. Polk's Army: The American Military Experience in the Mexican War*. College Station: Texas A&M University Press, 1997.

Yarinski, Amy Waters. *All for One and One for All: A Celebration of 75 Years of the League of United Latin American Citizens*. Virginia Beach, VA: Donning Company, 2004.

ELECTRONIC RESOURCES

Acosta, Teresa Palomo. "Chapa, Francisco A." Texas State Historical Association, *Handbook of Texas Online*, June 12, 2010. http://www.tshaonline.org/handbook/online/articles/fch50.

Anders, Evan. "Canales, José Tomas." Texas State Historical Association, *Handbook of Texas Online*, June 12, 2010. www.tshaonline.org/handbook/online/articles/fcaag.

Duke, Escal F. "San Angelo, TX." Texas State Historical Association, *Handbook of Texas Online*, June 15, 2010. http://www.tshaonline.org/handbook/online/articles/hds01.

Hormann, Matt. "When Patriotic Fevers Ran High." *Hometown Pasadena*, June 30, 2011. http://hometown-pasadena.com/history/when-patriotic-fevers-ran-high/28158.

League of United Latin American Citizens. http://lulac.org/about/history/.

Neeno, Timothy. "The Mexican Revolution and US Intervention, 1910–1917." *Military History Online*, January 8, 2010. http://www.militaryhistoryonline.com/20thcentury/articles/mexicanrevolution.aspx.

Smyrl, Vivian Elizabeth. "Thorndale, TX." Texas State Historical Association, *Handbook of Texas Online*, June 5, 2010. https://www.tshaonline.org/handbook/online/articles/hjt04.

US Customs and Border Protection. "United States Border Patrol: Protecting Our Sovereign Borders." https://www.cbp.gov/about/history.

Villahermosa, Gilberto. "America's Hispanics in America's Wars." *Army Magazine*, September 2002. http://www3.ausa.org/webint/DeptArmyMagazine.nsf/byid/CCRN-6CCS5U.

Wood, Andrew Grant. "Birth of the Modern Festival." In *Carnival in Veracruz*. Tulsa:

University of Tulsa, 2012. http://www.personal.utulsa.edu/~andrew-wood/carnival/chapter1.html.

FILMS AND DOCUMENTARIES

Cuellar, Linda, prod. *The Artistic Legacy of the Mexican Revolution.* Films for the Humanities and Sciences, Princeton, New Jersey, 2003.

Public Broadcasting Service. *The Hunt for Pancho Villa.* WGBH Educational Foundation, American Experience, Boston, Massachusetts 1993.

Index

Page numbers in italic text indicate illustrations.